H. P. LOVECRAFT
An Introduction to His Life and Writings

THE HIPPOCAMPUS PRESS LIBRARY OF CRITICISM

S. T. Joshi, *Primal Sources: Essays on H. P. Lovecraft* (2003)
S. T. Joshi, *The Evolution of the Weird Tale* (2004)
Robert H. Waugh, *The Monster in the Mirror: Looking for H. P. Lovecraft* (2006)
Scott Connors, ed., *The Freedom of Fantastic Things: Selected Criticism on Clark Ashton Smith* (2006)
Ben Szumskyj, ed., *Two-Gun Bob: A Centennial Study of Robert E. Howard* (2006)
S. T. Joshi and Rosemary Pardoe, ed., *Warnings to the Curious: A Sheaf of Criticism on M. R. James* (2007)
S. T. Joshi, *Classics and Contemporaries: Some Notes on Horror Fiction* (2009)
Kenneth W. Faig, Jr., *The Unknown Lovecraft* (2009)
Massimo Berruti, *Dim-Remembered Stories: A Critical Study of R. H. Barlow* (2010)
Gary William Crawford, Jim Rockhill, and Brian J. Showers, ed., *Reflections in a Glass Darkly: Essays on J. Sheridan Le Fanu* (2011)
Robert H. Waugh, *A Monster of Voices: Speaking for H. P. Lovecraft* (2011)
Donald Sidney-Fryer, *The Golden State Phantasticks: The California Romantics and Related Subjects* (2012)
William F. Nolan, *Nolan on Bradbury: Sixty Years of Writing about the Master of Science Fiction* (2013)
Steven J. Mariconda, *H. P. Lovecraft: Art, Artifact, and Reality* (2013)
S. T. Joshi, *Unutterable Horror: A History of Supernatural Fiction* (2014)
Massimo Berruti, S. T. Joshi, and Sam Gafford, ed., *William Hope Hodgson: Voices from the Borderland* (2014)
Robert H. Waugh, *The Tragic Thread in Science Fiction: Essays on David Lindsay, Olaf Stapledon, et al.* (2019)
Charles Hoffman and Marc Cerasini, *Robert E. Howard: A Closer Look* (2020)
Robert H. Waugh, *A Monster for Many: Talking with H. P. Lovecraft* (2021)
Ellen J. Greenham, After Engulfment: Cosmicism and Neocosmicism in H. P. Lovecraft, Philip K. Dick, Robert A. Heinlein, and Frank Herbert

Lovecraft Annual (2007–)
Dead Reckonings (2007–)

H. P. LOVECRAFT
An Introduction to His Life and Writings

Arthur S. Koki

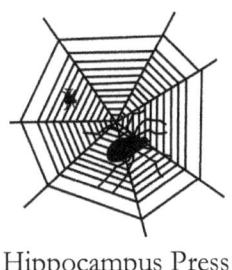

Hippocampus Press

New York

Copyright © 2022 by Cheryl Koki
Preface, additional notes and other editorial matter
copyright © 2022 by S. T. Joshi

Published by Hippocampus Press
P.O. Box 641, New York, NY 10156.
www.hippocampuspress.com

All rights reserved.
No part of this work may be reproduced in any form or by any means without the written permission of the publisher.

Cover illustration by Khoi Nguyen.
Cover design by Dan Sauer, dansauerdesign.com
Hippocampus Press logo designed by Anastasia Damianakos.

First Hippocampus Press Edition 2022
1 3 5 7 9 8 6 4 2

ISBN 978-1-61498-391-0 (paperback)
ISBN 978-1-61498-392-7 (ebook)]

Contents

Foreword, *by* S. T. Joshi 7
  I. Introduction 17
  II. From Childhood's Hour 21
  III. The Formative Years 49
  IV. A Protracted Season in Hell 95
  V. Home 145
  VI. The Story Thus Far 257
Bibliography 265
Index 275

Foreword

Arthur Sotir Koki, author of a 1962 master's thesis on Lovecraft, is something of a mystery man—not least because he changed his surname even before his thesis was completed. He was born on 9 March 1937 in Worcester, Massachusetts, the son of Sotir and Anna Koki, who emigrated to the United States from Albania. He spoke Albanian as a child, as he noted to his thesis advisor, the noted Hart Crane biographer John Unterecker: "I have the unique advantage of having spoken the language [Albanian] since childhood so the prospect of my achieving complete fluency in it is a likely, attainable goal."[1] In 1951 he began attending South High School in Worcester, graduating in 1955. Around this time he joined the Albanian-American Literary Society and also the Worcester Boys' Club.

Koki went on to attend Clark University in Worcester, where he received a B.A. in English in 1960. That fall he enrolled in a master's program in English and comparative literature at Columbia University. His attendance extended from September 1960 to May 1961, and the degree was granted on 28 February 1962, presumably when he submitted his 350-page thesis, "H. P. Lovecraft: An Introduction to His Life and Writings."

But already during his time at Columbia, Koki had changed his name to Arthur R[obert] Byron. His brother Philip changed his name

---

1. From a letter by Koki to Unterecker, found in the John Unterecker Papers relating to Hart Crane. I am indebted to Marcos Legaria for this and all my biographical information on Koki.

to Philip Adams. Possibly Koki and his brother did not wish to be saddled with a "foreign" name. Arthur's other brother, Alfred S. Koki, also became an educator: after receiving a master's degree in education from Worcester State College, he taught in the Worcester public school system for thirty-nine years.

Arthur did graduate work in linguistics at Temple University in Philadelphia and the University of Chicago before becoming a professor of English at Kutztown University in Kutztown, Pennsylvania (a city in southeastern Pennsylvania, near Allentown). This stint began in 1969 and lasted until 1988, when Koki retired at the unusually early age of fifty-one.[2] Possibly health considerations necessitated this move, since he died on 25 December 1989 at the Lehigh Valley Hospital Center in Allentown. (His obituary does not state the cause of death.) He does not appear to have published any books or articles in scholarly venues or, in fact, in any venues.

How Koki became interested in Lovecraft is unknown, but that interest dates well before he began his graduate work at Columbia. A previously unknown honors thesis, "H. P. Lovecraft," submitted to the Department of English at Clark University on 14 January 1960, is a 118-page text that anticipates many of the features of his M.A. thesis. Even at this early date, Koki had made the effort to investigate primary documents, especially Lovecraft's unpublished letters to his aunt Lillian D. Clark housed in the John Hay Library at Brown University. The trip from Worcester to Providence is not a long one, but Koki must have spent considerable time in Lovecraft's hometown absorbing the atmosphere of the city while also hunting up the research materials that would go into his two theses.

Koki's Columbia thesis is an impressive work, especially for its

---

2. During this period Koki was also a Fulbright scholar in Yugoslavia (1981–83) and received the Woodrow Wilson and the National Defense Foreign Language Fellowships.

time. While it contains a sprinkling of minor factual errors, it is on the whole a sound and surprisingly detailed account of Lovecraft's life. Its judgment on Lovecraft's work is somewhat rudimentary and occasionally off the mark (it is, for example, striking that he provides not even a cursory analysis of "The Dunwich Horror"), but Koki manifestly regards Lovecraft as a significant literary figure and not just a writer of pulp or popular fiction. His frequent quoting of French and Spanish scholars on Lovecraft suggests that Koki was aware that foreign critics had done more to address the distinctive qualities in Lovecraft's work than Anglo-American critics had.

As such, Koki's thesis stands as a pioneering work of Lovecraft scholarship. It was the second academic paper written on Lovecraft, following James Warren Thomas's severely biased account, "Howard Phillips Lovecraft: A Self-Portrait" (M.A. thesis: Brown University, 1950)—a text Koki apparently did not consult. It also preceded Barton L. St. Armand's "H. P. Lovecraft: The Outsider in Legend and Myth" (M.A. thesis: Brown University, 1966), although that work was purely critical, with no biographical discussion.

More significantly, Koki's thesis is the first extended treatment of the entire course of Lovecraft's life, preceding L. Sprague de Camp's *Lovecraft: A Biography* (1975) by more than a decade. There is considerable evidence that de Camp mined Koki for many facets of his own biography, as other scholars such as Kenneth W. Faig, Jr. and myself have done. Particularly valuable, for example, is Koki's transcript of a portion of the divorce proceedings between Lovecraft and his wife Sonia in 1929, which he found among the records in the Providence Superior Court.

Koki's thesis in some sense anticipated Lovecraft's burgeoning popularity, which began in the later 1960s with the proliferation of paperback editions of his work. Indeed, his thesis was written before Arkham House reissued Lovecraft's fiction in three volumes in 1963–65, so that he was forced to cite the earlier Arkham House omnibuses—*The*

Outsider and Others (1939) and *Beyond the Wall of Sleep* (1943)—when quoting from Lovecraft's fiction. Although he states at the very outset that Lovecraft "has a small, devoted following," he concludes by noting: "There are more hopeful signs of Lovecraft's growing importance than the stagily written articles in fanzines and elsewhere might suggest."

In his assessment of Lovecraft's life Koki is fair and even-handed. He is well aware of Lovecraft's racist tendencies (he could hardly help knowing of them, since they are embedded in Lovecraft's letters to his aunts, which was Koki's primary source of biographical information), but he places this aspect of Lovecraft's life and thought in proper perspective—as James Warren Thomas did not. Thomas was so offended by Lovecraft's views that he rashly declared the Providence writer "narrow and prejudiced and strait-laced and lacking in ordinary human feeling." Koki is more judicious, writing: "Granted that Lovecraft was (1) racially prejudiced, and (2) alienated from the majority of mankind, does this make him a less effective commentator on the life around him?" His answer is a qualified no.

Koki made good use of other documents, including the various memoirs of Lovecraft that had already been written up to that time. In particular, he consulted the original, unpublished text of Sonia H. Davis's memoir, "The Private Life of H. P. Lovecraft," rather than the abridged and altered versions that had appeared in print. It is also clear that Koki came into direct contact with several of Lovecraft's colleagues who were then living, including Ethel Phillips Morrish (Lovecraft's second cousin, who knew Lovecraft when he was a boy), Muriel Eddy, Wilfred B. Talman, August Derleth, Donald Wandrei, Bernice L. Barlow (R. H. Barlow's mother), Robert Bloch, Margaret Sylvester (then Margaret Ronan), Kenneth Sterling, and others. Even though Koki states at the outset that he established contact with Samuel Loveman (possibly through his advisor John Unterecker, who was surely acquainted with Loveman) and Frank Belknap Long, who like Loveman lived in New York City at the time Koki was writing his thesis, he does not appear to include many of their reflections about Lovecraft. Even so, the diligence that Koki exhibited was far greater than is customary for a twenty-four-year-old writing a master's thesis.

It is now a full sixty years since Koki submitted his thesis to Columbia University, and in that time Lovecraft's reputation has ascended far beyond what Koki could have imagined. Arthur Sotir Koki (or Arthur Robert Byron) would be gratified that his landmark work played its role in that ascension.

—S. T. JOSHI

A Note on This Edition

The editors have sought to present this thesis with a minimum of editorial alteration, but we have systematized Koki's citations of literary works to bring them in line with current practice—e.g., quotation marks without italics for short stories, short poems, essays, and other works; italics for novels, periodicals, and other book-length works. (Koki tends to use underscoring for all titles.) Koki's footnotes have been preserved largely unaltered; editorial footnotes are enclosed in square brackets. Footnotes are placed at the bottom of the page, rather than at the end of the chapter as in the thesis. Minor factual or spelling errors have been silently corrected.

H. P. LOVECRAFT
An Introduction to His Life and Writings

Submitted in partial fulfillment of the requirements for the degree of Master of Arts, Faculty of Philosophy, Columbia University

ABSTRACT

This essay is the first full length introduction to the life and works of Howard Phillips Lovecraft (1890–1937), the weird tales and fantasy author of Providence, Rhode Island. In approach this purview is frankly chary of much of the preexisting ana which has excessively and dangerously oversimplified Lovecraft the man, devising him to be, on the one hand, a misanthropic recluse, a human oddity, and, on the other, a benign person, whose equanimity was touched, but rarely, by indigestion or overambition. To arrive at a more balanced, complete view, this essay constructs Lovecraft's life largely from primary source materials: letters, birth and death certificates, wills, high school transcripts, psychiatric records, divorce petitions, medical reports, as well as interviews with those who knew Lovecraft personally.

Although my discussion of Lovecraft's fiction deals mainly with his work in the weird tales genre, comment is made on his adjunctive writings—juvenilia; essays, poetry, and short stories for Amateur Press publications; and, revision and ghost-writing labors. Thirty-eight of the fifty-two professionally published short stories are summarized and evaluated. The influence of other writers—notably Poe, Machen, and Lord Dunsany—on his style and conception of themes are discussed, as are the probable source influences for the Cthulhu Mythos, the unique creation of Lovecraft's work. The last chapter notes some of the bibliography which has come into existence since Lovecraft's death. The various articles and editions are hopefully interpreted as signs of a growing interest in his life and works, not only in America, but also on the Continent, especially in France.

I. Introduction

In recent years much ink has been spilled over American writers, past and contemporary, but as yet little has been spilled over H. P. Lovecraft. This is not to say that Lovecraft is all but forgotten. He has a small, devoted following. Early editions of his works now fetch prices upwards of a hundred dollars. The pulp magazines in which his stories originally appeared are today collector's items, as are the Amateur papers containing his verses, essays, and early tales.

The bibliography of critical writings on Lovecraft is very small at this time, but reaction to him has been refreshingly candid. Michel de Ghelderode, Belgium's distinguished playwright, is reported to have hailed him as one of America's four greatest writers, the other three being Poe, Bierce, and Whitman. Jean Cocteau has praised the French translations of Lovecraft's stories made by Jacques Papy, while André Billy, writing in *Le Figaro* on October 28, 1961, boldly titled his four-column article, "Lovecraft: Edgar Poe du XXe siècle." Lovecraft's detractors, Edmund Wilson for one, dismiss him as "quite second-rate." Opinions on Lovecraft as a person have also clashed sharply. One person who knew him as a young man said that Lovecraft was "crazy as a bedbug." Less puissant, more anodyne statements by his friends eulogize him as an unforgettable person, warm, affectionate. All these unreserved remarks are a sign of Lovecraft's vigor. It is difficult to remain indifferent to him. One admires him enormously or one loudly dooms him, his stories, and the monsters he raised therein for being puerile and unclean.

A word about those Lovecraftian monsters. They are not the werewolves and vampires of Hollywood creation who may be foiled by a dash of holy water or a golden crucifix resting peacefully between the heroine's inviting breasts. They are the blind idiot gods who created Man who in turn created gods in his own image. They are as much the monsters of the mind and spirit—the denial of goodness. That much of life is a denial of what we know to be true and beautiful, few will dispute. Perhaps this is the reason why the French, who have "chew'd bitter ashes," are so eagerly seizing Lovecraft's stories.

The majority of the letters to be cited in my study were written by Lovecraft to his aunt, Mrs. Lillian D. Clark, who lived with him in Providence. (In 1923 they were joined by another aunt of Lovecraft's, Mrs. Annie E. P. Gamwell.) These letters, along with those to Robert H. Barlow and Elizabeth Toldridge, totaling over a million words, are now part of the Special Collections Division of the John Hay Library at Brown University. Although Lovecraft carried on a voluminous correspondence with many people—a correspondence estimated at well over five million words—the letters to his aunt are particularly valuable because they were written to his closest relative and, more important, they were written to a person he knew intimately. With her his reticence, which so often caused him to adopt, by his own admission, an artistic pose, vanished, and he wrote with casual, colloquial ease. It is almost as if he were in the same room with her, chatting pleasantly.

Or perhaps not so pleasantly. Diana Trilling in an introduction to D. H. Lawrence's letters felt that Lawrence's letters were "so wonderful" and second only to Keats's because they were "so absolutely personal, so close to home, so miraculously without an eye to posthumous publication." Candor is desirable, but a surfeit of intimacy may, paradoxically, give us a lopsided picture and present us not a whole individual but a loathsome creature or a calloused soul. When Lovecraft wrote to his aunt he was aware of her limitations and thus dealt with subjects which interested her. He often neglected to speak

I. Introduction

of the philosophical and literary part of his life, while from a sense of *pudeur* he concealed his altruism. Thus one must proceed with the assumption that the Lovecraft correspondence to Mrs. Clark, although valuable, does not furnish us with the complete portrait of the man.

I would like to express my thanks to those who have aided me thus far in my research on H. P. Lovecraft. I am grateful to Dr. William H. Carter, Jr. and Dr. James Franklin Beard, Jr. of Clark University who supervised this study when it first took form as an essay in the English Honors program there.[1] Professor Thomas O. Mabbott of Hunter College very kindly talked over this paper with me, and also permitted me to read the Lovecraft letters in his possession. Several others allowed me free access to their Lovecraft correspondence. They are Mrs. R. Morrish, Margaret Ronan,[2] Samuel Loveman, Dr. Kenneth Sterling, George Kirk, and Edward Daas. I am also indebted to Samuel Loveman, Dr. Sterling, George Kirk, Frank B. Long, Jr., Donald Wollheim, Mrs. Muriel E. Eddy, Douglass Dana, and Edward Cole for talking to me about H. P. Lovecraft, their mutual friend.

My especial thanks to Jack Grill for permitting me to borrow from his extensive collection of Lovecraftiana. His constant interest and encouragement were deeply appreciated. I also wish to thank Lin Carter and Harrison Brown for lending me books.

The following correspondents have helped to fill in various gaps in my knowledge: James Wade, George W. Macauley, Robert Bloch, Dorothy C. Walter, Mrs. Mary Spink, Jacques Papy, George Wetzel, August Derleth, Donald Wandrei, Mrs. Sonia Greene Lovecraft Davis, and Alfred Galpin. For information concerning Robert H. Barlow, Lovecraft's literary executor, I am grateful to Mrs. Bernice L. Barlow, Dr. Ignacio Bernal, Mrs. Carmen Cook de Leonard,. Mary D. Parsons, Dr. Isabel Kelly, and Dr. H. Nicholson.

---

1. [Koki refers to his honors thesis, "H. P. Lovecraft" (Clark University, 1960).]
2. [I.e., Margaret Sylvester, who corresponded with HPL in the mid-1930s.]

Yvette Bessis of Éditions Denoël and John Bush of Victor Gollancz, Ltd. graciously answered my questions on French and British reaction to Lovecraft. I thank Samuel Draper, President of The American Friends of Michel de Ghelderode. Also, Dr. C. H. Jones of Butler Hospital; Mr. George Ford, Supervising Records Clerk, Department of Public Schools, Providence, R.I.; Dr. William L. Leet, physician to Lovecraft during his last illness.

Miss Martha Peck of the Special Collections Division, John Hay Library was most helpful in calling miscellaneous items of Lovecraftiana to my attention, as well as permitting me to photograph several of them.

Let me acknowledge thanks to Winfield Townley Scott for allowing me to read his book manuscript *Exiles and Fabrications* prior to its publication. My thanks also to Steve Rojcewicz for translating an article in *Prze Kroj*.

I was fortunate to have had as my adviser, Dr. John Unterecker.

II. From Childhood's Hour

> From childhood's hour I have not been
> As others were; I have not seen
> As others saw; I could not bring
> My passions from a common spring.
> From the same source I have not taken
> My sorrow; I could not awaken
> My heart to joy at the same time;
> And all I loved, I loved alone.[1]

Howard Phillips Lovecraft was born in Providence, Rhode Island on August 20, 1890, into a family whose ancestry, he wryly commented, was "lousy with clergymen but short on straight thinkers."[2] He was, however, proud, inordinately proud of his maternal lineage. The Phillipses could trace their ancestry to Sir Hubertus de la Feld, an Alsatian land owner and companion of William the Conqueror. They also claimed as their kith John Philips, poet and Milton biographer, and Ambrose Philips,[3] whose saccharine verses to children and "personal

---

1. "Alone," Edgar Allan Poe.
2. H. P. Lovecraft, MS. letter to Kenneth Sterling, dated May 25, 1936, Collection of Dr. Kenneth Sterling. Hereafter abbreviated to KS.
3. Miscellaneous papers and genealogical charts relating to the Phillips family, Collection of Mrs. R. Morrish. Hereafter abbreviated to RM.

pomposity that ill accorded with this infantile style," once moved Henry Carey to write a satiric poem about him and thereby, incidentally, coin a new word—"namby-pamby."[4] Howard's maternal ancestors had settled in Boston as early as 1620. The divergent branches may be traced through the Field, Mathewson, Rathbone,[5] Whipple, Place, and Phillips families. These progenitors of H. P. Lovecraft were sober, hardworking people in government and business. A degree of wealth and respectability accumulated, and the family stood like a shade tree, old and substantial despite some withering branches.

The influence which Ancestors have among the living is often strong. It is well at the outset to be aware, in a general way, of Lovecraft's heritage, because Lovecraft himself, from an early age, slowly garnered the riches of his past until his chief sustenance was pride of ancestry.

Howard's mother was Sarah Susie Phillips Lovecraft. She was one of three surviving daughters of Whipple V. Phillips, a successful real estate speculator. Prior to coming to Providence, he had prospered in Foster, Rhode Island, operating, among other ventures, a country store and a sawmill. His standing in the community was such that he was given the honor of selecting the name of a new adjacent town; he named the town Greene, after a Revolutionary hero who had hailed from Rhode Island. Whipple V. Phillips also founded a Masonic Lodge in Greene which continues to meet to this day.[6]

A search through the Phillips family papers furnishes several glimpses of the widespread activities of Howard's grandfather. His calling card gives two business addresses, one at Finsbury Circus, E.C., London, and the other at 30 Union Square, New York. Some letter-

---

4. *A Literary History of England*, ed. Albert C. Baugh, New York: Appleton-Century-Crofts, Inc., 1948, p. 908.

5. Rathbone or Rathbun, written both ways, sometimes by children of the same father. The family is believed to be of Saxon origin. See *The Rathbone Family Historian* 1, No. 7 (July 1892).

6. Mrs. R. Morrish, MS. letter to Arthur Koki, dated April 11, 1961, AK.

II. From Childhood's Hour

head stationery lists him as the proprietor of the Westminster Hotel in Providence. There is also a prospectus from the Snake River Company, an investment corporation directed by W. V. Phillips, which planned to sell 100,000 acres of farming and cattle raising land in Idaho. Shares sold at a thousand dollars each, "fully believing the investment will pay not less than 33⅓ per cent annually," according to the brochure.[7] Presumably this Aladdin dream failed for no further references to this cattle grazing empire are to be found.

An 1878 passport issued to Mr. Phillips, then forty-five years old, describes him as being five feet, ten inches tall, with black eyes, a prominent nose, dark complexion, oval face, and grayish black hair.[8]

His hair had turned white, his face florid, perhaps apoplectic, by the time his grandson Howard was born.[9] Howard was born in his grandfather's Victorian mansion at 454 Angell Street. The day of his birth, August 20, 1890 coincided with that of the nation's president . . . 418 miles S.W. of the terrace-perched structure in which Howard's first experimental wails were vociferously echoing, the cakes were going into the White House ovens. Benjamin Harrison was fifty-seven years old. And Edgar Albert Guest[10] was nine years old—this coincidence of birthdays Lovecraft came to accept with philosophic resignation and some humor.

Howard's father was Winfield Scott Lovecraft, a salesman for the Gorham Manufacturing Company of Providence, one of the country's largest silversmith firms.[11] His parents had come from Devonshire,

---

7. Miscellaneous papers of the Phillips family, RM.

8. Passport issued by Legation of United States of America at London, No. 104, on December 5, 1878, for Whipple V. Phillips, RM.

9. Mrs. R. Morrish, MS. letter to Arthur Koki, dated March 13, 1961, AK.

10, [Edgar A. Guest (1881–1959), British-born American poet whose verse, frequently published in newspapers, became a byword for triteness and conventionality.]

11. Sonia H. Davis, MS. "The Private Life of Howard Phillips Lovecraft," dated

England to Rochester, New York in 1827.¹² Since the personnel records of the Gorham Company are not retained beyond forty years, it is difficult to determine when he was first employed there. One may guess that he met his future wife during a return to the home office. His frank, engaging manner must have contrasted sharply with Miss Phillips's demure personality. Little is known of her early life, although a "Commonplace Book" she kept gives some clues, containing as it does her genealogy, as well as prayers, psalms, and extracts from such conventional poetry as *Hiawatha* and *Barbara Frietchie*, all dutifully copied in a spidery hand. There is also a tribute to her sister Emma, who died of diphtheria in 1865 at the age of five. Something of Sarah's own "artless simplicity," which she attributes to her sister, is perhaps seen:

> Little Emma was a child of great promise, her budding intellect already began to awaken fond expectations in the minds of her friends, while her artless simplicity of manners and sweetness of temper not only doubly endeared her to her parents but won the hearts of all who knew her.
> She manifested much patience during her sickness although suffering severely from difficult breathing and once in her childlike manner said to her mother, "I wish I could stop breathing a little while just to rest" at another time she roused up and said "mother the bible is a guide to youth."¹³

If, according to the popular notion, every woman seeks her father in her husband, Sarah Phillips must, at least, have seen in both (apart from their walrus moustaches) the same forehead, Roman nose, and clear resolute eyes, suggesting a bluff, hearty spirit.¹⁴ Inasmuch as both were businessmen meeting the public, the resemblance may have been one of temperament as well.

194-, Special Collections, John Hay Library, Brown University, Providence, Rhode Island. Hereafter, more simply, JHL.

12. H. P. Lovecraft, "Autobiography: Some Notes on a Non-entity," in *Beyond the Wall of Sleep*, collected by August Derleth and Donald Wandrei, Sauk City, Wis.: Arkham House, 1943, p. xi.

13. Sarah Susie (Phillips) Lovecraft, *Commonplace Book*, n.d., JHL.

14. Photograph of Winfield Scott Lovecraft, Collection of Jack Grill. Hereafter, JG.

II. From Childhood's Hour

Sarah Phillips and Winfield Lovecraft were married June 12, 1889; she was thirty-one years old and her husband thirty-five. The following year in August Howard was born.[15]

Two autobiographical pieces by Lovecraft cover this early period. One was his squib, "Autobiography: Some Notes on a Nonentity," which was published posthumously in 1943 in *Beyond the Wall of Sleep*. Another self-sketch was the letter he wrote to a magazine editor, Edwin Baird, in 1924. From these, plus other sources, we have a fair outline of Lovecraft's early years. When he was a few months old, his family moved temporarily to Auburndale, Massachusetts, probably because of a new territory assignment by his father, who was sent on the road through that state. Mrs. Lovecraft and Howard lived with the beautiful poetess Louise Imogen Guiney, whose gift for deeply felt religious poetry has earned her a small though secure place in American literature. It would be interesting to know about the friendship between Mrs. Lovecraft and the Catholic poetess, where and how they met, but in Grace Guiney's edition of her sister's letters, which cover a period from 1872 to 1920, no mention of Mrs. Lovecraft is found.[16] Oliver Wendell Holmes often visited the Guiney household, and on one occasion, at least, rode young Howard on his knee.

At the age of one Howard began talking and by two was familiar with the alphabet.[17] In 1893, the family returned to his grandfather's mansion.[18] It was located on the felicitous sounding Angell Street. Here Howard was captivated by Grandfather Phillips's stories of European trips he had taken.[19] When Howard was five, his mother, with

---

15. Sarah Lovecraft, *Commonplace Book*, JHL.
16. Louise Imogen Guiney, *Letters*, edited by Grace Guiney, 2 vols., New York, Harpers, 1926.
17. H. P. Lovecraft, MS. letter to Edwin Baird, dated February 3, 1924, JHL.
18. [Koki fails to mention that this return to the family home was the result of Winfield Scott Lovecraft's mental breakdown in April 1893.]
19. Ibid.

sadness on her part and anger on his, had his long tresses shorn.[20] His doll was given to a neighbor's daughter and his skirt was discarded for knee pants.[21] At the age of six he entertained himself in his grandfather's library, turning over illustrated volumes of sculpture and architecture. When he did begin to read, his taste steadily retreated from the present until, "Before I knew it the eighteenth century had captured me more utterly than ever the hero of 'Berkeley Square' was captured; so that I used to spend hours in the attic poring over long f'd books banished from the library downstairs and unconsciously absorbed the style of Pope and Dr. Johnson as a natural mode of expression."[22]

We are inclined to overlook the novelty of his enthusiasm. In his day the eighteenth century was passed over as a sleepy hollow between the peaks of Elizabethan drama and Romantic poetry. The past thirty years with their meticulous, often brilliant scholarship, have changed that attitude and today we recognize the period's special flavor. The Enlightenment was distinguished by a formal elegance in literary style, a tremendous control over subject matter, and a rationalistic approach to common experience. There is merit in these generalizations if one does not push them too far. I believe, however, that it is attributing too much to Lovecraft's youth to claim these as his prime reasons in the beginning for selecting the period. Precocious, undeniably so, he was after all only a boy who must have read Gay's *Fables* for pleasure first and laughed at Swift's grotesque humor. His attraction to Pope and Johnson may have initially come from hearing about their lives. All of the family read aloud to the boy. A weak child himself, Howard must have sympathized over Pope's deformity; and what youngster could fail to be moved by Thomas Babington Macaulay's truth-fiction account of Samuel Johnson[23]—

---

20. [This incident took place when HPL was six.]
21. Miss Dorothy C. Walter, MS. letter to Arthur Koki, dated March 3, 1959, AK.
22. H. P. Lovecraft, *Beyond the Wall of Sleep*, p. xi.
23. [In the essay "Samuel Johnson" (*Edinburgh Review,* September 1831), a review of a new edition of Boswell's *Life of Johnson;* the essay was reprinted in Macaulay's *Criti-*

II. From Childhood's Hour 27

Johnson with his lovable quirks, cursed by wretched eyesight, disfigured by scrofula, saving up scraps of orange peel. But stories aside, it was those eighteenth century books with their curious orthography and topography that bewitched him until, as he later wrote, he would "read nothing without the 'long ſ' ſo that his Taſte became completely that of the 18th Century and his firſt writing (or rather hand printing) performed at the age of five (script came at the age of seven) hath this ſelf-ſame long ſ as its most ſalient characteristic."²⁴ Did this orthography satisfy a peculiar need in Howard to read with an infantile lisping voice?

The first Lovecraft tale extant, "The Little Glass Bottle," dates to 1896 when Howard was six years old. Slightly under two hundred words, it is a humorous piece in which a Capt. Jones searches for treasure described in a map. It is all a hoax and the duped Captain, enraged at the unknown perpetrator, roars, "I'd like to kick his head off."²⁵ His next story, "The Secret Cave or John Lees Adventure," he wrote at the age of eight. A little boy, John Lee, and his sister are playing in their cellar when suddenly a portion of the wall dissolves, revealing a dark passageway. John fetches some candles and they enter the tunnel. They continue a great distance, discovering en route a strongbox and a boat, which John drags with him. Again part of a wall fades out and a torrent of water explodes around them. The girl is drowned. John pulls her body into the boat and, with the strongbox, he floats back to the cellar. There he bounds up the stairs and into the kitchen to tell his story to his parents. After the girl's funeral the box is opened and found to contain "a *solid gold* chunk worth $10,000 enough to pay for anything but the death of his sister."²⁶ The concatenation of horrors

---

cal and Historical Essays (1843). HPL owned a separate edition of the essay (*LL* 605).]
24. H. P. Lovecraft, letter to Baird.
25. H. P. Lovecraft, "The Little Glass Bottle," *The Shuttered Room and Other Pieces* by H. P. Lovecraft and Divers Hands, compiled by August Derleth, Sauk City, Wis., Arkham House, 1959, pp. 45–46.
26. Ibid., pp. 46–47.

which he compressed into this story makes it seem like a surrealistic nightmare. Except for the sentence quoted above, the whole tone is casual, matter-of-fact, contrasting with the actual happenings, as bizarre, in its way, as a gaily colored funeral awning. The psychoanalytically predisposed may see Howard's childhood sexual fantasies being expressed in his moving through dark sinuated tunnels and wombchambers, but more significantly one may conclude that Howard was an unusually sensitive and articulate child, an intelligent one, who was compelled to tell stories at an age when the overwhelming majority of children are clumsily holding onto thick pencils and tracing the letters of the alphabet.

It was near Howard's eighth year that the first shadow of unhappiness passed over him. In early April, 1898, his father suffered a mental and physical collapse.[27] The crisis erupted in Chicago, the territory Mr. Lovecraft covered for the Gorham Company. Alone in his hotel room, he suddenly began crying out that the chambermaid had insulted him and that his wife was being assaulted on the floor above. He was finally subdued, put under sedation, and returned to Providence, where the family committed him to Butler Hospital on April 25, 1898. His condition there was diagnosed as an organic brain disease of a progressively downhill type or, as the hospital physician lists it, "general paralysis of the insane."[28] Periods of lucidity were eclipsed by hallucinations which increased in force as he descended into madness. The once handsome features of the "drummer" now became flabby, the eyes lacklustre, and the tongue coated. Paralysis of the limbs set in and with it resultant loss over bodily functions. Death occurred on July 19, 1898. He was forty-four years old. After a private funeral service two days later, he was buried in the Phillips' plot at Swan Point Cemetery, adjacent to the spacious wooded acres of Butler Hospital.[29]

---

27. [As noted (see n. 18 above), this incident occurred in 1893.]
28. In private conversation with Dr. C. H. Jones, Administrator of Butler Health Center, 333 Grotto Avenue, Providence, R.I. on December 21, 1960.
29. "Deaths," *The Providence Daily Journal* (Thursday, July 21, 1898), p. 6.

II. From Childhood's Hour

The cause of death was listed as "general paresis."[30] This fact has led some to idly wonder whether he died of syphilis. At least one writer has so speculated in public. Dr. David H. Keller (credentials unknown), psychiatrist and weird tales writer, while acknowledging in one breath that at the end of the nineteenth century "the relation between paresis and syphilis was not clearly understood," said in the next that Lovecraft Sr. "was definitely syphilitic."[31] Keller then listed three so-called axioms of medical science: (1) Cerebral insults, in men forty or younger are almost always the result of syphilis, (2) the wife of a syphilitic is a syphilitic, (3) the child of a paretic is a syphilitic.[32] Dr. Kenneth Sterling (intern psychiatrist at Columbia Presbyterian) in a rebuttal to the Keller article briefly and succinctly demolished the latter's rash assumptions. Even if one were to grant axiom one, inaccurate though it is, the other two do not follow. Modern medical investigation refutes them. Cerebral insults may as easily be due to such non-syphilitic diseases as congenital aneurysms of the circle of Willis. Concerning the second "axiom," Sterling cites J. Earle Moore's *Modern Treatment of Syphilis,* which says that the spouse may escape infection in early syphilis while in the late stage the likelihood of infection is slight. Keller's third point, based on the obsolete Colles' Law of 1837, has been dispelled by research at Johns Hopkins Hospital, among other centers, where, of 155 children of untreated syphilitic mothers, over one-third showed no evidence of congenital syphilis.[33] Keller's whole hypothesis that the Lovecraft family was venerally diseased comes from his reading too much into the expression "general paresis." Dr. C. H. Jones, the present administrator of Butler Hospital, told me that "this term back in 1898 was a

---

30. Death Certificate: Winfield Scott Lovecraft (Bk. 20, p. 262). Issued by the City Registrar's Office, Providence, R.I.
31. David H. Keller, M.D. "Shadows over Lovecraft," *Fresco,* 8, No. 3 (Spring 1958), p. 21.
32. Ibid., p. 24.
33. Ibid., pp. 27–29.

catch-all or waste-paper-basket term. It was found within the following decade that a substantial portion of the patients who displayed the general paresis symptoms did in fact have syphilis, but there are a number of other conditions which show the same set of symptoms . . . Just sitting here I could name at least twenty other organic brain diseases."[34] In the 1890s people were not being operated on for brain tumors.

Neurosurgery came out of World War I. The Wasserman Test and neuropathological techniques had not yet been developed. Mr. Lovecraft's acute torture could only be noted as "a debilitating physical disease affecting his mentality."[35] Today psychiatrists would use the general term "chronic brain syndrome," and while no more helpful than "paresis" it at least has the virtue of modernity. Because the damage of Mr. Lovecraft's reputation has already been effected by Keller and others, I feel it is important to return to primary source material to obtain a clearer view of Mr. Lovecraft, one uncolored by outdated medical theories grown preposterous. As a traveling salesman for a distinguished company, he was a protector and breadwinner for his family rather than a *roué*, that type of salesman who has become the butt of a thousand smoking car jokes.[36]

After Winfield Lovecraft's death, Howard and his mother lived on in Whipple Phillips's gray mansion. Howard's frail health spared him two of the most distasteful chores of boyhood: attending grammar and Sunday School.[37] Daily education was secured through private tutoring;

---

34. Conversation with Dr. C. H. Jones on December 21, 1960.
35. Psychiatric record of Winfield Scott Lovecraft at Butler Hospital.
36. [It is now the general consensus that HPL's father did in fact have tertiary neurosyphilis. Kenneth Sterling's rebuttal to Keller chiefly emphasized the unlikelihood of HPL himself having congenital syphilis—a point subsequently proved by a Wasserman test given to HPL upon his own entry into the hospital in 1937, which was negative.]
37. [HPL in fact attended the Slater Avenue School for the school years 1898–99 and 1902–03. He also did sporadically attend Sunday school (at the age of five and at the age of twelve).]

II. From Childhood's Hour

the moment his lessons were out of the way, Howard was free to pursue his main interest, i.e. reading, in a desultory fashion, the books in his grandfather's study. He became slightly like a character that he was later to describe in a short story:

> He was the most phenomenal child scholar I have ever known, and at seven was writing verse of a sombre, fantastic, almost morbid cast which astounded the tutors surrounding him. Perhaps his private education and coddling seclusion had something to do with his premature flowering. An only child, he had organic weaknesses which startled his doting parents and caused them to keep him closely chained to their side. He was never allowed out without his nurse, and seldom had a chance to play unconstrainedly with other children. All this doubtless fostered a strange secretive inner life in the boy, with imagination as his one avenue of freedom.[38]

A photograph of Howard at the age of eight may reveal something of a "secretive inner life"—in this case, innocent reveries of childhood. His retrospective eyes seem to see past all he looks upon.[39]

After her husband's death, Mrs. Lovecraft came to look upon her son as a poetic genius. She took excessive and absurd measures to protect him:

> On their summer vacations at Dudley, Massachusetts, Mrs. Lovecraft refused to eat her dinner in the dining-room, not to leave her sleeping son alone for an hour one floor above. When a diminutive teacher friend, Miss Ella Sweeney, took the rather rangy youngster to walk, holding his hand, she was enjoined by Howard's mother to stoop a little lest she pull the boy's arm from his socket. When Howard pedalled his tricycle along Angell Street, his mother trooped beside him, a guarding hand upon his shoulder.[40]

---

38. H. P. Lovecraft, "The Thing on the Doorstep," *The Outsider and Others*, compiled by August Derleth and Donald Wandrei, Sauk City. Wis.: Arkham House. 1939. p. 217.
39. Photograph of H. P. Lovecraft, JHL.
40. Winfield Townley Scott. "His Own Most Fantastic Creation," *Marginalia* by H. P. Lovecraft et al., collected by August Derleth and Donald Wandrei. Sauk City, Wis.: Arkham House, 1944, pp 313–14.

He opened different avenues of make-believe. He avidly read the adventures of Old and Young King Brady, Detectives, in *Secret Service*, as well as the other dime thrillers of his day.[41] Against his tame life, their daring exploits jolted his imagination and he grappled on the lawn of 454 Angell Street with invisible arch villains, oblivious to the world around him. Across the street a neighbor observed the child's frenzied antics. Some thirty years later, when asked if he knew Lovecraft, this neighbor said, "Sure I remember him. He was crazy as a bedbug. He was always playing detective."[42]

As might be expected, Howard wrote a detective story. It was called "A Dead Man's Revenge." He was nine at the time. Divided into twelve chapters, each a brief paragraph, this juvenile effort despite its brevity tells an interesting though improbable story. A Rev. Dobson, following the deathbed wish of one of his parishioners, descends into the crypt after the funeral to lay a golden ball on an indicated spot. When he does not re-appear from the tomb, King John, a famous detective, is called into the case by Dobson's daughter. A thug offers to release her father for $10,000. King John gives chase and arrests the kidnapper in the name of the queen. Rev. Dobson, meanwhile, had escaped from his captors, who had kept him in a luxurious apartment beneath the tomb. King John married the girl.[43] A handful of other stories dating from this period are to be seen at the John Hay Library.

"The Beast in the Cave," a short story which is dated April 21, 1905, is a more sustained effort than these earlier tales, being some 1,700 words in length. One naturally looks for, and finds, an improvement here over "A Dead Man's Revenge." That story was plainly a hasty imitation of the popular detective stories, where a number of

---

41. H. P. Lovecraft, *The Shuttered Room*, p. 44. [The reference is apparently to the Providence Detective Agency, formed by HPL and his friends.]
42. Winfield Townley Scott. MS. Reportorial notes, deposited at JHL.
43. H. P. Lovecraft, *The Shuttered Room*. pp. 48–52. [The story's actual title is "The Mystery of the Grave-Yard."]

II. From Childhood's Hour 33

events are indiscriminately poured onto the page. In "The Beast the Cave" there is only one situation. A man, the narrator, is separated from a party of sightseers and becomes lost in the labyrinths of the Mammoth Cave. To accentuate his plight his torch goes out. He calls for help. Footsteps approach, yet there is something unnatural about the sound, for "when I listened carefully, I seemed to trace the falls of *four* instead of *two* feet." Thinking it a wild beast, he groups some rocks around for possible missiles. The strange patter of feet draws closer. "Most of the time, the tread seemed to be that of a quadruped, walking with a singular *lack of unison* betwixt hind and forefeet." Fear conjures up hideous shapes before the narrator, almost paralyzing him. As the panting beast stops a few feet away, he hurls a sharp edged rock at the thing. The beast falls to the ground, wounded and gasping. The narrator runs screaming through the labyrinth until he meets the guide who had been searching for him. Together they return to where the beast was felled. The penultimate page describes the loathsome appearance of the beast with its snow-white hair and its rat-like claws. They watched it go through its death throes. "For a moment I was so struck with horror at the eyes thus revealed that I noted nothing else. They were black, those eyes, deep jetty black, in hideous contrast to the snow-white hair and flesh. Like those of other cave denizens, they were deeply sunken in their orbits, and were entirely destitute of iris." In the last sentence, if one has not already guessed, "The creature I had killed, the strange beast of the unfathomed cave, was, or had at one time been a MAN!!!"[44]

Lovecraft later referred to "The Beast in the Cave" as "ineffably pompous and Johnsonese," yet he did concede that in it he had "achieved a new level of results in terms of fictional structure."[45] This makes "The Beast in the Cave" a transitional story. Told in the first person, it has a sense of immediacy lacking in the earlier stories. The

---

44. H. P. Lovecraft, "The Beast in the Cave," *Marginalia*, pp. 268–75.
45. August Derleth. *H. P. L.: A Memoir,* New York. Ben Abramson, 1945, p. 10.

viewpoint and action are not dispersed but focused on the hapless narrator. The image of horror which arises and dies in the narrator's mind as he awaits the padding animal creates an atmosphere of menacing terror. It is this mood of eerie suspense, in sum, which makes a successful weird tale. The diction is self-conscious at times, a little too literary even for this genre, but the criticism "ineffably pompous and Johnsonese" is too harsh, if Lovecraft meant by it a prose style so turgid that one reads the tale with a feeling of ennui.

It is difficult to pinpoint any one source or influence behind the story. In atmosphere it suggests Poe. The description of the beast recalls H. G. Wells' description of the bleached nocturnal Morlocks of *The Time Machine* (1895), degenerate subterraneans who practiced cannibalism on the Eloi race. Whatever story or author sparked Howard to write "The Beast in the Cave," he was nourishing his imagination from sources considerably above the level of the detective thrillers.

Infant prodigies are encountered frequently in music and mathematics, in literature practically never, since experience with reality is requisite. In taking cognizance of Howard's early writings, I do not suggest that he was a "marvelous boy" who should be eased into place close to Chatterton and Rimbaud. One glance at the obvious disparity between them would make such a claim sheer silliness. I merely point with some wonderment on my part at the alacrity with which he seized the horror genre as his area for aesthetic conquest. To trick out a metaphor, one may consider these early stories analogous in many ways to the Model-T's in the history of transportation. Though contraptions, they pointed to the shape of things to come.

It is interesting to see in most of these stories that Howard, using eighteenth century orthography, carefully hand-printed them and bound the leaves as in a chapbook. The outside cover generally bore the title, author, date, price, and, at the close of the book, there was a colophon with emblem. More often than not, he signed his name H. P. Lovecraft. The "H. P." bespoke a certain maturity beyond his years or ability.

II. From Childhood's Hour

By his ninth year his interests were centered on comparative mythology. This was not a sudden delight but one which had been nurtured for some three years when he first discovered and read Hawthorne's *Wonder Book* and *Tanglewood Tales*. Later he procured a copy of Bulfinch's *Age of Fable* and gave over all of his leisure time to the reading of that text. In a modest way he began collecting small plaster casts of Greek sculptural masterpieces, and in the company of his grandfather and uncle, Howard became a constant visitor to the classical art museums of Providence and Boston. He roamed the small hills and timothy fields along the Seekonk River where he envisioned:

> fragrant templed groves, faun peopled meadows in the twilight, and the blue, beckoning Mediterranean that billowed mysterious out from Hellas into the reaches of haunting wonder where dwelt Lotophagi and Laestrygoniana, and where Aeolus kept his winds and Circe her swine, and where in Thrinacian pastures roamed the oxen of radiant Helios.[46]

Before these impossibly beautiful deities the mild Baptist faith of his mother palled. The cross could only be a symbol of torture. By the age of ten:

> I was a genuine pagan, so intoxicated with the beauty of Greece that I acquired a half-sincere belief in the old gods and nature spirits. I have in literal truth built altars to Pan, Apollo, Diana, and Athena, and have watched dryads and satyrs in the woods and fields at dusk. Once I firmly thought I beheld some of these sylvan creatures dancing under oaks; a kind of "religious experience" as true in its way as the subjective emotionalism of Christianity and of equal valuelessness from an intellectual point of view. If a Christian tells me he has *felt* the reality of his Jesus or Jehovah, I can reply that I have *seen* the hoofed Pan and his sister of the Hesperian Phaedra.[47]

His passion for Greco-Roman mythology endured. It is seen in several of the tales written in the earlier part of his career, while the roots of

---

46. H. P. Lovecraft. MS. letter to Baird.
47. Ibid. [For "Phaedra" read "Phaëthusa."]

his own mythology, the Cthulhu Mythos, which I will explore in Chapter Four, owed something to it.

In 1902 he took up astronomy. Within four years he had purchased successively larger telescopes and had purchased sixty-one books on the subject.[48] The curator of the Brown University Observatory encouraged him to use the university telescope. The world's immensity refuted man's grandiose belief in his own importance.

> By my thirteenth birthday I was thoroughly impressed with man's impermanence and insignificance, and by my seventeenth, about which time I did some particularly detailed writing on the subject, I had formed in all essential particulars my present pessimistic cosmic view. The futility of all existence began to impress and oppress me; and my references to human progress, formerly hopeful, began to decline in enthusiasm.[49]

Writing had come easily to Howard. At the age of nine he put out his own science paper, *The Scientific Gazette*, written in longhand and distributed to his chums. In addition, he wrote how-to-do-it leaflets: "A Good Anaesthetic" by H. Lovecraft, Chemist, and "Lovecraft's Manual of Explosions—10 cents." From 1903 to 1909, between the ages of thirteen and nineteen, he first hand-lettered and later hectographed the *R. I. Journal of Astronomy*. He also contribute articles on astronomy to *The Providence Journal*.[50] However much it may have shattered his youthful optimism, this scientific period left him with many fond memories. In 1926 he looked back twenty-three years and wrote:

> Incidentally—it was this very day in 1903—Feb'y 12th—(which fell, however, on *Thursday*) that I bought the very first *new* book on *astronomy* that I ever owned. It was Young's "Lessons in Astronomy" & I got it at the R. I. News Co., for $1.25. Previously I had had only Grandma's copy

---

48. Ibid.
49. Ibid.
50. [HPL never contributed articles on astronomy to the *Journal*. His articles appeared in the *Pawtuxet Valley Gleaner* (1906–08?), the [Providence] *Tribune* (1906–08), and the [Providence] *Evening News* (1914–18).]

II. From Childhood's Hour 37

of "Burritt's Geography of the Heavens." As I returned in the evening darkness on the rear platform of an Elmgrove Ave. car—415, I think it was; one of the graceful J. M. Jones cars—I looked over the pictures & the chapter headings with perhaps the most delightful sense of breathless anticipation I have ever known. Most literally a strange cosmos of new worlds lay open before me![51]

Despite a frail physique he braved the frosty nights to study the Northern heavens. By his fourteenth birthday his health improved enough to allow him to attend Hope High School. Howard's transcript does not list his rank in class standing, but the numerical grades do confirm that he was an intelligent child. His average for the first year (1904–1905) was 81, with Latin his best subject (87) and Algebra (74) his poorest. During the first year he was absent 18 days and tardy 17 days. He was withdrawn at the end of the year. He re-entered the school in September, 1906, taking a full course: English—90, Algebra—75, Drawing—85, Latin Grammar—85, Latin Texts—90, Greek Texts—85, Plane Geometry—92, Physics—95. The attendance is recorded only for the first term. It lists him absent 6 days and tardy 25 days. Reasons for sickness or tardiness were not kept. In his third year at Hope High School (1907–1908), he cut down his program to three subjects: Chemistry—95, Intermediate Algebra—85, Physics—95. Attendance was not recorded. After the first quarter he dropped the algebra. He did not return to high school again.[52] The tardy record may be explained in two ways. First, Howard lived a good walking distance from the school. An adult can cover the distance in slightly over ten minutes. A child, particularly one moving in cold weather, would take twice as long. In that case, why didn't he leave his home earlier? Sec-

---

51. H. P. Lovecraft, MS. letter to Mrs. Lillian D. Clark, dated February 12, 1926, JHL.
52. High School Transcript: Howard Phillips Lovecraft, issued by Supervising Records Clerk. Central Records Office, Department of Public Schools, Providence, R.I., AK.

ond, we know that Howard made few friends during this period. He disliked children "on account of their freakishness and their disinclination to cast their playing into coherent narrative and dramatick channels."[53] Schoolboys, moreover, are capable of cruelty.

With his interest in astronomy, Howard indulged in the fanciful notion that he stood apart from the human race. "I looked on man as if from some other planet. He was merely an interesting species presented for study and classification . . . I could not help seeing the race in its cosmic futility as well as in its terrestrial unimportance."[54] I suspect that Howard deliberately timed it so that he would arrive at school just as the bell was ringing or a little later to avoid meeting the other children in the yard. Perhaps he had been given permission to do so. If punishment had been meted out to him he would not have indulged in the habit so often.

W. Paul Cook, who came to know both Lovecraft and his mother, asserted, "I shall always believe that it was his mother and not he that was sick—sick for fear of losing her sole remaining link to life and happiness. The result on the boy could only be to make him an invalid."[55] Mrs. Lovecraft, having lost through death her sister, her mother in 1896, her husband two years later, saw her father die March 28, 1904.[56] With the death of that venerable patriarch her already delicate health underwent a further deterioration. Perhaps this latest death in the family affected her most deeply. Mr. Phillips's love and affection for her and Howard, his largess, and the security of his home were removed forever. The house was sold and the estate was apportioned to his heirs. He left five thousand dollars to each of his daughters, Mrs. Lillian D. Clark, Mrs. Annie E. P. Gamwell, and Howard's mother. To

---

53. H. P. Lovecraft, MS. letter to Baird.
54. Ibid.
55. W. Paul Cook, *In Memoriam: Howard Phillips Lovecraft*, North Montpelier, Vt., Driftwood Press, 1941, p. 10.
56. Sarah Lovecraft, *Commonplace Book*.

his grandsons, Howard, and Phillips Gamwell, he bequeathed twenty-five hundred dollars each. All the rest and residue of the estate, both real and personal, was to be distributed to these five persons, with the condition. "share and share alike to them, their heirs and assigns forever."[57] It was a substantial award, but in Mrs. Lovecraft's case it had to be stretched to support her and Howard for the rest of their lives.

Mrs. Lillian Clark was the oldest of the three Phillips daughters. She was a tall, plain looking woman. Cheerful, calm, and optimistic, there was something of the owl in her appearance with her nose crooked into a little beak with nostrils just big enough for breathing and her eyes, large and pale, staring back from rimless glasses.[58] Her younger sister Mrs. Gamwell was still an attractive woman in her early forties when Whipple Phillips passed on. She was married to a Brown University graduate who was an editor and newspaper owner. They lived in Cambridge.[59] These two ladies frequently visited Howard and his mother, who had since taken the first floor at 598 Angell Street. Within its dim interior, smelling wistfully of camphor and furniture wax, Howard's somber clad aunts took tea and sometimes helped his debilitated mother with her household tasks. And Howard, who only vaguely remembered his father, now had three mothers to coddle and pet him.

To be sure, such coddling did not instill in him the measure of self-reliance to face life fully, accept it, and make the most of it. Yet these early years had their joys. He later characterized his high school years as a time when he hated to speak to any human beings, or even to see or be seen by one. As he grew into his late teens, however, he did manage to find some companions and, as the following letter will show, he cherished these moments of comradeship throughout his life.

---

57. Will of W. V. Phillips, dated, signed, and sealed on July 2, 1903, Clarke H. Johnson, Foster County, executor, RM.
58. Photograph of Mrs. Lillian D. Clark, ca. 1905, RM.
59. Mrs. R. Morrish, MS. letter to Arthur Koki, dated March 13, 1961, AK.

In a letter dated August, 1921, he described a visit from "the best friend of my youth—Deputy Sheriff Harold Bateman Munroe." The latter called on Lovecraft and together, in Munroe's Model-T, they drove down the Taunton Pike to the old quarry once owned by Lovecraft's grandfather. Here they "embarked on a pious pilgrimage to the tomb of our dead youth—Great Meadow Hill and the old clubhouse—which we deserted eight years ago."[60] As they walked along, they wondered whether the clubhouse would still be standing.

> Through the foliage we saw the antique "chimbly" . . . thrilled at the thought that at least one memorial of the old times remained—a sort of monument or headstone of our buried youth and hopes. Then through the opening in the new-grown trees we beheld the long deserted sight that neither of us had dared expect—*the old Great Meadow Country Clubhouse intact, in all the solid perfection of the old days!* We drew near, looked long, and tried the door. Aside from a broken lock, all was as ever, for in drowsy Rehoboth even relentless time sometimes nods and lets a few years slip away undevastatingly. There had been no decay, nor even vandalism. Tables stood about as of yore, pictures we knew still adorned the walls with unbroken glass. Not an inch of tar paper was ripped off, & in the cement hearth we found still imbedded the small pebbles we stamped in when it was newly wet—pebbles arranged to form the initials G.M.C.C. Nothing was lacking—save the fire, the ambition, the ebulliency of youth in ourselves; and that can never be replaced. Thus two stolid middle-aged men caught for a moment a visitation of the aureated and iridescent past—caught it, & sighed for the days that are no more.
> On the way back—the long way over which we used to sing "Sweet Elaine," "Dreaming," and "Down in de Co'nfield"—we speculated upon the possibility of reviving the G.M.C.C. . . .[61]

---

60. [Actually, the quarry owned by the Lovecraft family was in the Manton district of the West Side of Providence. The trip in question took HPL and Munroe east, to Rehoboth, MA.]

61. H. P. Lovecraft, MS. letter to Mrs. Annie E. P. Gamwell, dated August 19, 1921, JHL.

II. From Childhood's Hour

Lovecraft tended the letter with what was to become a characteristic refrain, a nostalgic note. Speaking of Munroe, he said: "He does not miss youth as I do. For him the dull routine of adult life is perfectly adequate."

Released from high school with slim prospects of a profession, he none the less luxuriated in his new freedom, reading until dawn and sleeping through the morning. The presence of nearby Brown University, which might have symbolized in Howard's mind a missed opportunity at higher education, seems not to have worried him. "I am singularly complacent about the training that this young man did not get," he said of himself.[62] Lovecraft claimed that these early high school years had so ruined his health that further schooling was out of the question.[63] W. Paul Cook, on the other hand, theorized that Mrs. Lovecraft wanted to keep her son by her side. I accept both explanations but would further speculate that financial considerations entered into the decision to keep Howard out of college. Economy was the watchword. Mrs. Lovecraft began having delusions of impending financial disaster. Howard accepted his curtailed education philosophically, saying, "After all, a cultivated family is the best school."[64]

Dr. Franklin C. Clark, his uncle, had a great influence on him. One might consider Howard as being his intellectual heir. A graduate of the College of Physicians and Surgeons, Brown University,[65] he was also an earnest student of literature. He gave shape and consistency to Howard's reading program. When he passed on, Howard eulogized him: "His influence on me from childhood upward was very strong and any precision which my English may possess is due largely to his

---

62. H. P. Lovecraft, MS. letter to Baird.
63. [In fact, HPL regretted his failure to get a high school diploma and to attend Brown University, referring to himself as a "non-university barbarian and alien."]
64. Ibid.
65. [The College of Physicians and Surgeons is the medical college of Columbia University, where Clark received an M.D. in 1872. Clark had received an A.B. from Brown in 1869.]

training. His retiring nature kept him from wider fame ... He is one who will not easily be replaced."[66]

Lovecraft's education, in the broad sense, was strongly influenced by the neighborhood in which he lived. The College Hill section of Providence was, and continues to be, one of the few spots in America wherein the beauty of pre-Revolutionary and colonial architecture may still be seen. The Hill was first settled in 1636 by Roger Williams, the religious leader and Indian trader, who, with his followers, had been exiled for heresy from Congregationalist Salem. In 1663 Charles II granted the hardy settlers a liberal charter "to hold forth a livelie experiment that a most flourishing civil state may stand and best be maintained ... with full liberty in religious concernments."[67] The fierce Indian fighting which commenced with King Philip's War in 1675 destroyed the town, but with the close of hostilities the settlers began the arduous task of rebuilding. Eighteenth-century Providence engaged in lively trade with the West Indies and Colonies, notably in rum and molasses. Substantial brick homes began to replace wood structures. By the outbreak of the Revolutionary War, College Hill was enhanced by a number of brick and wood houses in the full tradition of Georgian architecture. Below College Hill the complexion of the city changed with factories and shops gradually spreading in both directions along the waterfront. On the hill the merchants built their large homes, severe exteriors with opulent decorations for the interior; nervous embellishments that ran riot in pedimented door heads and across woodwork.

Providence architects borrowed from England, Italy, and Greece, but the overall trend was toward simplification of design and detail. "Gothick motives" were sparingly, judiciously copied from Horace Walpole's place at Strawberry Hill and Pope's villa at Twickenham. Lovecraft's favorite architectural period, not unexpectedly, was the

---

66. George W. Macauley, "Lovecraft and the Amateur Press," *Fresco*, p. 44.
67. *College Hill: A Demonstration Study of Historic Area Renewal*, Providence, R.I., 1959, p. 21.

II. From Childhood's Hour

Georgian and Federal period (1700–1835). It had a tendency toward lightness and variety in ground plans, elevations, and decorative detail. It was succeeded by the Victorian period (1865–1900) which was in turn restrained and held in check by the pre-existing sedate architecture. It was this attention and homage to the surroundings that prevented a clash of styles. With ten architectural periods to be seen, each street became a museum.[68]

H. L. Mencken, a favorite writer of Lovecraft's, praised Georgian architecture and the age that had created it:

> The Eighteenth Century, of course, had its defects, but they were vastly overshadowed by its merits. It got rid of religion. It lifted music to first place among the arts. It introduced urbanity into manners, and even made war relatively gracious and decent. It took eating and drinking out of the stable and put them into the parlor. It found the sciences childish curiosities, and bent them to the service of man, and elevated them above metaphysics for all time. Lastly and best, it invented the first really comfortable habitations ever seen on earth, and filled them with charming fittings. When it dawned, even kings lived like hogs, but as it closed even colonial planters on the banks of the Potomac were housed in a fashion fit for gentlemen . . . The Eighteenth Century dwelling-house has countless rivals today, but it is as far superior to any of them as the music of Mozart is superior to Broadway jazz. It is not only, with its red brick and white trim, a pattern of simple beauty, it is also durable, relatively inexpensive, and pleasant to live in.[69]

Ever since Lovecraft was a child he had crossed and recrossed the streets of College Hill until he knew every foot of it intimately. With an almost proprietary eye he had viewed it at all hours of the day and night, too, with the deliquescent moon shining on the balustrades and marble steps. It pleased and excited him to learn that Edgar Allan Poe had walked on Benefit Street in 1848 when he had wooed Mrs. Sarah

---

68. Ibid., pp. 23–70.
69. H. L. Mencken, "The New Architecture," *American Mercury*, 22, No. 86 (February, 1931), p. 164. [The article is part of Mencken's editorial column for the issue.]

Helen Whitman. One day they had strolled hand in hand across College Hill to Swan Point Cemetery where, under the shade of a cypress, Poe had proposed marriage.[70]

Lovecraft's devotion to College Hill caused him blindly to despise the unfortunate people who lived along the far slopes of the area. They were mainly Negroes who had settled there after the Civil War. At the turn of the century unsightly rows of cheaply constructed three-decker tenements were thrown up. They became, almost from the beginning, slums.[71] Some families pushed up the hill's edge into single family dwellings. Either because of the merciless tactics of landlords or the indifference of the tenants, those homes deteriorated and so they stand today, as they stood for Lovecraft, their windows patched with cardboard, their shutters swinging loosely on broken hinges above weeds growing lush through neglect.

Lovecraft, who thrilled at beauty, shrank from the tawdriness of this slum area close to the finest residential homes. He saw American democracy personified in the industry which was rupturing a leisurely pattern of life. The air was poisoned with smoke and the water polluted, a problem since 1874.[72] He hankered for eighteenth century England where attention had been paid to breeding and propriety. As for that age's slums, Gin Alley at least had a gusto, a wildly exuberant quality to recommend it, if one could believe Hogarth.

Lovecraft vented his spleen. His youthful, amused contempt for the Negro and other non–Anglo-Saxon races, later to descend into depths of bitterness, is first glimpsed in some jog trotting verses scribbled out, on three slips of butcher paper, at the age of fourteen.

---

70. Frances Winwar, *The Haunted Palace*, New York: Harper and Bros., 1959, pp. 327–49.
71. *College Hill*, p. 33.
72. Ibid.

DE TRIUMPHO NATURAE

The Triumph of Nature
Over Northern Ignorance

Lines dedicated to William Benjamin Smith
Tulane University, La.
Author of
"The Colour Line"
A Brief
In Behalf of the Unborn

The Northern bigot with false zeal inflam'd
The virtues of the Afric race proclaim'd;
Declar'd the blacks his brothers and his peers,
And at their slavery shed fraternal tears;
Distorted for his cause the Holy Word,
And deem'd himself commanded by the Lord
To draw his sword, whate'er the cost might be
And set the sons of Aethiopia free.

First with the South in battle he engag'd
And four dread years an impious warfare wag'd.
Then deaf to Nature, and to God's decree
He gave the blacks their fatal liberty.
The halls where Southern justice once had reign'd
He now with horrid negro rite profan'd.
Amongst the free in curs'd mock'ry sate
The grinning Aethiop, conscious of his state.

But reckless folly can no further run;
The will of Nature must in time be done.
The savage black, the ape-resembling beast
Hath held too long his Saturnalian feast.
From out the land, by act of far'way Heav'n,
To lingering death his numbers shall be driven.
Against God's will the Yankee freed the slave
And in the act consigned him to the grave.[73]

---

73. H. P. Lovecraft, MS. "De Triumpho Naturae," dated 1905, JHL.

Although he was but a boy at the time, one cannot explain away "De Triumpho Naturae" as an isolated instance of bigotry. Further investigation in this early period reveals a number of letters and scraps of doggerel, such as:

> On the Creation of Niggers
>
> When, long ago, the gods created Earth
> In Jove's fair image Man was shaped at birth.
> The beasts for lesser parts were next design'd;
> Yet were they too remote from humankind.
> To fill this gap and join the rest to Man,
> The Olympian host conceived a clever plan.
> A beast they wrought, in semi-human figure,
> Filled it with vice, and called the thing a NIGGER.[74]

Lovecraft's staid relatives must have encouraged him to give their common attitudes "lyric" expression. Most people censor their private thoughts before speaking. Certainly Howard indiscreetly wrote his down. It is painful and embarrassing to confront this racist problem in Lovecraft, obviously, but one must recognize it as characteristic of his social class.

There was, no less significantly, a gayer side to his youthful compositions. He wrote playful, innocuous verses to cheer up his morose mother.

> Dear Mother—
> If, as you start toward Lillie's festive spread,
> You find me snoring loudly in my bed,
> Awake me not, for I would fain repose
> And through the day in quiet slumbers doze.
> But lest I starve, for lack of food to eat,
> Leave here a dish of Quaker Puffèd Wheat,
> Or breakfast biscuit, which, it matters not,
> To break my fast when out of bed I've got

---

74. H. P. Lovecraft, MS. "On the Creation of Niggers," n.d., JHL. [The poem dates to 1912.]

> And if to supper you perchance should stay,
> Thus to complete a glorious festive day,
> Announce the fact to me by telephone,
> That whilst you eat, I may prepare my own.[75]

These attempts at jocularity must have brought, at best, a weak smile from Mrs. Lovecraft, whose distracted mind played with the uncertain future. She evinced great nervous anxiety, so that the slightest physical discomfort became a crisis. A toothache would set her to shrieking.[76] Miss Clara Hess, a next door neighbor of the Lovecraft's, said Mrs. Lovecraft talked to her continuously of her unfortunate son; who was so "hideous" and "ugly" that he fled from the sight of people and avoided walking the streets during the daylight when people could stare at him.[77] The unstable, unthinking Mrs. Lovecraft may well have impressed upon her son a belief in his "hideous" appearance.

In his early twenties Howard's soft features changed slowly though perceptibly into those of Mrs. Lovecraft. His small rounded chin broadened and his lips stretched into a thin, determined line. His voice retained its soft, almost girlish pitch. Ingrown hairs vexed him. Extremely sensitive to his appearance, he preferred the sequestered life, venturing out at night when he could amble through the deserted streets of Providence and the gravel paths of St. John's Cemetery. These nocturnal walks were sweet to him, a breathing spell. With the anguish that he experienced over his mother's ailing state and his own unhappy physical condition, and worry over distant financial problems, his life by 1914, to loosely borrow a title, was a long day's journey into a night largely unwashed by human sunshine.

He did not escape his dilemma through the easy exit of anacreontic or sentimental literature. These opiates he shunned for the writings

---

75. H. P. Lovecraft, MS. "To Mother," dated November 30, 1911, 3:30 a.m., JHL.
76. In private conversation with Mrs. Muriel E. Eddy on September 11, 1960.
77. August Derleth, "Addenda to H. P. L.: A Memoir," *Something About Cats and Other Pieces,* H. P. Lovecraft, et al. Sauk City, Wis.: Arkham House, 1949, pp. 247–52.

of Poe, Hawthorne, Bierce, and those other deep though narrow geniuses who confronted the malignant aspects of existence.

Lovecraft had not yet begun to write in any serious manner, but his tastes were formed. His was not the way of so many local colorists who wrote about the "nice people" in New England towns—those towns where the snow never turns to slush and people when they die do so with as little pain and suffering as possible.

III. The Formative Years

> Nothing really matters. Imagination is an amusement which one may draw from many sources—from all the reservoir of images & illusions deposited by the massed fancies of the race & the dreams & experiences of the individual.[1]

Lovecraft spent the winter of 1913–1914 indoors sequestered like a monk.[2] It was a practice he was to follow nearly every winter. He was not bored by these confinements since there were books and papers at hand and ample time to lie fallow, which is also important to a writer.

Sometime during the winter he had written a letter which appeared in Munsey's *All-Story Weekly*, an enormously successful adventure magazine published in New York and London. In this age of "vulgar taste and sordid realism," wrote Lovecraft, it was a relief to read this magazine "which has ever been and still remains under the influence of the imaginative school of Poe and Verne."[3] He had been a reader of *All-Story*, he confided, since its beginning in January, 1905.

If, in fact, man is unable to create living beings out of inorganic matter, to hypnotize the beasts of the forest to do his will, to swing from tree

---

1. H. P. Lovecraft, MS. letter to Elizabeth Toldridge, dated May 4, 1929, JHL.
2. [In fact, HPL sequestered himself for the entire period 1908–14.]
3. *All-Story Weekly*, 29, No. 223 (March 7, 1914).

to tree with the apes of the African jungle, to restore to life the mummified corpses of the Pharaohs and the Incas, or to explore the atmosphere of Venus and the deserts of Mars, permit us, at least, in fancy, to witness these miracles, and to satisfy that craving for the unknown, the weird, and the impossible which exists in every active human brain.[4]

Toward the close of his letter to the editor, he praised the stories of Edgar Rice Burroughs, a staple commodity in the magazine, but he could not resist the temptation to point out some scientific inaccuracies—a Martian year is 668⅔ solar days, not 687 as Burroughs stated in *The Gods of Mars*; also there are no tigers in Africa.

Either through this letter or some similar minor specimen of writing, Lovecraft's name came to the attention of Edward Daas of Milwaukee, Wisconsin.[5] Daas was an enthusiastic member of the United Amateur Press Association who never lost an opportunity to enlist young writers in the movement. He explained the history and the purpose of the Amateur Press to Lovecraft.

Simply put, the Amateur Press was an institution of primarily young people all over the country who edited, published, printed, or contributed to miniature journals. These publications were exchanged free among all the members. Many of the boys were printers' devils and cub reporters who looked on the amateur journals as an aid to self-improvement and a source of pleasure.[6] Others were schoolboys,

---

4. Ibid.

5. Cook, p. 53. Lovecraft's letter to *All-Story* was signed "Your obedient servant, H. P. L. Providence." Whether Daas obtained Lovecraft's name from the Munsey office is uncertain. Cook says Daas heard of Lovecraft "in connection with some contest or other." [Daas apparently heard of HPL through the several letters and poems he wrote for the *Argosy* in 1913–14 over the merits of the romance writer Fred Jackson. These items were also signed "Providence, R.I."]

6. Mr. George W. Macauley, MS. letter to Arthur Koki, dated November 16, 1959, AK. "Both of my sons helped out a fine education by following amateur journalism thru their school days," wrote Mr. Macauley, referring to one son Charles, now teaching at UCLA, and Robie Macauley, novelist and editor of the *Kenyon Review*.

III. The Formative Years

supplementing their education. Amateur Journalism has often been described as "a miniature world of letters."[7]

It is difficult to fix the birth of unorganized amateur journalism. Almost from the inception of the printing press in America samples of work were exchanged by boys. The first known amateur journalist in America was Thomas Gray Condie, Jr., of Philadelphia, who in 1797 printed a small weekly magazine called *Juvenile Port-Folio and Literary Miscellany*. Nathaniel Hawthorne's *Spectator* (1824) was composed in pen and ink. In 1862, Thomas Alva Edison, fifteen years old, had repaired a discarded hand press for his own use. The hobby grew considerably with the sale of inexpensive presses in 1867. Probably the first effort to organize into a society came in September, 1869, with a meeting at the home of publisher Charles Scribner. His son was elected president. By 1873 two hundred boys in America printed their own papers.[8] Two years later the first official organization of amateur journalism took place when sixty-five boys gathered in Philadelphia on July 4, 1876. The National Amateur Press Association, as it was called, elected a president and officers, and drew up a constitution. From the start the NAPA was open to dissension and politics over procedures and proxy votes. Rival organizations were formed either by disappointed office seekers, by those thinking to improve upon the NAPA, or by those who were unaware that the NAPA existed. The last was particularly true in the West and Southwest.

The United Amateur Press Association was organized in 1895, having as its distinguishing feature a more literary rather than journalist makeup. Its official organ was *The United Amateur*.[9] It was not at all unusual for a young man to belong to both the UAPA and the NAPA, as

---

7. Truman J. Spencer, *The History of Amateur Journalism*, New York, The Fossils, Inc., 1957, p. 3.
8. Ibid., pp. 2-17.
9. Ibid., pp. 71–85.

Lovecraft himself did. Amateur Journalism exists to this day, though it does not enjoy the wide membership it did from 1914 to 1940. The reasons for its decline are traceable to its democratic policy of allowing almost any level of writing to appear. Anyone collecting an anthology of bad writing could find in it an impressive amount of impossibly bad verse and illogical essays. "Amateur" which connoted to the founders of the movement a writer who wrote out of love [*amo*] and not for money, became associated with the more popular connotation, a mere dabbler. Yet there were many who wrote exceptionally well.

Lovecraft's entrance into Amateur Journalism preceded the outbreak of the Great War by six months. As an Anglophile he scoffed against the Woodrow Wilson administration which had considered itself "too proud to fight." From his pen came poems describing British courage in the face of German beastliness and essays on the superiority of the Anglo-Saxon race. There is even an unsubstantiated story that Lovecraft tried to make a dramatic contribution by enlisting in the British Army when England entered the war.[10] He detested President Wilson's procrastination. Writing to one of his aunts about The Old Man of the Mountains, which she had just visited, he said it was "highly interesting, but I dislike his long chin, which reminds me unpleasantly of my own ugly visage and of the visage of a once nefarious politician named Wilton—or Wilson—or something like that—who kept his country out of war for two years and out of good sense for eight years."[11] While he continued to write bellicose verse, he included very little of it in his own publication *The Conservative*, which he edited in 1915. (The printing was handled by a commercial press house in Malden, Massachusetts.) What little poetry appeared there by him was

---

10. Scott, "His Own Most Fantastic Creation," p. 318. [This account is false. Scott has confused it with HPL's attempted enlistment in the Rhode Island National Guard in 1917.]
11. H. P. Lovecraft, MS. letter to Mrs. Annie E. P. Gamwell, dated August 19, 1921, JHL.

III. The Formative Years 53

of a pastoral sort. Some of his best smiling satire ran in *Tryout*, edited by C. W. Smith of Haverhill, Mass. (The longest continuously published Amateur journal, *Tryout* began in 1914 and ended in 1948 with Mr. Smith's death at the age of ninety-five. During those thirty-four years, three hundred numbers were issued.)[12] In February, 1917, after apologies to W. Raleigh, Esq., appeared "The Nymph's Reply to the Modern Business Man":

> If all the world and love were young,
> And I had ne'er before been "stung",
> I might enough a dullard prove
> To live with thee and be thy love.
>
> But promised "autos", Love's rewards,
> Turn out too often to be Fords;
> And though you vaunt your splendid yacht
> 'Tis but a row-boat, like as not!
>
> Your silks and sapphires rouse my heart,
> But I can penetrate your art—
> My seventh husband fool'd my taste
> With shoddy silks and stones of paste!
>
> I like your talk of home and touring;
> They savour of a love enduring;
> But others have said things like that—
> And led me to a Harlem flat!
>
> So, dear, though were your pledges true
> I should delight to dwell with you;
> I still must as a widow rove,
> Nor live with thee, nor be thy love![13]

Lovecraft called his magazine *The Conservative* to indicate his preference in literature. He wished to avoid what he considered, on the one hand, the chaotic nature of much modern writing and, on the oth-

---

12. Spencer, n.p.
13. Lewis Theobald, Jr. (pseud.), "The Nymph's Reply to the Modern Business Man," (*Tryout*, February, 1917) *The Lovecraft Collectors Library*, ed. George Wetzel, 1955, IV, 27.

er, the remnants of Victorian sentimentality. He railed against modern architecture, free verse, and the trend toward simplified spelling, which he considered one of "the most pernicious literary crimes of this unsettled age."[14] His Amateur friends, formed through correspondence, shared his conservative viewpoints. Among them was Samuel Loveman, a Cleveland poet and friend of Ambrose Bierce and Hart Crane. Loveman's ornamental style and melancholic tone dated his poetry to the Yellow Book nineties; in that period he might have achieved recognition. He was at Camp Gordon during the war when he received a flattering letter from Lovecraft. Loveman replied, letters were exchanged, and friendship established.[15] Another early correspondent was Maurice W. Moe, an English high school instructor from Appleton, Wisconsin. In 1911 Moe had won a UAPA laureateship for his essay, "Why I Am Not a Free Thinker."[16] Although an orthodox Christian, Moe and Lovecraft shared common ground in their approach to literature.

When America entered World War I, Lovecraft sat it out at home in Providence. On the margin of his "Pacifist War Song—1917," he wrote, "It is not my fault that my 'military service' was with pen rather than sword. I did my best to enlist in the R. I. National Guard in the spring of 1917, but could not pass the physical examination. Have been in execrable health—nervous trouble—since the age of two or three."[17] Further information on this enlistment episode is lacking in the correspondence deposited at the John Hay Library. Recently I came into possession of a Lovecraft letter, where, among other things, he elaborates on the quotation above and gives us the cynical attitude which he had adopted at this stage of the war.

---

14. H. P. Lovecraft, "The Simple Spelling Mania" (*United Co-operative*, December, 1918), *The Lovecraft Collectors Library*, V, 5.
15. Samuel Loveman, *Something About Cats*, p. 229.
16. Spencer, p. 120.
17. H. P. Lovecraft, MS. "Pacifist War Song—1917," JHL.

III. The Formative Years 55

Realising the utter inconsequentiality of one man more or less in this insignificant world, I lately endeavoured to justify my hitherto useless existence by ending it in the Army. Specifically, I attempted despite my frail & nervous physique to enlist in the R.I. National Guard; trusting to the sheer force of psychological stimulus to keep me alive and on my feet until a Hunnish missile might gracefully dispose of me. Since I have no actual *disease* or abnormal organs, I nearly passed the physical tests by judicious restraint in answering questions; but my mother & family physicians were finally able to frustrate my belligerent ambitions and bring about my rejection for physical disability. I presume they will do the same thing when the draft occurs; though for mine own part I think I could do much worse than quietly extinguish (if not distinguish) myself in a more or less effulgent blaze of martial glory! I am told that a week of camp life & its hardships would probably wreck my constitution forever; but who can tell until it is attempted? And besides, what is the life or health of one weakling, when thousands of sturdy & useful young men are to be killed, crippled, and disfigured in a few months? Verily, 'tis amusing to make so great a stir about a little matter like this, when in the interminable recesses of ethereal space all mankind is but a superfluous atom! My despised theories of ultimate & absolute truth are (or ought to be) quite comforting in this hour of stress & trial![18]

This same cynicism touched many between parades of furled pomp. As one historical writer put it, the Great War closed forever the "good years"—after plumbing and before taxes—bringing new problems of "preparedness, taxes, war, Bolshevism, disillusionment, depression, Fascism . . ."[19] Something of the old confidence was gone. It may have buckled on April 13, 1912,[20] when ten cent's worth of ice sank the unsinkable *S. S. Titanic.*

Not all of Lovecraft's writing during and after the war reflected despair. Much of it approached the light satire of the Augustans, but a dozen of his essays expounded his belief that the earth was part of a

---

18. H. P. Lovecraft, MS. letter to Maurice W. Moe, dated May 30, 1917, AK.
19. Walter Lord, *The Good Years,* New York, Harper and Bros., 1960, p. 342.
20. [Actually 15 April 1912.]

mechanistic universe. He plucked this string loudly, monotonously to readers who could behold World War I as an example of human folly. "Human thought, with its infinite varieties, intensities, aspects, and collisions, is perhaps the most amusing yet discouraging spectacle on our terraqueous globe,"[21] he began one article. He went on to consider the role of Christianity in European civilization. He granted that it had served in restraining the animalistic longings of the lower classes, but it had claimed excessive credit for having done so. "Christianity ... claims to have civilized Europeans; whereas in cold truth it is Europe which has civilized Christianity." While disparaging the claims of Christianity he chided the rationalist for pulling down what he could not replace. Both were to be shunned. "The spectacle of Christians and idealistic atheists in mortal combat is indeed grotesque—one thinks of such things as the battles of the frogs and the mice, or of the pygmies and the cranes." The pessimistic philosophy was preferable to the "feverish, pathological struggle and agony of the Christian mind, coping desperately with the mythical shadows and problems it has invented."[22] "A Confession Unfaith" (1920), "Nietzscheism and Realism" in 1921, "Some Causes of Self-Immolation," among other essays, elaborated on this theme.[23] It was a topic he liked to return to and play with.

There was a real connection between Lovecraft's family problems, the uncertain state of the world, and his insistent exposition of atheism. It all profoundly stirred his fiction.

Mrs. Lovecraft's steady disintegration necessitated her confine-

---

21. H. P. Lovecraft, "Idealism and Materialism—A Reflection," *The Shuttered Room*, p. 85. [Published in the *National Amateur* ("July 1919" [actually spring 1921]).]

22. Ibid., p. 94.

23. ["A Confession of Unfaith" was published in the *Liberal* (February 1922); "Nietzscheism and Realism" (extracts of letters to Sonia H. Greene) in the *Rainbow* (October 1921); "Some Causes of Self-Immolation" was written long after HPL's initial entry into amateur journalism; it dates to 13 December 1931.]

III. The Formative Years 57

ment to Butler Hospital on March 13, 1919. The hospital records, according to Winfield T. Scott, listed her as "a woman of narrow interests who received, with a traumatic psychosis, an awareness of approaching bankruptcy." The records also take note of "an Oedipus Complex, a psychosexual contact with her son."[24] "Oedipus Complex" is an oversimplified, vulgarized term. Taken out of context, as Scott took it, it is completely meaningless. It is not possible, however, at this time to look into Mrs. Lovecraft's complete mental history.[25]

From her room in the hospital, Mrs. Lovecraft sent her son notes and little gifts, and he replied with long and delightful letters about his increasing activity in Amateur Journalism.

In November of that year Lovecraft saw his short story "Dagon" published in one of the Amateur magazines, *Vagrant*. The story opens on an hysterical level. The narrator, an American merchant marine officer, is on the verge of committing suicide. He has been driven to this desperate act by an unnamed horror which he witnessed. His packet had been struck by a German sea-raider. Taken prisoner with the rest of the crew he later escaped in a rowboat and drifted aimlessly. One morning he awoke to find himself "half-sucked into a slimy expanse of hellish black mire which extended about me in monotonous undulations as far as I could see." The atmosphere was a wet blanket putrid with the stench of rotting fish. He guesses that he is on an island which has been volcanically thrown up. On the fourth day he sees a cyclopean monolith chiseled with hieroglyphics and aquatic symbols of frogs, fishes, eels, octopi. In bas-relief are depicted hideous semi-human creatures, but the narrator, not up to describing them, suggests

---

24. Scott, p. 319.
25. Mrs. Lovecraft's psychiatric record is presumably stored in one of several old files in the cellar of Butler Hospital. Sometime in the near future, according to Dr. C. H. Jones, these files will be brought upstairs, checked over, and deposited in the hospital's private library. [Susie Lovecraft's medical records were apparently destroyed.]

that they "would have excited the envy of a Doré," and that they were "grotesque beyond the imagination of a Poe or a Bulwer." That night, with the moonlight reflected on the waters surrounding the slimy monolith, the officer recounts: "Then suddenly I saw it. With only a slight churning to mark its rise to the surface, the thing slid into view above the dark waters. Vast, Polyphemus-like ... it flung its gigantic scaly arms [around the monolith] ... bowed its hideous head and gave vent to certain measured sounds. I think I went mad then." Shocked into insanity, the narrator dreams of the day when such beasts will rise above the waves and pull down the last of the puny, war-exhausted humans. "Dagon" ends with the outburst: "The end is near. I hear a noise at the door, as of some immense slippery body lumbering against it. It shall not find me. God, *that hand!* The window! The window!"[26]

The hysterical pitch which opens "Dagon" is a poor beginning. It is one which most writers avoid for the obvious reason that it is difficult to maintain beyond a few pages, and it too often destroys suspense by hinting directly at the climax. The one scene that remains in the reader's memory is Dagon fulsomely embracing the monolith.[27] His half-human figure recalls the ancient legends of abominable rites which primitives committed with animals. Dagon's counterparts are found throughout middle eastern mythology, the Babylonians, for example, having worshipped him under the name of Odacon. Despite his clumsy body he is cunning, tracing the naval officer to his hospital bed in San Francisco.[28]

Lovecraft vividly declared his disgust with all sea creatures in his fiction and in actual life. Perhaps no fact has been recorded more frequently by Lovecraftians than his detestation of fish. "He believed,"

---

26. H. P. Lovecraft, "Dagon," *The Outsider,* p. 6.
27. [It is not Dagon itself who embraces the monolith but a monstrous worshipper of Dagon (who presumably resembles that god).]
28. [HPL almost certainly intended the narrator's sight of Dagon outside his hospital window as a hallucination.]

III. The Formative Years

wrote one correspondent, "that an odd, macabre relationship existed between fish and men."[29] When a friend of his ordered a steam clam dinner, Lovecraft, in a rare display of mild profanity, withdrew, saying, "While you are devouring that *God-damn* stuff, I shall cross the street and eat a sandwich. Please excuse me."[30] These incidents can be multiplied. In attempting a possible answer one may pay reference to the psychologists, whose theories are thought provoking, to say the least. There is a case reported where a patient's fear of fish, particularly its odor and the slimy secretion if its skin was traceable through analysis to an overstrenghened fear and disgust of the semen at pollution. The psychologist calls to our attention that the fish is a gross sexual symbol used in fertility rites and in Dionysian mysteries.[31] He sidesteps it as an early Christ and Christian symbol.[32] I do not propose to search for phallic symbols behind every monument and spiral staircase.

If Lovecraft's fish phobia has become his most famous idiosyncrasy, the most quoted words of Lovecraft are:

> All of my stories, unconnected as they may be, are based on the fundamental lore or legend that this world was inhabited at one time by other races who, in practising black magic, lost their foothold and were expelled, yet live on outside ever ready to take possession of this earth again.[33]

This raises the possibility that Lovecraft had a mythology in mind from the start, as early as 1919,[34] if we stretch the meaning of "outside" to

---

29. Mrs. Muriel E. Eddy, MS. letter to Arthur Koki, dated June 30, 1959, AK.
30. E. Hoffmann Price, "The Man Who Was Lovecraft," *Something About Cats*, p. 284.
31. R. Eisler, "The Fish As Sexual Symbol," *The Psychoanalytic Review* 6, 460–64 (1919).
32. For fish symbolism in Christianity see C. R. Morey's "The Origin of the Fish Symbol," *The Princeton Theological Review* 8, 93–106 (1910); 9, 268–89 (1911).
33. H. P. Lovecraft, *Best Supernatural Stories of H. P. Lovecraft*, Cleveland and New York, World Publishing Co., 1945, p. 8. [This "quotation" is not by HPL but by Harold S. Farnese, who thought he was quoting—from memory—a passage from one of HPL's nonextant letters to him.]
34. ["Dagon" was written in 1917. It is extremely unlikely that HPL had devel-

include creatures like Dagon which hibernated in primordial slime beneath the sea. The other possibility would be that as he wrote he reintroduced material which had appeared in some of his previous stories, thus giving an overall unity to the canon of his fiction. This is by no means uncommon among supernatural story writers. R. W. Chambers in *The King in Yellow* has as a connective device a dreaded book whose perusal draws the unfortunate reader into insanity. Arthur Machen's *The Three Impostors* employs the same characters. Both books were known to Lovecraft. He once listed them as among his favorite ten stories in weird literature.[35]

Sam Moskowitz has called "Dagon" "well within the scope of present-day science fiction."[36] It would take strenuous reasoning to fit it in that category. I forgo for the moment genre definitions, except simply to say that a science-fiction story is a science-fiction story when it has some science in it; the plot is founded upon a plausible development of scientific theory. The areas of weird-fantasy and science-fiction overlap at times, but they are not synonymous.

After his debut into the fantasy genre, Lovecraft awaited the reaction of the Amateur members. Most readers were impressed with the story, but one fellow Amateur wrote in *The Transatlantic Circulator*[37] to

---

oped the notion of a pseudomythology at this time.]

35. "The Favorite Weird Stories of H. P. Lovecraft," *The Fantasy Fan* (October, 1934) p. 22. The complete list runs as follows: Algernon Blackwood, "The Willows"; A. Machen, "The White Powder"; "The White People"; "The Black Seal"; E. A. Poe, "The Fall of the House of Usher"; M. P. Shiel, "The House of Sounds"; R. W. Chambers, "The Yellow Sign"; M. R. James, "Count Magnus"; A. Bierce, "The Death of Halpin Frayser"; A. Merritt, "The Moon Pool."

36. Sam Moskowitz, "A Study in Horror: The Eerie Life of H. P. Lovecraft," *Fantastic Science Fiction Stories* 9, No. 40 (May 1960).

37. [Koki seems to imagine that the Transatlantic Circulator was an amateur magazine; in fact, it was the name of a group of Anglo-American amateurs who exchanged manuscripts and commented on them. The group was in existence around 1920–21.]

III. The Formative Years

say that while "Dagon" evoked a feeling of horror, still it was too far removed from ordinary life and people, it lacked humor or moral content and, furthermore, it appeared that Mr. Lovecraft was taking an unwholesome view of life when he allowed a fetid monster to crawl over God's fair dominions. Lovecraft welcomed this challenge. He took pen in hand and laid low his adversary in three brilliant letters. He opened by declaring that the imaginative writer such as Blake, Poe, and Lord Dunsany devoted himself to art in its most essential shape:

> It is not his business to fashion a pretty trifle to please the children, to point a useful moral, to concoct superficial "uplift" stuff from the mid-Victorian holdover, or to rehash insolvable human problems didactically. He is a painter of moods & mind-pictures, a capturer and amplifier of elusive dreams and fancies—a voyager into those unheard of lands which are glimpsed through the veil of actuality but rarely, and only by the most sensitive.[38]

He then went on to defend his view of the universe and his reasons for doubting the existence of immortality. Aware that he had been inordinately serious, that he had put too much of his inner feelings into the letters, he brought the third epistle to a close on a note of sprightly good humor.

> I am not by any means such a "solemn cuss" as Mr. W[ickenden] infers from my somewhat archaic prose style—in fact, I have an idea that my respected foe would find me almost human if dealing with me less indirectly! As proof I will enclose a page from *The National Tribute*. Note that I am capable of even a *hearty laugh* at an amateur convention.[39]

The noticeable influence of this period from 1919 to 1922 was Lord Dunsany. "Polaris,"[40] "Beyond the Wall of Sleep," "The White

---

38. H. P. Lovecraft, MS. letter to the editor of *The Transatlantic Circulator*, dated June, 1921, JHL. [The quotation in fact comes from an essay, "The Defence Reopens!" (April 1921).]
39. H. P. Lovecraft, MS. letter to the editor of *The Transatlantic Circulator*, dated September, 1921, JHL. [From the essay "Final Words" (September 1921).]
40. ["Polaris" was written in the summer of 1918, more than a year before HPL read Lord Dunsany's work.]

Ship," "The Doom That Came to Sarnath," "The Statement of Randolph Carter,"[41] "The Cats of Ulthar," "The Quest of Iranon," and "The Other Gods" are marked by Dunsanian terse sentences, dreamy atmosphere, and oriental-sounding kingdoms at the edge of the world.

"Polaris" suggests immediate parallels with Dunsany's "The Wonderful Mirror."[42] "Polaris" begins apprehensively but with no threats of imminent suicide this time. The stars with their mellifluous names are ominously described:

> glittering Cassiopeia ... Arcturus winks ruddily ... Coma Berenices shimmers weirdly afar off ... the Polar Star leers down ... winking hideously like an insane watching eye which strives to convey some strange message, yet recalls nothing save that it once had a message to convey.[43]

The narrator recalls that many years ago during the night of the Great Aurora he had looked out and beheld the city of Olathoë, located on the plateau of Sarkia, between the peaks of Noton and Kadiphonek. After a number of visits to the city as an omniscient uncorporeal presence, he takes on bodily form, but apparently his body had already existed back in this city for he is regarded as an old friend. A crisis has reached Olathoë. The squat, yellow Inuto race is moving against them. The narrator, though a scholar, has the sharpest eyesight and is sent to watch the narrow pass behind the Noton peak. Should the Inutos attempt to cross through, he is to sound the alarm. As he waits he is lulled into a 26,000-year sleep by the pale Polar Star. Now living in the present he is tormented over the possible reality of this experience. He cannot sleep when the Polar Star shines and wonders whether the Eskimos are the descendants of the dreaded Inutos.

"Beyond the Wall of Sleep" may be considered Lovecraft's first

---

41. ["Beyond the Wall of Sleep" and "The Statement of Randolph Carter" are not usually considered pastiches of Dunsany.]
42. [Koki means "The Wonderful Window," in *The Book of Wonder* (1912).]
43. H. P. Lovecraft, "Polaris," *The Outsider*, p. 7.

III. The Formative Years

science-fiction tale. The apparatus introduced is central to the story, though crudely described. This story deals with an intern in a mental hospital who succeeds in penetrating the thought process of a dying lunatic whose behavior had excited his curiosity. Fitting a special transmitter over the subject's head and a receiver over his own, the intern tunes in with his "radio" on the patient's wavelengths of intellectual energy. Weird melodies are heard and he gazes on forgotten scenes of enchanted mountains and grottoes. As the patient's life ebbs, a voice speaks to the intern:

> I am your brother of light ... You and I have drifted to the worlds that reel about the red Arcturus, and dwelt in the bodies of the insect philosophers that crawl proudly over the fourth moon of Jupiter. How little does the earth-self know life and its extent! How little, indeed, ought it to know for its own tranquility![44]

Dislocations of time and space preoccupied Lovecraft's fancy.

"The White Ship" is a Dunsanian pastiche. A lighthouse keeper is beckoned aboard a ship which transports him to lands of happiness and close to places like Thalarion where only demons and mad things walk among the bones of those who looked eidolon Lathi in the face. When their barque plunges over a cataract the captain cries, "The gods are greater than men, and they have conquered."[45] The lighthouse keeper awakes back at his post. Washed on shore is a blue bird which had led their ship, the only tangible proof of his adventures.

"The Cats of Ulthar" is a simple tale of revenge. An old cotter and his wife who had a reputation for killing cats were visited one night by a small army of felines. The next day all the cats in the village walked around sleek, fat, and purring contentedly. A week later when the cotter's house was broken into by the burgomaster, two cleanly picked skeletons were on the floor. Another early story of revenge is "The

---

44. H. P. Lovecraft, "Beyond the Wall of Sleep," *Beyond the Wall of Sleep*, p. 38.
45. H. P. Lovecraft, "The White Ship," *Beyond the Wall of Sleep*, p. 27.

Doom That Came to Sarnath." The men of Sarnath waged war on the inhabitants of Ib, whose appearance was hateful to them. The Ibians were green, soft as jelly, had bulging eyes, pouting, flabby lips, and curious eyes and were without voice. Their dead bodies were pushed into the lake and all their monuments, save one, were destroyed. One sea-green stone idol in the image of Bokrug, the water lizard, was taken away by the Sarnathians. Sarnath flourished into a metropolis. This is described in a style so close to Dunsany's as to be almost a parody:

> On the ground were the halls as vast and splendid as those of the palaces, where gathered throngs in worship of Zo-Kalar and Tamash and Lobon, the chief gods of Sarnath, whose incense-enveloped shrines were as the thrones of monarchs. Not like the eikons of other gods were those of Zo-Kalar and Tamash and Lobon.[46]

The feast celebrating the thousandth year of Ib's destruction was a thing of gaudy splendor. At the height of the revels the Ibians rose from the depths of the lake and took possession of the banquet halls. The Sarnathians fled from the city, wild-eyed, and reduced to idiocy.

In "The Doom That Came to Sarnath" the full weight of the Dunsanian influence is felt, from the minor detail of green people and green monoliths—Dunsany's favorite color which he usually embodies in demi-god statues—to the vibrant colorations of Sarnath's gardens and buildings. Done persistently it becomes self-conscious. One is reminded how W. Somerset Maugham, as a young man, went to the British Museum and noted down the names of jewels, the sensual feel of textiles and the hues of mosaics and old enamels. "Fortunately," he wrote, "I could never find an opportunity to use them and they lie there yet in an old notebook ready for anyone who has a mind to write nonsense."[47] Maugham further regretted the effect of King James Bible on speech and language:

---

46. H. P. Lovecraft, "The Doom That Came to Sarnath," *Beyond the Wall of Sleep*, p. 22.
47. W. Somerset Maugham, *The Summing Up*, New York, International Collectors Library, 1938, pp. 24–25.

III. The Formative Years 65

The plain, honest English speech was overwhelmed with ornament. Blunt Englishmen twisted their tongues to speak like Hebrew prophets. There was evidently something in the English temper to which this was congenial, perhaps a native lack of precision in thought, perhaps a naive delight in fine words for their own sake, an innate eccentricity and love of embroidery, I do not know; but the fact remains that ever since, English prose has had to struggle against the tendency to luxuriance.[48]

This luxuriance is explained in Dunsany by this diligent reading of the Scripture carried to the exclusion of newspapers and ephemeral publications. Lovecraft easily imitated the style but gave it up after 1922, returning to it briefly in 1926 for the novelette, *The Dream-Quest of Unknown Kadath*. Later in his career he acknowledged to a friend that "Dunsany is, as you say, dangerous to imitate. That was my own fatal error in 1919–20–21 as you will see from my many effusions of that time."[49]

Lovecraft had first read Dunsany in 1919, and in October of that year heard him lecture in Boston at the Copley-Plaza ballroom. "I sat in the front row," he wrote, "absorbing all the details of my new idol. He is 6 feet four inches tall, & reads his work without any of the dramatic stresses & modulations which one might expect."[50] Lord Dunsany's popularity in America was as much due to his personality as to his writings. Edward John Moreton Drax Plunkett, 18th Baron Dunsany had served with honor in the Boer War and World War I, where he was severely wounded, returning from the conflict with a glass eye—which eye, Lovecraft hastened to say in an essay, did not in the least efface Dunsany's "wholesomely and delicately handsome" face.[51] Lovecraft was also attracted to Dunsany's concept of life as by his style and figure. In his myth-making book, *The Gods of Pegāna*, Yonath, the

---

48. Ibid., p. 35.
49. H. P. Lovecraft, MS. letter to Richard Ely Morse, dated July 28, 1932. Manuscript Division, New York Public Library. Hereafter, NYPL.
50. H. P. Lovecraft, MS. letter to Robert H. Barlow, dated March 14, 1933, JHL.
51. H. P. Lovecraft, "Lord Dunsany and His Work," *Marginalia*, p. 154.

true prophet utters this final truth: "And the end and the beginning of my knowing, and all of my knowing that there was, was this—that Man Knoweth Not."[52] Such a statement is sufficiently cryptic to be variously interpreted. To one reader Dunsany was not delighting in agnosticism but rather was telling men to be humble before mystery and pay homage to ancestral wisdom. This had contemporary relevance to a world emerged from war, where there still existed "helpless and ignorant nations grown insolent with pride and power."[53] Lovecraft, on the reverse, saw Dunsany's plays and stories as a confirmation of his own nihilism. Man is a plaything of the gods, who are themselves only the dreams of MANA YOOD SUSHAI.

> Be not too wildly amorous of the far
> Nor lure thy fantasy to its utmost scope[54]

cautioned Walter de la Mare, a writer of great versatility, whose supernatural creations were studied and admired by Lovecraft. De la Mare's influence on him is not as readily discernible as Dunsany's though Lovecraft's enthusiasm for de la Mare did not diminish. He considered de la Mare's novel *The Return* (1910) one of the best efforts in the psychic vampire motif, i.e. the spirit of a dead person taking over a living body. Such tales as Poe's "Morella" and "Ligeia," Guy Endore's "Lazarus Returns," and H. G. Wells' "Dispossession" would come under this heading. Since *The Return* furnished Lovecraft with the idea for one of his earliest stories, "The Tomb," it might be well to briefly consider both.[55]

---

52. Lord Dunsany, *The Gods of Pegāna*, Boston, J. W. Luce Co., n.d., p. 53.
53. Ethel G. Sturtevant, "Dunsany on Gods and Men," *Columbia University Quarterly*, 21, No. 197 (July 1919).
54. Walter de la Mare, "The Imagination's Pride," *Collected Poems*, New York: Henry Holt and Co., 1941, p. 142.
55. ["The Tomb" was written in 1917; HPL did not read *The Return* until at least 1926. The novel may have influenced HPL's *The Case of Charles Dexter Ward* and later stories on the psychic possession theme.]

III. The Formative Years

The Return opens in the mild September afternoon with Arthur Lawford quietly strolling through an English graveyard. He pauses to read the inscription on a headstone which is set off from the other graves. It is the grave of Sabathier, a Huguenot who had committed suicide in 1739. Lawson swoons over the plot. He awakens exhilarated, full of energy, and sprints home. There he discovers in the mirror that his face has altered its features (into those of Sabathier as he discovers later) and his voice has changed its timbre. At first his wife takes him for an imposter, but when she is persuaded that he is in her husband, she is caught between deserting him or continued fidelity to this changeling whose presence will arouse gossip. She is enraged at the predicament and cannot help thinking that this metamorphosis must have come about because of some malefic action he perpetrated in the past. Even the sight of him combing his hair irritates her. "Her forehead grew suddenly cold, the palms of her hands began to ache, she had to hasten out of the room to avoid revealing the sheer physical repulsion she had experienced."[56] The rest of the novel details the struggle of Lawson's will against Sabathier's as the Huguenot's homeless spirit tries to take complete control over Lawson's mind and body. The length and leisurely pace of the book permit de la Mare a close delineation of character and inspection of motives. There are scenes of quiet tenderness between Lawson and his teenage daughter and with Grisel, whose sympathy and love for him gives him the strength to weather this crisis. After some time he regains his old appearance and we are left with the merest hint that perhaps the transformation existed only in Lawson's imagination which exercised a strong hypnotic or telepathic power over the others.

The central character of Lovecraft's "The Tomb" is Jervas Dudley, a wealthy young man, a dreamer from childhood days who spent many hours of his youth before the burial vault of the Hydes. "The abode of

---

56. Walter de la Mare, *The Return*, New York: Alfred A. Knopf, 1922, p. 116.

the race whose scions are here inurned had once crowned the declivity which holds the tomb, but had long since fallen victim to the flames which sprang up from a stroke of lightning."[57] He likes to lie down before the tomb or sniff around the padlocked door. The odor of the place at once repels yet bewitches him. He hears voices, a mélange of New England dialects reaching to the Puritans. Jervas opens the vault, inspects the coffins, and lies down in one. When he leaves the vault, his sober mien abruptly vanishes and he goes among the townsfolk "with the easy grace of a Chesterfield or the godless cynicism of a Rochester," drinking and writing jestful songs:

> Young Harry, propp'd up just as straight as he's able,
> Will soon lose his wig and slip wider the table:
> But fill up your goblets and pass 'em around—
> Better under the table than under the ground!
>   So revel and chaff
>   As ye thirstily quaff:
> Under six feet of dirt 'tis less easy to laugh![58]

Although Jervas frequently enters the tomb, his physical body is seen resting outside the tomb. The climax is a melodramatic spectacular. With lightning and thunder playing around him, he sees the old Hydes mansion rise before his eyes. An elegant eighteenth century ball is in progress when a thunderbolt cremates the house and Jervas. He awakes in the custody of two men who had trailed him under orders from his worried father. A box which was unearthed by the lightning is opened and found to contain among its contents a porcelain miniature of a certain Jervas Hyde who exactly resembles Dudley Jervas. From this it appears that the homeless, ghoul spirit had taken possession of Dudley in an attempt to force him into the tomb where he could be reunited with his ancestors.

---

57. H. P. Lovecraft, "The Tomb," *The Outsider*, p. 140.
58. Ibid., p. 144. [The song (titled "Gaudeamus" [let us delight]) was written some years before the story.]

III. The Formative Years

The Return was the catalyst for "The Tomb" but Lovecraft turned the theme to his own use. When de la Mare begins his tale, it is in light and he gives us a leading character who is a likeable, successful businessman; Lovecraft moves his story through darkness and presents us with a madman. His opening sentence is an echo from Poe's "The Black Cat": "In relating the circumstances which have led to my confinement within this refuge for the demented, I am aware that my present position will create a natural doubt of the authenticity of my narrative."[59] Jervas is a typical Poe character, wealthy and dissolute. *The Return* and "The Tomb" are fantasies in that they are not meant to be literally believed, yet *The Return* achieves plausibility in terms of the allegorical validity which clings to the story. The phenomenon of the facial change is not so difficult to accept; one almost hopes to find scientific evidence to explain it.

Weird tale literature falls into two schools. One is exemplified by de la Mare, where the horrors or supernatural occurrences are played down, hinted at, against a background of everyday life. The founder and consummate practitioner of the other is Edgar Allan Poe. Neither approach is superior to the other. If the tyro follows de la Mare and fails he becomes prolix and dull. If he fails after Poe he becomes ridiculous with his concretion of terrors. From the commercial viewpoint there are no two ways about it. Better than ninety-five percent of commercially successful fiction falls into a certain basic pattern which has as its first requirement a warm and likeable lead character—not a superman or lunatic.

In terms of bulk, the fictional works of Lovecraft in the 1917–1922 period were small compared to the rest of his writing. Most of this was non-fiction, a large part of it devoted to literary criticism. The United Amateur Press Association inaugurated a Critic's Bureau to aid members with their submissions. Lovecraft served on the Bureau, gen-

---

59. Ibid., p. 140.

erously offering his assistance. Much of his work was mechanical as he corrected spelling, punctuation, and awkward phraseology. When faced with impossibly bad poetry or prose, he offered assistance and encouragement.

In writing for the Amateur journals, Lovecraft, besides his own name, used a variety of pen names: Humphrey Littlewit, Richard Raleigh, John J. Jones, Albert Frederick Willie, Henry Paget-Lowe, Ames Dorrance Rowley, Ward Phillips, Edward Softly, Augustus T. Swift,[60] Lewis Theobald, Lawrence Appleton, and Archibald Maynwaring.[61] The use of aliases was a common practice in Amateur history; it was used as early as 1885, especially by puzzle makers of cryptograms, acrostics, and anagrams.[62]

His activity in the UAPA formed a bridge from his previous insularity to the world at large. It was not an abrupt transition since most of Lovecraft's contact with the members was through correspondence and the pages of their little journals. His letters and articles presented him in the best light before he came to actually meet some of them in person at their yearly convention.

His writing interests did not flag with his mother's confinement to Butler Hospital. He added her on his list of correspondents. In one letter he thanked her for "some small primroses ... The Weekly Review, the banana, and the most captivating cat picture, which I shall give a permanent place on the wall."[63] And yet, while he did not experience any noticeable periods of creative sterility, his fictional writing did take on a darker pessimism as he left the dream realm of Dunsany and wrote

---

60. [Augustus T. Swift is not a Lovecraft pseudonym but an actual individual living in Providence, R.I., who wrote two letters to the *Argosy* in 1920 praising the work of Francis Stevens.]

61. George T. Wetzel, "The Research of a Biblio," in *H. P. Lovecraft: Memoirs, Critiques, & Bibliographies*, ed. George T. Wetzel, North Tonawanda, New York, 1955, p. 44.

62. Spencer, p. 137.

63. H. P. Lovecraft, MS. letter to Mrs. W. S. Lovecraft, dated February 24, 1921, JHL.

III. The Formative Years

steadily in the Poesque tradition. An only child, babied by his mother, who saw in him a poetic genius, it was impossible that he could remain unaffected by her unhappy condition. There was little to cheer about in the world, too. These anxieties he released into his stories.

Much of the material for these stories came from reading other writers in the supernatural horror genre. Various ideas for possible story plots came to him at all hours of the day; he put them into small notebooks which he kept on him. He was subject to nightmares and these gave him something to think about during the day. One story from this early period, "The Statement of Randolph Carter," is an almost literal transcription of a dream which he had on the night of December 29, 1919.[64] In the dream he was Randolph Carter while the poet Samuel Loveman played the part of Harley Warren.[65] Both men in the story are scholar occultists. Warren is in possession of a malevolent book in Arabic script[66] which furnishes the location for an opening to the underworld. He makes the descent while Carter remains above ground with a telephone hookup. Far below, Warren is assailed by fiends which defy all description. He screams out to Carter to close the opening and leave, but Carter is reluctant to abandon his friend. Warren's voice is cut off and after a pause another voice is heard. From the description of the sound it made one may imagine it to have been some sort of protoplasmic glob—"the voice was deep; hollow; gelatinous; remote; unearthly; inhuman." It calls up to Carter over the telephone: "You fool, Warren is DEAD!"

"The Statement of Randolph Carter" was published in *The Vagrant*,

---

64. [The dream probably dates to early to mid-December 1919, as HPL had already written the story when he wrote about the dream in a letter to Rheinhart Kleiner (27 December 1919).]
65. H. P. Lovecraft, MS. letter to Elizabeth Toldridge, dated October 1, 1929, JHL.
66. [The book "was written in characters whose like I never saw elsewhere"—and the narrator was familiar with Arabic, so the book could not have been written in that language.]

May, 1920. Not all of his early tales saw immediate publication. The Poesque "Arthur Jermyn," though written in 1920, was not published until 1924 when it appeared in the April issue of *Weird Tales*.[67] The story begins apocalyptically. "Science, already oppressive with its shocking revelations, will perhaps be the ultimate exterminator of our human species . . ."[68] It chronicles a history of scholarship and insanity in the Jermyn family. The last survivor of this English family, Sir Arthur, set fire to his clothing when he learned that his great-great-great-grandfather had married a white ape princess in the Congo. The reader suspected as much since the Jermyns had marked simian characteristics. Lovecraft was again drawing on the belief that some primitive men in wild orgiastic rites had committed bestiality, giving rise to such monsters as Dagon and the Abominable Snowman, whom the white apes here suggest. Another aberration theme which Lovecraft came to use was the compulsion toward cannibalism in some individuals. "The Picture in the House" (1920) is impaired by a clumsy ending, but his description of the area around the town of Arkham, modeled after Salem, is a minor tour de force where melody, foreboding atmosphere, and mood coalesce to present a scene which might have left Poe's hand.

> But the true epicure in the terrible, to whom a new thrill of unutterable ghastliness is the chief end and justification of existence, esteems most of all the ancient, lonely farmhouses of backwoods New England; for there the dark elements of strength, solitude, grotesqueness and ignorance combine to form the perfection of the hideous.
>
> Most horrible of all sights are the little unpainted wooden houses remote from travelled ways, usually squatted upon some damp, grassy slope or leaning against some gigantic outcropping of rock. Two hundred years and more they have leaned or squatted there, while the vines have crawled and the trees have swelled and spread. They are almost hidden now in lawless luxuriances of green and guardian shrouds of shadow; but

---

67. [It had previously appeared in the amateur journal the *Wolverine* (March and June 1921).]
68. H. P. Lovecraft, "Arthur Jermyn," *The Outsider*, p. 121.

III. The Formative Years 73

the small-paned windows still stare shockingly, as if blinking through a lethal stupor which wards off madness by dulling the memory of unutterable things.[69]

It is in such a house that the narrator takes refuge during a storm. The owner of the place is an old, senile gentleman who relishes looking at Pigafetta's *Regnum Congo,* an illustrated account of Africa. With intemperate pride the old man gazes on a plate showing a cannibal butcher shop with limbs and quarters hanging on the walls. His voice now almost a low, husky whisper, the old man is oblivious to the raging storm, so engrossed is he with the prints. At the peak of the storm a tiny drop of blood splatters from the floor above onto the open book. At that instant the story ends for "A moment later came the titanic thunderbolt of thunderbolts; blasting that accursed house of unutterable secrets and bringing the oblivion which alone saved my mind."[70] Of all possible endings this is the least satisfactory. Was the narrator struck insensible by a thunderbolt? Probably. But what of the house and the old man? The story may have ended with a struggle taking place between the two after the discovery of dripping blood, or the narrator might have fled and brought the police to the house.

By early 1921 Mrs. Lovecraft's condition at the asylum had worsened. Lovecraft's letters to her steered clear of any unpleasantries. He had heard that Brown University's drama group was planning to stage a few productions at Butler Hospital and he hoped they might present something by Lord Dunsany. "Not *those kind,* here, dear," she penciled in the margin. In that same letter he described a banquet of the United Amateur Press Association which he attended in Boston. Everything went smoothly, "Even the face was almost at its best." He had bought a new suit for the occasion. "The excellence of my attire permitted me to be absolutely unconscious of my appearance—to forget that I was

---

69. H. P. Lovecraft, "The Picture in the House," *The Outsider,* p. 127.
70. Ibid., p. 131.

visible, as it were—which is the secret of all enjoyment in public." He gave a speech entitled "Amateur Journalism: Its Possible Needs and Betterment," in which he urged expansion of the present literary board and the exercising of greater selectivity in accepting manuscripts for publication. He was painfully aware that there were too many interlopers in the Association who could neither write nor evaluate stories in any intelligible fashion. He backed up his belief by referring to his favorite period, the eighteenth century:

> All brilliant periods of literature have corresponded with the existence of dominant coteries . . . down through the ages to the coffee house circles of Dryden and Addison and the literary club of Dr. Johnson. In truth, the ideal of utter democracy in the arts is a false and misleading one.[71]

His talk evoked "fairly thunderous applause," and five people told him afterwards that his was the best speech of the evening. "Probably my freedom from embarrassment, which Houtain said was unusual in one who had never addressed a banquet before, was due to that immaculate suit." Then, referring to the Providence store[72] where he had purchased his suit, he said: "To think I owe my post-prandial triumph to a set of Jews! . . . Pardon the egotism which doubtless animates this narration—I thought the incident might interest you since such a role is so diametrically opposite to my usual scheduled routine." Toward the end of the banquet, he was called upon to join in some singing, but "Anglo-Saxons, however, have a sense of fitness and dignity; and I gently declined the insistent invitation."[73]

According to Winfield T. Scott, Lovecraft did not visit his mother during her final illness.[74] He was, says Scott, "a fearful and selfish young man. But it was not his fault. His mother had herself to

---

71. Manuscript, JHL.
72. [I.e., The Outlet, founded by Joseph and Leon Samuels.]
73. H. P. Lovecraft, MS. letter to Mrs. W. S. Lovecraft, dated February 24, 1921, JHL.
74. [What Scott meant was that HPL did not go into Butler Hospital itself when visiting his mother. Instead, he met her on the grounds.]

III. The Formative Years

thank."[75] Just how Scott knew that Lovecraft avoided seeing his mother is not explained. The fact that he wrote letters to his mother does not mean that these took the place of visits. He was growing into an active letter writer from his work with the UAPA, ready to write letters for the slightest reasons.

Mrs. Lovecraft died on May 24, 1921, at the age of sixty-three. She was buried beside her husband at Swan Point Cemetery. Her mental condition is not recorded on the death certificate. Cause of death was a kidney disease, cholecystitis cholangitis.[76]

It is difficult to know how much Mrs. Lovecraft meant to her son. It is not to be denied that she did much in his early years to cast him into the young man he was. There is nothing, to my knowledge, in the John Hay correspondence to show that he was disconsolate over her death. But a few days after her death, Frank B. Long, Jr. received a letter from Lovecraft which began, "Although I have always prided myself on my coldly scientific, detached position in life, I nevertheless feel strangely moved and saddened. Yesterday my mother died." "Of course he was genuinely heartbroken," said Long, "but it was part of his pose not to show it. He played the role of stoic right to the end."[77]

If her passing grieved him and left a void in his life, that void was quickly filled by the keen interest he took in Amateur Journalism. Even before her death he had publicly stated what Amateurdom had done for him:

> This is a case in which overstatement would be impossible, for Amateur Journalism has provided me with the very world in which I live. Of a nervous and reserved temperament, and cursed with an aspiration which far exceeds my endowments, I am a typical misfit in the larger world of endeavour, and singularly unable to derive enjoyment from ordinary mis-

---

75. Scott, p. 328.
76. Death Certificate: Sarah Susan Lovecraft (Bk. 27, p. 158) Issued by the City Registrar's Office, Providence, R.I.
77. From private conversation with Frank B. Long, Jr. on January 25, 1961.

cellaneous activities. In 1914, when the kindly hand of Amateurdom was first extended to me, I was as close to the state of vegetation as any animal well can be—perhaps I might best have been compared to the lowly potato in its secluded and subterranean quiescence. With the advent of the United I obtained a renewed will . . . and I found a sphere in which I could grow and feel that my efforts were not wholly futile . . .

What Amateur Journalism has brought me is a circle of persons among whom I am not altogether an alien—persons who possess scholastic leanings, yet who are not as a body so arrogant with achievement that a struggler is frowned upon.

What Amateur Journalism has given me is life itself.[78]

The year after his mother's death his first story for a professional magazine was published in *Home Brew,* which proclaimed itself "America's Zippiest Pocket Magazine." It was edited by George J. Houtain and his wife. He was a flamboyant Brooklyn lawyer whose enthusiasm outdistanced his literary judgement. As an active member and officer in the UAPA he roped in several members to contribute to his new publication: Lovecraft, James F. Morton, Jr., Rheinhart Kleiner, and later Frank B. Long, Jr., among others.[79] The magazine quickly fell into a stereotype. The first issue containing the editorial "Let Us Be Serious For A Moment—Is Prohibition a Flat Failure?" appealed to Government to make good on prohibition enforcement or repeal the Eighteenth Amendment. This topic was raised in every issue. Blue laws, KKK, the efficacy of monkey glands, and movie gossip were played up. There were titles which belied the bland puerility of the articles ("Boudoir Talks with the Girls," "Why I Love Wild Women," "The Scandals of Broadway") and the equally callow vignettes of Josiah Pitts Woolfolk, better known as Jack Woodford. Woodford had not yet found his mark writing about "dainty and desirable" nymphomaniacs who had

---

78. Quoted from a February 1921 speech. Taken from the pages of an amateur publication, *The Boy's Herald*, Western Springs, Ill., 1937, JHL. [The speech was titled "What Amateurdom and I Have Done for Each Other."]

79. In private conversation with Frank Belknap Long, Jr. on January 25, 1961.

"narrow hips ... perfect breasts, with pink ornaments erect."[80]

All in all it was a strange magazine for abstemious Lovecraft professionally to appear in. The first installment of his "Herbert West—Reanimator" appeared in the first issue of *Home Brew* in February, 1922. The story is a variation on the Frankenstein theme and as such it may be considered a science-fiction tale, albeit the "science" is incidentally described. We have our earnest, mad scientist in the person of Herbert West, "a small, slender, spectacled youth with delicate features, yellow hair, pale blue eyes, and a soft voice,"[81] who has made a nuisance of himself at Miskatonic University where he has been trying with only brief success to revive dead animals through chemical solutions. Nevertheless, he feels he is ready to move on to humans. The grave of a recent drowning victim is opened and the corpse brought to an isolated farmhouse which serves as West's clandestine laboratory. A solution is injected into the cadaver's arm. After three quarters of an hour it rouses up and emits some hellish sounds which sends West and his faithful assistant running into the night. In their haste a lamp is upset. Next morning the paper relates that the old farmhouse burned down; elsewhere it notes that a new grave showed signs of disturbance. This troubles West who had patted the mound smooth. In Chapter Two, "The Plague-Demon," West attempts the same experiment, this time using Dr. Allan Halsey, dean of Miskatonic, who succumbed to an epidemic which raged through Arkham. But this experiment also fails since the body is not quite fresh enough. The brain cells had been damaged. Dr. Halsey escapes and before he is captured kills fourteen victims, chewing some of them beyond recognition. In Chapter Three the subject for the experiment is Buck Robinson, "The Harlem Smoke," killed in a boxing match. He too revives and escapes. When he returns, West empties his revolver into Robinson, now reduced to

---

80. Jack Woodford, *Unwilling Sinner,* New York: Woodford Press, 1952, p. 186.
81. H. P. Lovecraft, "Herbert West—Reanimator," *Beyond the Wall of Sleep,* p. 59.

"a gigantic misshapen thing . . . glassy-eyed, ink-black apparition nearly on all fours, covered with bits of mould, leaves, and vines, foul with caked blood, and having between its glistening teeth a snow-white, terrible, cylindrical object terminating in a tiny hand."[82]

The fourth victim is a "heaven-sent gift," a salesman who conveniently drops dead from a heart attack in front of West's door. He is restored to life long enough to scream out "Help! Keep off, you cursed little tow-head fiend—keep that damned needle away from me!" before collapsing into dissolution.[83] World War I offers a rich field for Dr. West's experiments. His magnum opus comes when a surgeon major is decapitated in an airplane crash. The major, who had secretly studied the theory of reanimation under West, proves an admirable specimen with his splendid nervous system, West sets eagerly to work

> in a room full of classified charnel things, with blood and lesser human debris almost ankle-deep on the slimy floor, and with hideous reptilian abnormalities sprouting, bubbling, and baking over a winking bluish-green spectre of dim flame in a far corner of black shadows.[84]

Mercifully his malpractices cease and something approaching poetic justice is achieved when West's past victims, led by the major (replete in uniform and wax head) pounce on Dr. West and tear him to pieces.

Most stories suffer in retelling, but no injustice is done to "Herbert West—Reanimator," one of Lovecraft's least successful stories, perhaps even his worst story, excluding, of course, the juvenilia. Since the story appeared in six installments each episode ended on a climax and this tedious repetition on a theme diluted any possibility at horror. After the first chapter the events in the preceding episodes were recapitulated, and this accretion slowed the tale. The science in the story was of the elementary cookbook sort with syringes and vats filled with

---

82. Ibid., p. 67.
83. Ibid., p. 69.
84. Ibid., p. 72.

pulpy reptilian tissue, never ascending to the Gothic romance school. It is in the diction that the story falls badly, disastrously as the just-cited quotation shows. Chaucer in "The Knight's Tale" spoke of knights who "Up to the ancle foghte they in hir blood," but he was employing exaggeration which was characteristic of the saga and the romance. Lovecraft's precedent here was bad popular writing. He too often failed to appreciate the tremendous control which lay beneath the surface of Poe's best writing, a difficult writer, by all odds, to emulate, and one whose poetical style and learning make it hard to place him in the American tradition, however influential he may have been on Hayward, Aiken, Cabell, and, if Levin is correct, Faulkner.[85] There may have been something, after all, in Simms' advice to Thomas Holley Chivers:

> Poe, who wrote in jerks & spasms, only, & in intervals of passion or drink, contended for fugitive performances. This was his excuse & apology, only, for his own shortcomings. Do not allow his errors to wreck you as they did himself. Give him up as a model & as a guide. He was a man of curious genius, wild & erratic, but his genius was rather curious than valuable—bizarre, rather than great or truthful.[86]

Lovecraft did not produce any noteworthy stories in 1922, but he did enter a period of increased social activity. Travel for the first time in his life became important. In August, Alfred Galpin, Jr., an Amateur, invited Lovecraft to come and spend a month with him at Cleveland, Ohio. Lovecraft went and thoroughly enjoyed himself meeting some of his correspondents. Galpin was an undergraduate at the University of Wisconsin. He first began corresponding with Lovecraft in 1917 while an English student of Maurice W. Moe's. Lovecraft wrote him "coyly paternal" letters under the nickname of Grandpa Theobald. When they met face to face Lovecraft's shy reserve evaporated and his

---

85. Harry Levin, *The Power of Blackness,* New York, Vintage Books, 1960, p. 160.
86. *The Letters of William Gilmore Simms,* ed. Oliphant, Odell, Eaves, Columbia, South Carolina, South Carolina Press, 1958, III, 170.

personal warmth and conversation eased from Galpin's mind the initial shock of Lovecraft's appearance, "the strange half dead, half arrogant cock of his head weighed down by his enormous jaw, the rather fishy eyes belied by his animated and friendly manner when he began to speak—but with what a strange high-pitched voice!"[87] Besides Galpin, Lovecraft was also met by Moe, George Kirk, and Samuel Loveman, who introduced his friend Hart Crane to him. The two were apparently polite though not cordial to each other. Lovecraft, who was a luminary in the United Amateur's world, had his small circle of admirers—a fact which must have impressed the cigar smoking Crane not at all. During this visit Lovecraft's health perked up. He was

> free from melancholy . . . look so well that I doubt if any Providence person would know me by sight! I have no headaches or depressed spells—in short, I am for the first time being really alive & in good health & spirits. It's the companionship of youth & artistic taste that keeps one going![88]

There was so much to see and do in Cleveland that he couldn't find time to answer all the mail that had been forwarded to him. "This may be an appropriate time," he wrote to his aunt, "to get rid of about twenty uninteresting correspondents!" Lovecraft also began to take an interest in music—an art that he had referred to as his "only aesthetic blind-spot."

> I am learning to appreciate music—Galpin has given me a record of a Chopin nocturne . . . which was especially potent in evoking imaginative images. Tonight, Galpin, Crane, I, & a fellow I have not yet met are going to a concert held in the museum building. Great Days![89]

The following month, September, 1922, found Lovecraft stopping over in New York City to visit a few Amateur members with whom he

---

87. Alfred Galpin, "Memoirs of a Friendship," *The Shuttered Room*, pp. 194–195.
88. H. P. Lovecraft, MS. letter to Mrs. Lillian D. Clark, dated August 9, 1922, JHL.
89. Ibid.

III. The Formative Years

had been corresponding.⁹⁰ One of these was Mrs. Sonia H. Greene. She was a large handsome woman of Junoesque appearance who had come to America from Russia as a little girl, had been married at the age of sixteen, widowed seven years later, and now had a daughter and a position as a hat designer in a fashionable Fifth Avenue store. She was seven years older than Lovecraft.⁹¹ The two had met the previous year at a Boston convention of the Amateur Journalists. Mrs. Greene, recalling that meeting, said of Lovecraft, "I admired his personality but, frankly, first, not his person."⁹² But the initial reserve was expunged by their subsequent correspondence and the articles which Lovecraft sent to her Amateur paper, *The Rainbow*.

Lovecraft stayed on in New York for a month. His letters, long and bubbling over with enthusiasm, were filled with information about his New York friends, Frank Belknap Long, Jr. James F. Morton, and Rheinhart Kleiner. He described his trips to the museums, the zoo, and his favorite intellectual pursuit, examining fine Colonial houses and other antiquarian sites. He also enjoyed browsing through secondhand book stores for a bargain:

> Am going to write you presently—but just now I can't resist bragging about the book bargain secured yesterday—Ovid's Epistles in black letter, printed in *1567*, when Shakespeare was only 5 years old, for only $2.00!⁹³

Something more than casual friendship toward Lovecraft began to stir within Mrs. Greene's breast. When he asked her, "How can any woman love a face like mine?" she replied, "A mother can, and some who are not mothers would not have to try very hard."⁹⁴ If "Grandpa

---

90. [HPL had first visited New York in April 1922.]
91. Davis, MS., p. 14.
92. Sonia H. Davis, "Lovecraft As I Knew Him," *Something About Cats*, p. 234.
93. H. P. Lovecraft, postcard to Mrs. Lillian D. Clark, dated September 26, 1922, JHL.
94. Davis, *Something About Cats*, p. 236.

Theobald" was aware of Mrs. Greene's affection, his correspondence to his aunts gives no clue. He admired her for her financial success and her ability to enter easily into the workaday world and become a part of it. "Mrs. Greene and her hats," he wrote, "Good profits—just now she's getting $60 for a couple whose raw material costs only $20. Forty simoleons for labour which isn't in the least repulsive."[95]

In that same letter we find a passage which was typical of Lovecraft's attitude toward the racially mixed population of New York City. We have already seen several examples of his race bigotry, but the following quotation is significant in that it prophesied, pathetically so, the anguish and rage that New York was later to inflict upon him.

> We had made an engagement to visit McNeil in his Hell's Kitchen studio, and in due time we proceeded to keep it.
> Hell's Kitchen is the last remnant of the ancient slums—and by ancient I mean slums in which the denizens are not sly, cringing foreigners; but "tough" & energetic members of the superior Nordic stock—Irish, German, & American. The slinking Dago or Jew of the lower East Side is a strange furtive animal . . . It was odd to see slums in which the denizens are Nordic . . . with shapely faces, & often light hair & blue eyes.

Lovecraft took leave of New York and returned to Providence. Mrs. Greene wrote to tell him how much she missed him, and "His appreciation of this led us both to more serious ground."[96] They continued to correspond daily.

Owing to pressures in his business life, William B. Dowdell resigned in November, 1922, from the presidency of the National Amateur Press Association and the Executive Judges appointed Lovecraft in his place. According to Truman Spencer, the Shakespearian scholar and indefatigable biographer of the Amateur movement, "President Lovecraft, excelled by no President in intellectual power, laid great

---

95. H. P. Lovecraft, MS. letter to Mrs. Lillian D. Clark, dated September 29, 1922, JHL.
96. Davis, p. 237.

III. The Formative Years

stress upon the literary side of amateur journalism and sought diligently to arouse a spirit of honest, intelligent criticism of the work of author and editor."[97] He was not greatly interested in recruiting as much as improving the existing group. Twenty-seven new members were secured during his seven month term and forty-six issues of Amateur journals appeared. In his farewell message he reaffirmed what he considered their goal to be:

> Our primary purpose, if we are to claim a place of unique merit in the world, must be to promote artistic self-expression for its own sake. I believe every effort should be made to keep the National to its proper goal of aesthetic and intellectual encouragement.[98]

The work of the UAPA and NAPA, plus his almost daily letters to Mrs. Greene cut into his professional short story writing, although he did not consider himself a professional in 1923. That year he wrote four stories: "The Lurking Fear,"[99] "The Rats in the Walls," "The Unnamable," and "The Festival." "The Lurking Fear" was serialized in four installments in *Home Brew*. In suspense it was an improvement over "Herbert West—Reanimator," although he still wrote of "nocturnal darkness ... pitchy darkness."[100] The theme was rich enough for future variations.

The deserted Martense Mansion atop Tempest Mountain in the Catskills is haunted by an unknown lurking fear which stalks from its lair when there is thunder. Once this unseen monster wiped out a hamlet of squatters who lived near the mansion. The investigator who tells the story sleeps at the mansion one night with two assistants. He is awakened by a shriek to find both men gone. A shadow of a name-

---

97. Spencer, p. 70.
98. Ibid. [The quotation is from "The President's Annual Report" (*National Amateur*, September 1923).]
99. ["The Lurking Fear" was written in November 1922.]
100. H. P. Lovecraft, "The Lurking Fear," *The Outsider*, p. 247.

less monstrosity on the fireplace chimney flits and disappears. The narrator next calls on Arthur Munroe, a reporter, and the two minutely explore the deserted village. Overtaken in the late afternoon by a storm, they find shelter in a deserted cabin. Munroe peers out of the window when lightning flashes nearby. After a time, when Munroe fails to leave the window, the narrator turns him around and discovers "Arthur Munroe was dead. And on what remained of his chewed and gouged head there was no longer a face."[101] After this episode, the narrator feels that the Lurking Fear is the ghost of Jan Martense, who was murdered by his family in 1762. The narrator bases his feeling on local tradition and research into the Martense family history. He digs in Martense's grave. "God knows what I expected to find."[102] Finding a tunnel beneath the coffin, he crawls along it with his pocket light and inches up against a thing with claws and eyes. A lightning bolt at that moment providentially heaves the narrator above ground. Where another would have fled this region, the narrator, at the risk of unhinging his sanity completely, is possessed with "a mad craving to plunge into the very earth of the accursed region, and with bare hands dig out the death that leered from every inch of the poisonous soil."[103] Further prowling shows the Martense property to be honeycombed with weird molehills. At night a lightning storm calls forth the occupants—dwarfed, deformed ape-like creatures. The shrieking horde rushes along, some sucking the juices from twisted roots while the stragglers are killed and eaten by their species. The narrator shoots one. He notes that it has one eye blue, the other brown, a characteristic of the old Martense family. A few days later the burrows and their inhabitants are exterminated with dynamite charges.

Included in the story is a history of the Martenses' degeneration

---

101. Ibid., p. 248.
102. Ibid., p. 250.
103. Ibid., p. 252.

III. The Formative Years

from their early solitude in the Catskill region, where they brooded and heard voices in the thunder. They intermarried with the menial class on the estate. Insane, cannibalistic, living underground, every descendant of a once proud Dutch family, in less than two hundred years, regressed to "a filthy whitish gorilla thing with sharp yellow fangs and matted fur."[104] The Martense clan living on to old age and corruption suggests that other story of protracted life and woe, Huxley's *After Many a Summer Dies the Swan* (1939) and the Fifth Earl of Gonister. The manner in which the Martenses dispatched their victims, by chewing up their hearts, is a motif which Lovecraft, with apparent fondness, often uses in his stories. It touches the fear of violent death, yes, and mutilation, disfigurement, and obliteration of identity as well, but the power of this motif may also reside, in part, in another area: in certain primitive aggressive tendencies not entirely shed by moderns—the child who invariably munches off the head of his animal crackers, first; or, the frequency with which the head is singled out in expressions denoting passion, anger, and hostility these are but two tame examples.

Cannibalism and atavism are also the subject for Lovecraft's next short story, "The Rats in the Walls." This title writes Peter Penzoldt is not a choice one because it suggests that rats haunt the castle. Thus it appears to reveal too much to the reader. Penzoldt submits M. R. James' "The Rats" as a better title since it leaves more play for the reader's imagination.[105] James, of course, was a master at this, viz., "After Dark in the Playing Fields" and "Oh, Whistle, and I'll Come to You, My Lad." Lovecraft did not trouble over titles since "The Rats in the Walls," like most of his later tales, appeared in *Weird Tales* magazine, which was given to major supernatural horror stories. The readers automatically expected something beyond the tameness of rodents in the wainscoting. While I agree with Penzoldt that a catchy title

---

104. Ibid., p. 254.
105. Peter Penzoldt, *The Supernatural in Fiction*, London: Peter Nevill, 1952, p. 13.

would have enhanced Lovecraft's stories, I believe he overstates his case when he writes, "The title of any piece of literature is unfortunately largely responsible for its success or failure. If we know nothing of a book, the title determines whether we shall buy it."[106] Many famous books have as title the plain homely name of hero or heroine.

The prosaic titled "The Festival" has the narrator visiting the land of his Puritan ancestors in Arkham, Massachusetts to take part in a festival which is held once every century at Christmas. An old man in Puritan garb leads him into a church, down a crypt, and through catacombs "maggoty with subterraneous evil."[107] There is a conclave of hybrid winged creatures whose appearance suggests but does not approximate crows, vampires, bats, and decomposed human beings. These creatures, among other horrors, unnerve the narrator into attempting suicide. He flings himself into a greasy underground river. At dawn he is pulled out half frozen in Kingsport Harbour. He recalled seeing a copy of Abdul Alhazred's *Necronomicon* at his guide's house. He asks permission to look at the copy owned by Miskatonic University in an effort to riddle out his nightmare. In the *Necronomicon* he reads:

> For it is of old rumour that the soul of the devil-bought hastes not from his charnel clay, but fats and instructs *the very worm that gnaws;* till out of corruption horrid life springs, and the dull scavengers of earth wax crafty to vex it and swell monstrous to plague it. Great holes secretly are digged where the earth's pores ought to suffice, and things have learnt to walk that ought to crawl.[108]

The nature of the creatures is akin to the soft, pasty night watchman in R. W. Chambers's "The Yellow Sign" who, apparently dead for months, decays into a putrescent heap.[109]

---

106. Ibid.
107. H. P. Lovecraft, "The Festival," *The Outsider*, p. 135.
108. Ibid., p. 137.
109. [HPL didn't read *The King in Yellow* until 1927.]

III. The Formative Years

"The Festival" reintroduced items which had been incidentally mentioned in previous stories. Besides a lengthy quotation from the *Necronomicon*, we learn a little about the history of this strange book of unholy incantations, namely that Olaus Wormius translated it into Latin. Arkham is modeled after Salem in general features. It lies across the bay from Marblehead, which Lovecraft called Kingsport in his stories. He drew maps laying out the street plan of Arkham.[110] It does not correspond with the streets of actual Salem, except in having a harbor to the north. Lovecraft also gave Arkham a large university, Miskatonic, while, of course, Salem has nothing of the kind. Lovecraft saw Salem as the seat of weirdness. It was more redolent of the sinister than any other part of the United States. Here the lugubrious colonists settled between the eating sea and the dark green woods. Repression and fear festered. "To me there is nothing more fraught with mystery & terror than a remote Massachusetts farmhouse against a lonely hill," Lovecraft wrote. "Where else could an outbreak like the Salem witchcraft trials have occurred?" he asked.[111] The power he had in vividly depicting the brooding New England landscape came from direct sense experience.

In May, 1923, he went visiting Newburyport and Salem. Early American architecture and furniture had ever been a source of aesthetic enjoyment to him. These locales also gave him background for his tales of horror. In his treatment of setting he went beyond Poe. In a letter to one of his aunts he described laconically but vividly an incident which occurred when he knocked at the door of a splendid brick house of Colonial design which had arrested his attention.

> My summons was answered simultaneously by two of the most pitiful and decrepit-looking persons imaginable—hideous old women more sinister than the witches of 1692, and certainly not under 80. For a moment I believed them to be Salem witches in truth; for the peculiarly sardonick

---

110. Lovecraft's plan of Arkham (photograph), *Marginalia*, p. 279.
111. H. P. Lovecraft, MS. letter to Elizabeth Toldridge, dated October 9, 1931, JHL.

face of one of them, with the furtive eyes, sneering lips & a conspicuously undershot lower jaw, intensify'd the impression produced by their incredible ages . . . utterly nondescript bundles of brownish rags form'd their attire. The "ell" in which they dwelt was in a state of indescribable & dreary squalor; with heaps of rags, books, cooking utensils, & the like on every hand . . . what a study they would both have made for a Poe, a Baudelaire, or a Goya! . . . Yes, it was the old, old New England story of family decay & aristocratick pauperism—a case like that of the poor Salem Nicholses, but infinitely worse.[112]

In July, Mrs. Greene came to Providence and the two went on an outing to Narragansett Pier and Point Judith. They were together again in Boston in November. There was still no indication from Lovecraft that he was contemplating marriage. He was not in a financial position safely to do so.

Lovecraft undertook ghostwriting and revision work in a modest way to supplement his allowance. Most of his clients had met him through the Amateur organizations. One person who contracted him was David V. Bush. And here began Lovecraft's strangest literary alliance, more incongruous than his writing for *Home Brew*. Looking more like a bouncer with his bald pate, tiny bright eyes, and prognathous jaw jutting defiantly, David V. Bush lectured extensively across the United States on the power of positive thinking. Working from Bush's lecture notes and suggestions, Lovecraft ghost-wrote these platitudes, anecdotes, and scraps of popular philosophy into books and pamphlets which enjoyed brisk sales. In the preface of most of them Bush apologized if his writing was not a literary masterpiece, but he was eager to bring these works before the public with all speed. The titles of some of them give us an idea of this man's scope: *Psychology of Sex: How to Make Love and Marry, Spunk, Character Analysis, The Law of Vibration and Its Uses, Applied Psychology and Scientific Living*. Bush was a kind of Geritol for those tired white haired, dyed haired ladies who crowd the matinee

---

112. H. P. Lovecraft, MS. letter to Mrs. Annie E. P. Gamwell dated May 1, 1923, JHL.

III. The Formative Years

theatres every afternoon. Successful love and gracious living. If we are to believe Bush, he was a Christlike figure healing the sick. A crippled woman was brought before him. World famous surgeons had failed to help her but the act of Bush laying his hands on her leg did the trick and "She threw down her crutches and walked."[113] He took all sickness as his province. From "A" (Any Specific Disorder) to "W" (Worry) no distress was too great. Cancer could be cured by prayer as well as bed wetting—"You will sleep dry tonight, rest in peace and be dry in the morning."[114]

In his inspirational, sentimental, patriotic, and didactic verses Bush out-guested Edgar Guest. The bulk of this was fortunately published before Lovecraft was hired. What could Lovecraft have done with alteration-defying verses like "Work and Sweat," "Grit Your Teeth and Bear It," or, if I may include one stanza from my favorite, "Though You're Struggling in the Cellar You Can Climb Up to the Top"?

> There's an elevator running
>   From the cellar to the top,
> And the man who may board it—
>   Here it comes—now on its hop!
> There'll be stops to make a plenty;
>   There'll be floors that "floor" you oft;
> But the man with grit and gumption
>   In the end will mount aloft![115]

For reasons which have not been clearly explained to my satisfaction, Lovecraft quite suddenly married Mrs. S. H. Greene. One may facetiously suggest that he became infected with David V. Bush's grit and gumption philosophy. The money he was earning from revision work helped to bolster his confidence, of course. Besides working with

---

113. David V. Bush, *Applied Psychology and Scientific Living*, St. Louis, Mo.: David V. Bush Pub., 1913, p. 44.
114. David V Bush, *Affirmations and How to Use Them*, Chicago, Ill., 1923, p. 81.
115. David V. Bush, *Inspirational Poems*, St. Louis, Mo.: David V. Bush Pub., 1921, p. 55–56. [HPL probably did revise this book.]

Bush, he was doctoring manuscripts for would-be poets and aspirants of slick magazines. "The Temple," "The Picture in the House," "The Hound," "Arthur Jermyn" in late 1923 and early 1924 were sold to *Weird Tales* magazine, a pulp magazine of overall mediocrity paying low wordage rates but one promising to be a ready market place for his stories. Through *Weird Tales* he ghostwrote "Imprisoned with the Pharaohs" for Harry Houdini.

Samuel Loveman thought Lovecraft had married Mrs. Greene out of a sense of obligation for the interest and encouragement she took in his work. Frank Belknap Long, Jr. said Lovecraft believed it befitted a proper gentleman to take a wife.[116] In a small way he may have been attracted by her name, a distinguished one in Rhode Island. It was Lovecraft's grandfather, half a century earlier, who had chosen this name for a rural Rhode Island town. There was even, coincidentally, an S. H. Greene & Sons Corporation at Clyde, Rhode Island which, after one hundred years of business, declared bankruptcy and passed into temporary receivers on February 21, 1924.[117]

On March 2, 1924, Lovecraft made the move to New York and the next day he and Mrs. Greene were married. In his autobiographical letter to Baird (February 3, 1924), he had referred to "the coming spring when finances will decree a final disintegration landing me in all probability in New York." He also mentioned that Mrs. Greene had taken some of his manuscripts to a Miss Tucker, editor of a publication called *The Reading Lamp*. Miss Tucker had been enthusiastic and had suggested something about a "reviewing proposition" for Lovecraft. Perhaps this happy prospect of a steady writing position gave him that extra ounce of confidence to migrate to New York and get married.

It is important to remember that that lengthy autobiographical let-

---

116. In private conversation with Samuel Loveman on September 14, 1959, and Frank Belknap Long, Jr. on January 25, 1961.
117. "Century-Old Firm Fails," *New York Times* (February 22, 1924), p. 25.

III. The Formative Years

ter to Baird was written exactly one month before his marriage. For a man who was soon to become a bridegroom, a protector, and breadwinner, the tone of the whole letter was a singularly negative one. "I no longer desire anything but oblivion," wrote Lovecraft one month before his marriage, "and am thus ready to discard any gilded illusions or accept any unpalatable fact with perfect equanimity . . . Happiness I recognize as an ethereal phantom whose simulacrum comes fully to none and even partly to but a few, land whose position as the goal of humanity is a grotesque mixture of farce and tragedy." More surprising is the fact that his "nearly six-foot, chalk-white Nordic type—the type of the master-conqueror," as he referred to himself, was to marry a Jewess and live in a city with a teeming, mixed population.

On March 2, 1924, after having stayed up all the previous night typing the manuscript of the story he had ghostwritten for Houdini, Lovecraft set out for New York, only to lose the typescript en route. On March 3, 1924, he and Mrs. Greene were married. In a letter to Frank Belknap Long, Jr. he described the event:

> I am glad the Big Event didn't make you faint! Analysts, I presume, might have foreseen it in the growing congeniality of the United's President and Official Editor; but even the most gradual evolutions seem sudden when their ultimate results become manifest. The projected move to New York . . . discussion . . . and lo! That becomes finally precipitated which must have been years in a slow unconscious preparation! We thought we'd give the world a knockout, so didn't tell a soul—not even my aunts—till it was all over and we were about to depart for Philadelphia on a Colonial honeymoon. Later came the notifying, the approval of both of Grandpa's daughters, and the happily coincidental visit of Mrs. Gamwell to friends in Hoboken, N.J., which puts her very much in touch with us here. You'll see her Sunday, Sonny, if you're a good boy and come over! Grandpa means to settle here and do some cash-corralling in local pastures unless—as a subsequent paragraph will develop—a thunderbolt comes out of WEIRD TALES' office and lands me in ugly, modern, crassly repellent CHICAGO . . . damn the possibility.
>
> The traditional felicity of approaching matrimony was considerably alloyed by a heavy worry of a wholly unconnected nature. What worry, you ask? I'll shed light . . . and impart the sad news that I LOST, just be-

fore taking the New York train, the entire typed manuscript of my Houdini story . . . My Gawd! Think of the rush-typing done . . . and now all the fruits thereof were gone! It remained, then, for me to get the thing retyped somehow . . . Thus on my wedding morn, I hastened to the READING LAMP office, where Miss Tucker was damn generous in letting me use the whole stenographick force in one mad effort to replace the lost text. No use—before it was half done, the hour for more momentous steps had arrived and I had to meet the bride-elect in the final license-ring rush . . . The license stuff! Dead easy! We beat it to the Brooklyn borough hall and got the papers with all the coolness and *savoir faire* of an old campaigner . . . you ought to have seen your old Grandpa, Sonny! Brigham Young annexing his 27th, or King Solomon starting in on the second thousand had nothing on the Old Gentleman for languid fluency and casual conversation! Then we prepared for the historical spectacle of the execution—hopping a taxi and proceeding at once to the place de la Guillotine.

And what was that place? Why, Sonny, how can you ask such a question of an old British Colonial ever faithful to His Majesty, King George the Third! Where was it that Richard Lord Howe, Admiral of His Majesty's fleet worshipped from 1776 to 178.3—and where H.R.H. the Prince of Wales (later the Prince Regent and finally King George IV) was a communicant whilst a midshipman with the fleet? Where, indeed, can one find most strongly Old Theobald's traditional and mythological background—a background intensified by the marriage of his parents in Boston's venerable St. Paul's? Yes, Sonny—of course you guessed it! St. Paul's Chapel, Broadway and Vesey Streets, built in 1776, and like the Providence 1st Baptist design'd after St. Martin's-in-the-Fields. GOD SAVE THE KING! I'll give you a booklet of the place if you want it.

In the Church's parsonage we hunted up the resident curate, Father George Cox, who upon inspecting the license was more than willing to perform the soldering process. Having brought no retinue of our own, we availed ourselves of the ecclesiastical force for purposes of witnessing . . . With actors thus arranged the show went off without a hitch. Outside, the antient burying ground and the graceful Wren steeple; within, the glittering cross and traditional vestments of the priest—colourful legacies of OLD ENGLAND's gentle legendry and ceremonial expression. The full service was read; and in the aesthetically histrionick spirit of one to whom elder custom, however intellectually empty, is sacred, I went through all the various motions with a stately assurance which had the stamp of antiquarian appreciation if not pious sanctity. Your Grandma, needless to say, did the same—and with an additional grace. Then, fees,

III. The Formative Years

thanks, congratulations, inspection of Colonial pictures in Father Cox's study, and farewells! Two are one. Another bears the name of Lovecraft. A new household is founded!

We had intended to depart for Philadelphia at once, but the fatigue of the preceding heavy programme prompted us to defer this melilunar pilgrimage till the morrow. Tuesday afternoon, after changing the name card in the door of Parkside and notifying the tradesmen of the new cognomen, we did get started for the Quaker City; leaving from the magnificently ROMAN Penn, Station . . . Arriving at the Broad St. Station about 6 P.M., we stopt at the Robert Norris Hotel—a new but reasonable hostelry which performs the marvel of harmoniously combining a Gothic exterior with a Colonial interior. Signing the register "Mr. and Mrs." was quite easy despite total inexperience. Being obliged to get that damned Houdini manuscript done instantly, we finished the evening at the only publick stenographer's in town which was then open—that at the Hotel Vendig, where for a dollar we obtain'd the use of a Royal machine for three hours. Grandma dictated while Grandpa typed—a marvelous way of speeding up copying. She had the absolutely unique gift of being able to decipher the careless scrawl of my rough MS.—no matter how cryptically and involvedly interlined.

The next day "we saw Philadelphia right" by rubberneck bus—folder and views are enclosed. That evening we had to do typing again at the Vendig truly a most practical and industrious honeymoon—and at length we drifted back to N. Y. with the finished MS.[118]

Mrs. Lovecraft's account of their marriage and honeymoon in *Something About Cats* agrees with her husband's here. Having discussed this phase of their life, she must have been aware that readers would inwardly ask whether she had consummated her marriage with this strange man, this Outsider, who never felt at home for lack of a powdered periwig and a lace-trimmed coat. Mrs. Lovecraft deflected this query in oblique fashion by stating that after they had finished typing the Houdini manuscript they were "too tired and exhausted for honeymooning or anything else."[119]

---

118. H. P. Lovecraft, MS. (typescript carbon copy) to Frank Belknap Long, Jr., dated March 21, 1924, JHL.

119. Davis. p. 239.

And thus began Lovecraft's New York exile. It was the period, according to some of his friends, in which the often selfish, finicky young man of these letters was "tried in the fires" to emerge "pure gold."[120]

---

120. Cook, p. 15.

IV. A Protracted Season in Hell

> "By the way, do you have any of Lovecraft?"
>
> "Is that a sex book?"
>
> Lantry exploded with laughter. "No, no. It's a man."
>
> She riffled the file. "He was burned, too. Along with Poe."[1]

Mrs. Greene's courtship and marriage to Lovecraft seems to have had all the daring and precision of a well-executed chess game. We cannot record the opening moves exactly since their correspondence seems regrettably to have been destroyed.[2] Enough can be learned from other sources to suggest that she played her part with aplomb, drawing out this reluctant suitor, checking, and checkmating him, much to his friends' surprise.[3]

It was recently suggested to me that Lovecraft was tricked or embarrassed into matrimony. When he had stopped over in New York to visit Mrs. Greene, she kept him talking until the morning hours. When he got up to leave, she persuaded him to sleep over, she in her bed and he upon the sofa. When they awoke that afternoon, Mrs. Greene was very upset at what the neighbors might think of a casual acquaintance

---

1. Ray Bradbury, "Pillar of Fire," *Planet Stories* 3, No. 46 (Summer 1948).
2. Mrs. Sonia H. Davis, MS. letter to Arthur Koki, dated March 11, 1961, AK.
3. Rheinhart J. Kleiner, "A Memoir of Lovecraft," *Something About Cats,* p. 221.

sleeping with her. He could only make amends to her injured pride by acquiescing to marriage. The story of this ruse, if my source is correct, came from Lovecraft himself. A good man is hard to find by all accounts so one need not be too critical of Mrs. Greene in search of a gentle mate.

In the early stages of their friendship Lovecraft gave her a book which he admired tremendously. It was George Gissing's *The Private Papers of Henry Ryecroft*.[4] I wonder what she made of this extraordinary book in praise of solitude, English flora, English weather, and cooking? Of statements like: "The truth is: do not much enjoy anything nowadays which I cannot enjoy alone"?[5] Or, further on: "I have always been too self-absorbed; too critical of all about me; too unreasonably proud. Such men as live and die alone, however much in appearance accompanied"?[6] One critic expressed the common reaction to this book when he wrote: "Read cold, as it were, without reference to the author, it can scarcely be anything but repellent."[7] Yet Lovecraft chose to present Gissing's dream as his own calling card. If you really want to know how I feel and think, read this; you may not enjoy it, or me, but then I have given you fair warning, Lovecraft was in effect saying to Mrs. Greene. During their honeymoon in Philadelphia he must have had occasions to echo *Ryecroft* in praise of the honest workmanship of early architecture with our present day "complicated machinery . . . destroying all simplicity and gentleness in life."[8]

Like Ryecroft, who had settled down to a comfortable life after hack writing, Lovecraft expectedly entered New York, pinning his future bliss on a joyous wife with a bank account.

---

4. Davis, p. 242.

5. George Gissing, *The Private Papers of Henry Ryecroft*, New York, E. P. Dutton, 1927, p. 131.

6. Ibid., p. 149.

7. Walter Allen, *The English Novel*, New York, E. P. Dutton, 1958, p. 343.

8. Gissing, p. 203.

IV. A Protracted Season in Hell

When their honeymoon came to a close, Mr. and Mrs. Lovecraft returned to 259 Parkside Avenue. Lovecraft awoke the next morning to face the task of finding work. Mrs. Tucker, for one, had offered to see if she could find him a writing position with some magazine chain. There was also the possibility of working for *Weird Tales*,[9] though the thought of moving to Chicago was distasteful to him.

> This I can hardly contemplate without a shiver—think of the tragedy of such a move for an aged antiquarian just settled down to enjoy the reliques of venerable New-Amsterdam! SH [Mrs. Lovecraft] wouldn't mind living in Chicago at all—but it is Colonial atmosphere which supplies my very breath of life. I would not consider such a move, big though the proposition would be if genuine, without previously exhausting every effort of rhetorick in an effort to persuade them to let me edit at long distance.[10]

He did not flatly reject the *Weird Tales* proposition. He vacillated. He made several tries on his own, visiting employment bureaus, waiting for long periods of time, hours sometimes, to speak with employers. A sorry business at best. The morning was spent at job-hunting. The afternoon he kept for culture: "Stopped off at another museum! ... What's the use of living in a big town if you don't use the advantages thereof? I mean to soak up all the artistic and scientific stuff this burg has to offer."[11]

A few days later, on September 14, 1924, Hart Crane, now living in New York, in a letter to his mother and grandmother commented on the peripatetic Mr. Lovecraft:

> Dear Grace and Grandma: I have just come back from a breakfast with Sam [Loveman], and he has left to spend the rest of the day with the widow of Edgar Saltus (whom you must have heard him talk about enough to identify) I have been greeted so far mostly by his coattails, so

---

9. [HPL appears to have been offered the editorship of *Weird Tales*.]
10. H. P. Lovecraft, MS. letter to Mrs. Lillian D. Clark, dated March 21, 1924, JHL.
11. H. P. Lovecraft, postcard to Mrs. Lillian D. Clark, dated September 10, 1924, JHL.

occupied has Sambo been with numerous friends of his ever since arriving; Miss Sonja Green (sic) and her piping-voiced husband, Howard Lovecraft (the man who visited Sam in Cleveland one summer when Galpin was also there), kept Sam traipsing around the slums and wharf streets until four this morning looking for Colonial specimens of architecture, and until Sam tells me he groaned with fatigue and begged for the subway!"[12]

On September 18, 1924, an editor from *Weird Tales* came to New York to speak to Lovecraft. A new magazine in the horror genre was planned and Lovecraft was to be its New York editor. His salary of forty dollars a week would soon be sent to him. He was calm, free at last, he supposed, from the annoyance of answering advertisements. But the proposed horror magazine never materialized.[13] Why? Lovecraft did not say. A lack of self-assurance or ambition may be suspected. One is again reminded of his credo: "I shall never amount to anything because I don't care enough about life and the world to try. Heigho!" It is significant that on this very same September 18th—a day full of promise Lovecraft again took refuge from reality and wrote from an art museum: "Am at the Metropolitan! Eternal beauty! To immerse oneself in its strongest solution, & grow drunken with its poignant intensity is the only way for a man of taste & sensitiveness to forget life & reality, & postpone the hour of self-sought oblivion!"[14]

Here note should at last be taken of Mrs. Lovecraft's daughter, a strange, enigmatic girl, voiceless, faceless, nameless, she is never mentioned by Lovecraft for all his copious letters. His wife refers to her child only twice; once to say that the girl was nineteen at the time of Mrs. Lovecraft's marriage to Lovecraft;[15] the second time to say that

---

12. Hart Crane, *Letters*, ed. Brom Weber, New York, Hermitage House, 1952, p. 187.
13. [In fact, J. C. Henneberger, former owner of *Weird Tales*, had proposed that HPL edit a humor magazine, the *Magazine of Fun*.]
14. H. P. Lovecraft, postcard to Mrs. Lillian D. Clark, dated September 18, 1924, JHL.
15. Sonia H. Davis, MS. "The Private Life of Howard Phillips Lovecraft," 194-, n.p., JHL.

IV. A Protracted Season in Hell

the daughter later served as Paris correspondent for several newspapers.[16] The girl had an independent, headstrong temper equal to her mother's. Three or four months after her mother's second marriage, she moved out.[17] None of Lovecraft's friends with whom I have spoken know of her present whereabouts. She could, if located, undoubtedly tell something about the Lovecrafts' early marital life.[18]

Six months of marriage and job-hunting had swiftly passed by leaving the Lovecrafts worried over the future. Finances were low. Mrs. Lovecraft left, or lost, her job on Fifth Avenue, but she quickly found another. Lovecraft returned to the drudgery of answering "those beastly advertisements."[19] Harry Houdini, in a letter to him, offered to assist him in finding a position on his return to New York, promising to put him in touch with "someone worthwhile."

He was still revising and ghostwriting for David V. Bush. He despised Bush and said so in his letters, calling him "that eternal pest,"[20] and "one of my dumbest revisionist clients."[21] He opposed the positive Bush, who so glibly taught others to sing hosannas before their burning houses. Bush could be especially silly in an effort to be daring. He would give septuagenarians a chance to revel in their desiccated flesh by advising them to spend at least an hour each day in the sun's rays, nude—"even if it is not customary in your house to go undressed." The conclusion of this exercise is to get down and crawl on hands and knees along the floor.[22]

---

16. Davis, "Lovecraft As I Knew Him," p. 237.
17. In private conversation with Samuel Loveman on November 5, 1960.
18. [Sonia's daughter Florence (1902–1979) later married John Weld and became a well-known journalist in New York.]
19. H. P. Lovecraft, MS. letter to Mrs. Lillian D. Clark, dated September 30, 1924, JHL.
20. H. P. Lovecraft, MS. letter to Mrs. Muriel E. Eddy, dated July 21, 1924, JG.
21. H. P. Lovecraft, MS. letter to Elizabeth Toldridge, dated October, 1932, JHL.
22. David V. Bush, *How to Put the Subconscious Mind to Work,* Chicago: David V.

The revision tasks out of the way, Sundays, for Lovecraft, became a day of letter writing:

> A day of gloom & nerves—more advertisements to answer. It has become such a psychological strain that I almost fall unconscious over it! Monday I went in vain to a publishing house, whither I was sent by one of the agencies I had consulted, and later visited other agencies—with as little result. After that, to get the taste out of my mouth, I made another lone exploration trip; this time covering the entire length of Colonial Hudson St., where some marvellous houses & corners still lurk unimpaired.[23]

There can be no doubt but that these first six months of marriage and family responsibilities were among the most trying in Lovecraft's life. Accustomed from boyhood to a life of relative seclusion and leisure, he was ill-prepared for this new role which called for so radical an alteration of his character. After September his efforts to find employment nearly ceased, though he did occasionally compose long letters requesting interviews. Rheinhart Kleiner, one of his closest friends, aptly described them as "the sort of letters a temporarily straitened English gentleman might have written in an effort to make a profitable connection in the business world of the day before yesterday."[24] A brief excerpt from one of these letters will illustrate this:

> Dear Sir—
> If an unprovoked application for employment seems somewhat unusual in these days of system, agencies, and advertising, I trust that the circumstances surrounding this one might help to mitigate what would otherwise be obtrusive forwardness. The case is one wherein certain definitely marketable aptitudes must be put forward in an unconventional manner if they are to override the current fetish which demands commercial experience and causes prospective employers to dismiss unheard the application of any situation-seeker unable to boast of specific profes-

---

Bush Pub., 1924, pp. 378–79.
23. H. P. Lovecraft, MS. letter to Mrs. Lillian D. Clark, dated September 30, 1924, JHL.
24. Rheinhart Kleiner, pp. 225–26.

IV. A Protracted Season in Hell

sional service in a given line...⁲⁵

And so the letter continued for six hundred words.

In October of 1924, Mrs. Lovecraft was suddenly taken ill with gastric spasms. She was rushed to the hospital where Lovecraft visited her the next afternoon before leaving for a downtown tour of the bookstalls with Kleiner and Samuel Loveman. He knew now that with the breadwinner ill they would have to give up their Parkside apartment, but, as he bragged to his aunts, "being of haughty & imperial instincts, I will proceed to play blithely on the lyre whilst Rome burns."[26]

Mrs. Lovecraft left the hospital after two weeks. On November 10th, Lovecraft accompanied her to Somerville, New Jersey, where she was to enter a rest home. He then proceeded on to Philadelphia to continue his explorations of the Quaker City. "I am entranced beyond words!" he cried jubilantly, "I must stay over another day." The colonial atmosphere, the leisure and good breeding which he seemed to find there, reminded him of his own Providence and, conversely, increased his rancor against New York:

> I regretted the departure, for Philadelphia has an atmosphere peculiarly suited to an old gentleman like me. None of the crude foreign hostility & under breeding of New York—none of the vulgar trade spirit & plebeian hustle. A city of real American background—an integral & continuous outgrowth of a definite & aristocratic past instead of an Asiatic hell's huddle of the world's cowed, broken, inartistic, & unfit. What a poise—what a mellowness—what a character in the preponderantly Nordic faces![27]

The Lovecrafts expected to move to less expensive quarters by December first. His wife sold her piano and most of her books and

---

25. H. P. Lovecraft, MS. undated, JHL.
26. H. P. Lovecraft, MS. letter to Mrs. Lillian D. Clark, dated November 4–6, 1924, JHL.
27. H. P. Lovecraft, MS. letter to Mrs. Lillian D. Clark, dated November 17, 1924, JHL.

furniture, while Lovecraft had his own family belongings packed and placed in storage; it was another strain on their budget, but he was loath to sacrifice anything that reminded him of Providence.

Although the imminent breakup of the household was uppermost in his mind, he did not cease writing fiction. He read aloud one evening, to several of his friends, his recently completed "The Shunned House." The story was enthusiastically received and he was gratified. "I'm glad my style isn't going to seed; for writing, after all, is the essence of whatever is left in my life, & if the ability or opportunity for that goes, I have no further reason for—nor mind to endure—the joke of existence."[28]

In writing this macabre tale, Lovecraft looked back to Providence. In the story, the house with its conspicuous cellar is described with sufficient clues so that a reader may with a little sleuthing find the actual house to be 135 Benefit Street. It was on this street, as Lovecraft tells us in the beginning of the story, that Edgar Allan Poe walked while courting Mrs. Helen Whitman.

The story relates a curious series of deaths which occurred in the grim house. Legends told of smoke from the chimney curling into ghoulish shapes. The narrator's uncle, Dr. Whipple, put into his hands notes which he had made while investigating the histories of the families who had lived there. This immediately immerses Lovecraft in his favorite device of weaving out genealogies which here cover half the story. From this recitation, a pattern emerges of healthy people falling sick and anemic, raving before a monster invisible to others and, most curious, crying out in bursts of French even though they had no previous knowledge of that language. Tracing back into the history of the area, the narrator and his uncle discover that a French Huguenot, Etienne Roulet, and his wife had lived and were buried on the site of the house. Etienne, a secretive, swarthy creature who spent his time

---

28. Ibid.

IV. A Protracted Season in Hell

"reading queer books and drawing queer diagrams,"[29] had been grudgingly accepted into the Providence community during the time of the Salem witchcraft panics of 1690. The evidence mounts that the ghoul-monster of the malefic Frenchman has been rising from the cellar ground to feed off the hapless tenants, drawing out their breath and blood and leaving them like crushed husks. The monster, grown into "a kind of semi-putrid congealed jelly,"[30] is destroyed, but not before it has taken the life of Dr. Elihu Whipple.

"The Shunned House" is one of Lovecraft's best stories; a consistency of tone is maintained and suspense upheld as the story recedes into the past before the forward shift in time and the confrontation of the monster. Frank B. Long Jr. said the story is "so far removed in theme from our familiar world of radios and politicians and adding machines that it does not touch, at any point, the ancillary stream of modern writing."[31]

Since the weird tale is removed from our everyday world, it requires, if it is not to collapse into messy ludicrousness or obscenity, the author's utmost discretion. "The Shunned House," as in no previous Lovecraft story, is richly embroidered with circumstantial details. Dr. Whipple apparently was suggested by Lovecraft's real uncle, Dr. Franklin Chase Clark. The actual house I have noted before, though it may be interesting to add that nearby St. John's Cemetery, founded by "elect" Episcopals in 1722, has, among its graves, the grave of the famous French Huguenot Gabriel Brenon entombed under the nave of the chapel of the church.[32] The Huguenot in the story is Etienne Roulet whom the narrator connects with one Jacques Roulet (either they

---

29. H. P. Lovecraft, "The Shunned House," *The Outsider*, p. 155.
30. Ibid., p. 162.
31. H. P. Lovecraft, *The Shunned House*, pref. Frank B. Long, Jr., Athol, Massachusetts, Recluse Press, 1928.
32. *History of Providence County Rhode Island*, ed. Richard M. Bayles, New York, W. W. Preston & Co., 1871, 293.

were relatives or the same person is not clear) who "in 1598 was condemned to death as a daemoniac but afterward saved from the stake by the Paris parliament and shut in a madhouse." A victim of lycanthropy, "he had been found covered with blood and shreds of flesh in a wood, shortly after the killing and rending of a boy by a pair of wolves."[33] This werewolf episode may strike the reader as bizarre and out of keeping with the preceding narration so calm and circumstantial. Yet the story of Jacques Roulet has its basis in fact. There was in 1598 a French peasant by this name who, believing himself a werewolf, tore a boy to pieces. He was captured and charitably committed to an asylum.[34] The account is given in John Fiske's *Myths and Myth Makers*, a book owned by Lovecraft,[35] though he does not refer to it by title in his story, saying instead that he gleaned the story from a book of "morbid horror which tells of the creature Jacques Roulet, of Caude," and so on.

It is Fiske in *Myths and Myth Makers* who elaborated on these cases of lycanthropy and cannibalism in Western Europe. Popular folk tales discounted, the numerous records of such acts of perversity are so adequately documented that they cannot be argued away. The relevance of these cases to us lies in pointing out in vivid and horrible fashion how delicate growing civilization is, where even among landscapes of pastoral calm or urban complexity arpeggios of cruelty explode.[36] The whole phenomena of sickness in the midst of health, atavism in families and races fascinated Lovecraft. He had described it in all the stories written after his Dunsany period.

Excellent as "The Shunned House" is, it was not immediately accepted for publication. Lovecraft hoped to have it published separately

---

33. "The Shunned House," *The Outsider*, p. 155.
34. John Fiske, *Myth and Myth Makers*, Cambridge, Mass.: Riverside Press, 1902, pp. 114–15.
35. Mary Spink, MS. "List of Books in Howard Phillips Lovecraft's Library," n.d., JHL.
36. Fiske, pp. 94–140.

IV. A Protracted Season in Hell

in a chapbook. Eventually it was.[37] But for present needs a check for seventy-five dollars from Mrs. Gamwell allowed him and his wife to stave off moving another month at least. In that period Mrs. Lovecraft found it necessary to take a well-paying position in Cleveland.[38] She did not explain why this long-distance move was necessary, but in any case she left. She wanted Lovecraft to come with her but he preferred New York where at least he had some friends. She next wrote to his two aunts, suggesting that one of them come to New York and keep house for their nephew. They declined and thought it best that she sell or store her remaining furniture and find a suitable apartment for her husband. She did so. Lovecraft was moved to 169 Clinton Street in Brooklyn. She sent him weekly checks from Cleveland; every three or four weeks she visited him for a few days. The rest of the time—to Lovecraft's content—their marriage was carried on by correspondence.

When Aunt Lillian took a trip through the Southland, he wrote to her at great length on all the important historical sites she would encounter. He concluded the letter with an invitation to his aunt to stop off in Brooklyn on her way home and see his quarters at 169 Clinton. He had furnished it with his Providence heirlooms, making it into a bit of 454 Angell Street. With the shades lowered he had created a "perfect ... parlour-study atmosphere." He asked his aunt to "come and see, before some new and unexpected shock destroys everything, or before I go stark mad with the uncertainty of things and the inability to continue a quiet programme of solitary nocturnal writing."[39] His aunt was unable to visit him, though she later wrote, inquiring solicitously whether he had gotten a job, if he was eating enough, and how his wife was. No, he had no work, but he was keeping his eyes open for a pos-

---

37. [The story was rejected by *Weird Tales*—the first rejection he received from the magazine. The sheets of the booklet (1928) was printed by W. Paul Cook, but were not bound or distributed at the time.]

38. Davis, p. 241. [Sonia first moved to Cincinnati, then later to Cleveland.]

39. H. P. Lovecraft, MS. letter to Mrs. Lillian D. Clark, February 26, 1925, JHL.

sible proof-reading or envelope-addressing stint; and as for his dietary programme, "Bosh!—I *am* eating enough!" His more-or-less daily menu consisted of:

1 loaf bread	0.06
1 medium can beans	0.14
¼ lb. cheese	<u>0.10</u>
	0.30¢

If this isn't a full-sized, healthy day's quota of fodder for an old gentleman, I'll resign from the League of Nation's dietary committee! It's good sound food, & many vigorous Chinamen live on vastly less. Of course, from time to time I'll vary the "meat" course by getting something instead of Heinz beans—canned spaghetti, beef stew, canned beef, &c. &c. &c.[40]

His wife had given up her job in Cleveland because of certain "quibbling executives and insidious inferiors," but quickly, after a brief return to Brooklyn, found another position, this time as a governess to "an intelligent & amiable child" in New Jersey.[41] Weekends were spent with her husband, seeing that he was properly clothed and fed.

The itch to write persisted. His next short story turned to the nearby Red Hook district of Brooklyn for its setting. "The Horror at Red Hook" continues the theme of degenerate humans communicating with spectral powers, though this becomes almost secondary as Lovecraft's revulsion at this neighborhood, too close for comfort, drives him lengthily to describe its stinking alleys and slums on the waterfront. The place "is a babel of sound and filth, and sends out strange cries to answer the lapping of oily waves at its grimy piers and the monstrous organ litanies of the harbour whistles."[42] Yezidi Kurds, possibly the last survivors of the Persian devil-worshippers, infiltrate Red Hook. A grotesque sight with their squinting features and squat,

---

40. H. P. Lovecraft, MS. letter to Mrs. Lillian D. Clark, dated April 2, 1925, JHL.

41. [This appears to have been a short-term position—not in New Jersey, but in Saratoga Springs, NY, around April 1925.]

42. H. P. Lovecraft, "The Horror at Red Hook," *The Outsider*, p. 101.

IV. A Protracted Season in Hell

heavy bodies encased in flashy American dress, they are led in secret rites by "the arch fiend," Robert Suydam. Suydam is a type character who appears variously named throughout Lovecraft's work; he is the Faustian figure of old and wealthy stock who, in questing for occult knowledge, overreaches himself and is destroyed by the very demons whom he summoned from the cold wastes beyond our universe. (Crude symbolism is given by having him and the Kurds conduct their profane rituals in an abandoned Roman Catholic cathedral.) Typical too is the fact that though the agents of evil are either killed, arrested, or dispersed, the "victory" of good over evil is no victory at all. It is a mere respite. The Evil Ones are preparing to assault repeatedly until theirs is the final victory. Near the end of "The Horror at Red Hook," "the evil spirit of darkness and squalor broods on . . . prowling bands still parade on unknown errands past windows where lights and twisted faces unaccountably appear and disappear. Age old horror is a hydra with a thousand heads . . ."[43]

The story, which Lovecraft freely acknowledged to be one of his poorest, is one of spectacular effect rather than of eerie atmosphere, which is the real test of an effective weird tale. As Lovecraft pictures it, Red Hook is like a rotten log kicked over to reveal its squirming grubs and arachnids. Extraterrestrial horrors do not pose a unique threat since to live there is in itself a hell on earth.

The original manuscript of "The Horror at Red Hook" may be consulted in the Manuscript Collection of the New York Public Library. Its twenty-four pages are written on the backs of advertising circulars and Amateur members' letters to him, most of them dating to 1921. This first and final draft shows few changes and those made are concerned with diction rather than plot. In his corrections, there is a slight preference for words of Latin derivation. A few words substitute a more precise and therefore more effective word for a general term,

---

43. Ibid., pp. 111–12.

showing that Lovecraft has reached a clearer visualization of thought.

Word used originally	Replaced by
house	villa
existed	dwelt
old	elderly
thing	entity
strange	odd
began	commenced
kidnapping	stolen child
cabin	statesroom
hideous	singular
him	its noisome bulk

These often concrete yet slightly dated words are the cothurni of Lovecraft's prose which lifts it above common usage to a level appropriate to the story's dark and ancient horrors. Linked with this sensitivity to word values is his fulminant period of composition. The story, 6,500 words long, required only one day (August 2, 1925) to set down.[44] This knack of dashing off a story undoubtedly developed from his writing in the Amateur publications and from hack revision chores. He was also a tireless letter writer. This celerity is often difficult for us now to appreciate or understand since it is absent for the most part in present-day writers who are expected to ponder and ho-hum indecisively while blocking out their topic, writing it, and letting it "cool-off" before revising it once or several times. As a competent story teller one might have expected Lovecraft to continue writing steadily or with white heat speed in short periods to earn something better than bread and butter money.

His scathing "The Horror Red Hook" helped to purge some of the discontent which Brooklyn percolated in him. But it seemed to him that he was being continually beset by fresh problems. Thieves broke

---

44. H. P. Lovecraft, MS. "The Horror at Red Hook," dated August 2, 1925, Manuscript Division, New York Public Library, hereafter, NYPL. [According to HPL's 1925 diary, the story was written on 1–2 August 1925.]

IV. A Protracted Season in Hell

into his apartment and stole most of his clothing. Then there were the rats[45] to contend with:

> Upon our arrival we found the *second* invader caught. I took him out to the nearest rubbish container, said the burial service, and returned to retire.
>
> Traps are only 2 @ 5¢ and it does not pay to bother with repulsive details when one can avoid them at 2½ per experience. I throw them away without removing the corpus delicti, a thing I should hate to do with a costlier bit of mechanism . . . I can't find any of their holes, else I would make attempts at barricading & fortification. Of course we keep all food in tin, but even so, rodents will rove![46]

Despite the jesting spirit, and, however trivial these rat catching incidents may strike one, to an excruciatingly sensitive person like Lovecraft the problem loomed large, threatening his sanity.

The long boredom of his exile was relieved by weekend visits from his wife as well as by frequent all night gatherings with Rheinhart Kleiner, James Morton, Samuel Loveman, and Frank B. Long Jr. Occasionally they were joined by Everett McNeil, an author of juvenile books, Hart Crane and his friend and fellow poet e. e. cummings.[47]

Hart Crane, whom Lovecraft had met three years before in Cleveland, was the only eminent author Lovecraft knew in New York. His attitude toward him was ambivalent. In 1923 he had written to Samuel Loveman: "And so the delectable Crane is now wallowing in the underworld of New York? Good idea, your going there, but don't get in his Bohemian, near-Oscar-Wilde sort of circles! Gawd, how I hate that swinish Heliogabalan type!"[48] Yet to the end of his life, as his letters show, he remained interested in Crane, appreciative of his poetry without understanding it, and censurous of his life without meaning it. As a New Englander he felt obliged in the presence of Loveman and

---

45. [Actually mice.]
46. H. P. Lovecraft, MS. letter to Mrs. Lillian D. Clark, dated July 6, 1925, JHL.
47. [HPL never met e. e. cummings, but heard of him from Hart Crane.]
48. H. P. Lovecraft, MS. letter to Samuel Loveman, dated April 29, 1923, Collection of George Kirk.

Long to spit out an occasional word or two against young Crane, who with his freewheeling attitude was ready to raise hell at the drop of a hat. In his letters to his aunts, where no mask was necessary, Lovecraft's attitude was one of brotherly concern.

Crane never became a member of the Kalem Club, so called because the surnames of all the original members began with K, L, or M. An intimate group of five or six, they usually met at the home of Frank B. Long, Sr.[49] There, seated around the dining room table, which the Longs' maid heaped with coffee, cake, and ice cream, the conversation ran high into the morning. Mainly they discussed literature and occasionally read aloud their little works in progress. In the beginning these gatherings were exhilarating to Lovecraft, the closest he would come to Will's Coffee-house. The Kalem Club may be considered the first semi-professional society in the country given to discussing problems of science-fiction and fantasy writing.[50]

Two new members were added to the Kalem Club after its inception. One was George Kirk, a bookdealer, who lived on the floor above Lovecraft at 169 Clinton Street. "In beliefs he & I are exactly as one," Lovecraft wrote, "for despite a stern Methodist upbringing he is an absolute cynick & sceptick, who realises most poignantly the fundamental purposelessness of the universe."[51] Lovecraft, with all his erudition, said Kirk, did not dominate the Kalems' conversation. When he did speak, however, it was like "an encyclopedia falling open and speaking up to you."[52] At home Lovecraft did not encourage familiarity. He respected his own and other's privacy. When he or Kirk wished to go out, they would tap

---

49. [Actually, the weekly meetings alternated among the homes of all the Kalem members.]
50. L. Sprague de Camp, *Science-Fiction Handbook,* New York, Hermitage House, 1953, p. 135.
51. H. P. Lovecraft, MS. letter to Mrs. Lillian D. Clark, dated November 4–5, 1924, JHL.
52. In private conversation with George Kirk on March 12, 1961.

IV. A Protracted Season in Hell 111

out a code on the stovepipe that ran through their tiny apartments, and in a few minutes they would meet outside Lovecraft's door. Walking was Lovecraft's chief recreation. At one time he and Kirk planned to walk all around Manhattan Island in one evening; they never did, though the amount of walking they did was considerable. Kirk and Lovecraft were never molested in their night strolls. Possibly their nondescript clothing had something to do with it.[53]

The other new member was Wilfred B. Talman, a student of journalism at Columbia. Called by Mrs. Frank B. Long Sr., "the most practical of the Kalems,"[54] he has sketched Lovecraft with a benign countenance. "A man of splendid intellectual energy," Talman called him Lovecraft's behavior was democratic and affable; as proof, he pointed to Lovecraft's civility toward Domingo, a Portuguese waiter at Jacques Restaurant.[55]

Long remembered Lovecraft as having a "thoughtful appearance, sad eyes, and what was to become the most prominent lantern jaw I have ever seen. He was precise in his diction; generally serious—quite the reverse, I think, from Sonia."[56] Samuel Loveman recollected that Lovecraft was "fairly serious, but not cynical or jaded, though there were times when he reminded me of those chickens Hawthorne described in *The House of the Seven Gables*."[57] The passage alluded to runs:

> ... the hens were now scarcely larger than pigeons, and had a queer, rusty, withered aspect, and a gouty kind of movement, and a sleepy and melancholy tone throughout all the variations of their clucking and cackling. It was evident that the race had degenerated, like many a noble race besides, in consequence of too strict a watchfulness to keep it pure. These feathered people had existed too long in their distinct variety; a

---

53. Ibid.
54. Wilfred B. Talman, MS. letter to Arthur Koki, dated February 17, 1961, AK.
55. Ibid.
56. In private conversation with Frank B. Long, Jr., on January 25, 1961.
57. In private conversation with Samuel Loveman on September 14, 1959.

fact of which the present representatives, judging by their lugubrious deportment, seemed to be aware. They kept themselves alive, unquestionably, and laid now and then an egg, and hatched a chicken; not for any pleasure of their own, but that the world might not absolutely lose what had once been so admirable a breed of fowls.[58]

All ages and places were alike of no significance to Lovecraft. Fortunately he could dream of the past. In point of time he belonged back with the Georgians—in a sleepy English village, the meadow, the woods. "The affairs of 1925 et seq." he wrote, "are not likely to make any considerable impression upon me. They are not the especial section of the endless kaleidoscope display of useless patterns which most happens to interest me."[59] The patterns did, however, provide him with an endless source of amusement, and his letters grew into a compendium on the vanity of human wishes. The pretentiousness of the nouveaux riches, the foppish, garish dress of the lowest classes, the campaign hokum of a cheap, jovial politician were all clearly seen and etched sharply by this man who stood on the fringe of human activity like an emissary from another planet.

He was generally neglectful as to national current events, but the colorful Scopes trial, with its religious and scientific issues, engrossed him. As a professed scientific sceptic, there was no question of his stand. Not even his empathy for the South's colonial beauty, gentility, and hostility toward the Negro could prevent him from observing:

> As for the Scopes business—it really was a revelation to me to learn how perfectly & naively mediaeval the Tennessee mind has remained. Obviously logic & information can produce no effect upon a psychology so entrenched in its backwardness, & one might as well let the locality alone until it develops naturally in the course of succeeding generations. The only thing calling for active steps is the task of curbing poor old

---

58. Nathaniel Hawthorne, *The House of the Seven Gables*, A. L. Blunt, 1851, p. 108.
59. H. P. Lovecraft, MS. letter to Mrs. Lillian D. Clark, dated September 28–30, 1925, JHL.

IV. A Protracted Season in Hell 113

> Bryan before he organizes political machinery in less benighted parts of the Union for stifling science. Catholics & mossbacks all over the country would be only too glad to abet him in this issue.[60]

There was no need to curb Bryan, for six days after this letter was written, Bryan died.

> Unfortunate soul! He meant well, dense as was his ignorance; & I have no doubt but that his alarm at the expansion of human thought was a profound, altruistic, & genuinely frantic passion. His compact little mind was hardened into a certain primitive type of pioneer psychology & could not bear the strain of national cultural development. Life must have been a hell to him as all the securities of his artificial world cracked one by one under the pressure of time & scientific discovery—he was a man without a world to live in, & the strain proved too much for this mortal to bear. Now he is at rest in the eternal oblivion which he would have been the first & loudest to deny. Requiescat in Pace![61]

It seemed characteristic of Lovecraft to take a superior position of pitying his more energetic and brilliant contemporaries. It was doubly ironic that he failed to see how his strictures of Bryan could apply to himself. "Artificial world," aside, how well could Lovecraft "bear the strain of national cultural development"? Lovecraft, by identifying himself so strongly with his English-American-Protestant ancestry often failed to achieve flexibility, to correct his bias and move toward a center point of view in his human relations. To be sure, an attachment to one's family, ethnic group, or community is not by any means a strange condition, and up to a point maybe desirable. It appears more than likely in fact that mankind in society will always retain some social overexaggeration of the importance of his background. But sociocentrism became an absurdity with Lovecraft when, according to Mrs.

---

60. H. P. Lovecraft, MS. letter to Mrs. Lillian D. Clark, dated July 20, 1925, JHL.
61. Ibid.

Lovecraft, "soon after our marriage he told me that whenever we had company he would appreciate it if 'Aryans' were in the majority."[62]

In the racially-mixed crowds of New York he would actually become livid with rage. On a Fourth of July trip to Pelham Park, Lovecraft wrote:

> We came to the end of the line—& disillusion! My Pete in Pegāna, but what crowds! And that is not the worst—for upon my most solemn oath, I'll be shot if three out of every four persons—nay, nine out of ten—weren't flabby, pungent, grinning, chattering *niggers!* Help! It seems that the direct communication of this park with the ever thickening Harlem black belt has brought its inevitable result, & that a once lovely Southside park is from now on to be given over to Georgia camp-meetings & outings of the African Methodist Episcopal Church. Maw Lawdy, but dey was some swell high-yaller spo'ts paradin' round' dat afternoon! Wilted by the sight, we did no more than take a side path to the shore & back & reentered the subway for the long homeward ride—wishing to find a train not too reminiscent of the packed hold of one of John Brown's Providence merchantmen on the middle passage from the Guinea Coast to Antigua or the Barbadoes.[63]

This attitude toward minorities increased Lovecraft's longing to return to Providence. His ponderous transplanted furniture, plus the family's paintings, clocks, and books were a constant and painful reminder of his true home. The tie with Providence was kept strong by his regular letters to his aunts and his daily subscription to the *Journal,* this latter supplying him with fresh topics for conversation. The report of the destruction of a colonial dwelling was sure to provoke an angry outburst as well as recollections to scenes of his younger and better days on Angell Street.

> The tearing down of that Abbot house in 1900 was a crime which ought to have brought the death penalty on its instigators & perpetrators. It was the absolutely last relic of the *original* Providence—the 17th centu-

---

62. Davis, p. 242.
63. H. P. Lovecraft, MS. letter to Mrs. Lillian D. Clark, dated July 13, 1925, JHL.

IV. A Protracted Season in Hell

ry agricultural village of Mr. Williams, with its feuds & Indian wars—and was in fairly decent shape when destroyed. Its demolition was sheer obtuseness and careless vandalism—may it be a shunned example to warn the publick against permitting similar vandalism in the future.[64]

August Derleth in a recent essay set out to dispel three popular Lovecraftian myths, *viz.*, (1) Lovecraft died of starvation, (2) he committed suicide, and (3) he was racially prejudiced. The first two are not myths at all, but simply pseudo-myths, i.e. allegations so completely erroneous that only the laziest readers could believe them. (On two occasions I have met with booksellers who engage in this petty Lovecraftian mythmaking to enhance the value of their Lovecraft books.) The third point of Derleth's essay, that of Lovecraft's prejudices, merits further attention. According to Derleth, Lovecraft disliked those who were insensible to the beauties of old New England. It disturbed him to see such individuals buying his favorite antiquarian haunts. Derleth said, "These foreigners were of various nationalities and races, and Lovecraft disliked them all impartially." His dislike was not so much racial prejudice as it was fear for change, "which represents to all of us the passing of the familiar, and is in fact symptomatic, more deeply, of a basic insecurity which is associated with the passing of the familiar aspects of life which have come to signify security for those of us who are prone to such reactions."[65]

There is validity in the idea that the "passing of the familiar" may leave one with a nostalgic pang, if not momentary anger, as in Lovecraft's case. It does not, however, fully explain the problem. In the first place, the amount of destruction that went on in Lovecraft's neighborhood was negligible—several homes were taken for Brown University dormitories, an addition to the Rhode Island School of Design, a faculty parking lot, an extension for a cemetery. New members of the Col-

---

64. Ibid.
65. August Derleth, *Some Notes on H. P. Lovecraft*, Sauk City, Wis.: Arkham House, 1959, pp. 6–7.

lege Hill community were respectable and respected business and professional people. No gauderies on the order of Lord Timothy Dexter were committed. The Colonial homes that Lovecraft cherished are still to be seen and admired.[66]

The foreign intrusion, if such it was, was slight, although in Lovecraft's active mind it may have taken on the proportions of an invasion. It is probably nearer the truth, as Frank B. Long. Jr. has suggested to me, that Lovecraft's hatred of the well-to-do foreigner, especially the Jew, was jealousy, just that; a jealousy born out of the bitter realization that immigrants, seemingly without breeding or discourse, had come to America and acquired riches while he, Howard Phillips Lovecraft, had watched helplessly as his family's wealth deteriorated because his parents were overcome by growing inertia and insanity.[67] W. Paul Cook claimed that Lovecraft lived with but one ambition: "to repatriate the property [old estate of his grandfather] before he died and restore it as it was in his grandfather's day."[68] But how seriously can we take this ambitious program? As for Lovecraft's own business acumen, we have seen what ill fruit his attempts at employment seeking produced. Nor can nostalgia or fear of change explain his hatred for the Negroes, except to suggest that they reminded him of his boyhood days at Grandpa Phillips's sumptuous home, where, in those carefree, taxless times, there were four Negro servants, colorful ornaments of an era now irretrievably lost,

To our mid-century mind, racial prejudice has taken on a decidedly sinister cast and at its very mention one is apt to see the insane clown

---

66. See Robert C. Achorn's "When a Neighborhood is in Trouble," *The Worcester Evening Gazette* (December 1, 1959), p. 6. College Hill, with its 1,700 homes, some 300 of which date back to the 1700s and early 1800s, is about to begin a redevelopment program, saving the best buildings, replacing the rest. This "ambitious and imaginative program [may] serve as a blueprint for cities across the nation."

67. In private conversation with Frank B. Long, Jr., on September 14, 1959.

68. Cook, p. 4.

IV. A Protracted Season in Hell

Hitler exhorting the masses with his race supremacy doctrines; one perceives the translation of his evil: Belsen, Buchenwald, Auschwitz wherein thousands were tortured and exterminated. The misery and the shame. Closer to us, we are today experiencing the tragic attempts at racial integration. Hitler had not come on the scene when Lovecraft was writing. Colonialism, with the lofty aim of "the white man's burden," was a force in the world, albeit waning; yet to an Anglophile like Lovecraft it was still bright. He accepted it because he embraced the belief imbedded in the core of colonialism, namely, the white man was fit to rule by virtue of his mental and physical superiority.

Granted that Lovecraft was (1) racially prejudiced, and (2) alienated from the majority of mankind, does this make him a less effective commentator on the life around him? Are we to dismiss his letters as the complaints of a cantankerous fool, out of sorts with the world? It is entirely possible that Lovecraft as an outsider enjoyed a unique vantage point. He could write on the follies of certain groups because he experienced no inhibitions or shameful feelings over his prejudices. Dean Swift said of himself that he hated mankind but heartily loved John, Thomas, and Henry. We regard this confession with approbation. It indicates the temper of his satiric genius. Lovecraft would have concurred with him that "the bulk of your natives [are] the most pernicious race of little odious vermin that nature ever suffered to crawl upon the surface of the earth."[69] As an outsider, Lovecraft could very often be objective and substantive, keenly aware of the validity of Huxley's formulation that "a little ruthless laughter clears the air as nothing else can do; it is good for us every now and then, to see our ideals laughed at, our conceptions of nobility caricatured; it is good for human pomposity to be made to look mean and ridiculous ... it is very good for most of us to be made uncomfortable."[70] Under his crit-

---

69. Jonathan Swift, *Gulliver's Travels*, "Voyage to Brobdingnag," ch. 6.
70. Aldous Huxley, *The World of Aldous Huxley*, ed. Charles Rolo, New York: Universal Library, 1947, p. vii.

ical gaze, Lovecraft spoke on the tawdry scenes around him, the dress fashions of his day, for example:

> I think I have developed an eye for the difference between the clothing a gentleman wears & that which a gentleman doesn't. What has sharpened this sense is the constant sight of these accursed & filthy rabbles that infest the N. Y. streets, & whose clothing presents such systematic differences from the normal clothing of real people along Angell St. & in Butler Ave. or Elmgrove Ave. cars that the eye comes to feel a tremendous homesickness & to pounce avidly on any gentleman whose clothes are proper & tasteful. And so pining for the sight of a Swan Point car full of regular men, I have resolved to dress like Butler Ave. or not at all. Confound it, I'll be either in good Providence taste or in a bally bathrobe!!! Certain lapel cuts, textures, & fits tell the story. It amuses me to see how some of these flashy young "boobs" & foreigners spend fortunes on various kinds of expensive clothes which they regard as evidence of meritorious taste, but which in reality are their absolute social aesthetick damnation—being little short of placards shrieking in bold letters: "I AM AN IGNORANT PEASANT," "I AM A MONGREL GUTTER-RAT," or "I AM A TASTELESS & UNSOPHISTICATED YOKEL." And yet perhaps these creatures are not, after all, seeking to conform to the absolute artistic standard of gentlefolk. Possibly their object is entirely different; involving a recognition of their non-membership in the cultivated part of the community, & a desire simply to dress in accordance with the frankly different standard of their own candidly acknowledged type & class—as a Breton or Catalan peasant affects the grotesque finery of his kind, regardless of the attire of general European society. Sonny & I have frequently discussed the possibility of the rise of a definite plebeian American costume, & we think we can already see evidences of it. Its present visible signs are tight, waist-fitting coats, with narrow lapels & buttons near together; extremely low-cut waistcoats approximating evening waistcoats & probably derived from the rabble's ignorant admiration of the dress-suited heroes of their favourite cinemas; & exotick & effeminate "pastels" tones of colour—purple, lavender, & the like. The whole general trend of this growing peasant garb is toward the conspicuous & the feminine—infallible marks of a decadent slave stock as opposed to the classically subdued & loosely but finely hung

IV. A Protracted Season in Hell

garments characteristick of a genuinely refined & wholesomely masculine ruling or conquering class or race-stock. The phenomenon is a perfect parallel of the degradation of the Roman toga into the fussy gaudiness of the Byzantine mob. Eventually as the whole civilization decays, this artistic corruption will spread to the upper classes as well as the herd; but for the present it is possible to divide clothing pretty clearly into what a gentleman wears & what he doesn't. Better by far to wear the frayed & tattered rags of something with taste, than to sport the newest & freshest suit whose cut & texture bear the ineffaceable stigmata of plebeianism & decadence.[71]

The weather turned cold. The leaves of summer crinkled and fell to the ground. Lovecraft broke his daytime solitude to venture out in search of a woolen suit. He admitted that a gentleman should always be dressed in good taste but he should never be conscious of his clothing. "In my prime I could never have gotten so excited over clothes but exile & old age make trifles dear to me."[72] The subsequent anxiety that Lovecraft experienced in finding the correct suit invites some comparison with the central situation in Nikolai Gogol's short novel *The Overcoat* where the protagonist, Akaky Akakyevitch, a petty clerk, scrimps and saves to purchase a magnificent overcoat. On one level the story has been symbolically interpreted as a grotesque fantasy of human inconsequence. From a psychoanalytic standpoint, if we recall Freud's dictum that in dreams clothes and uniforms stand for nakedness and also that a cloak or hat is symbolic of the male organ, then Akakyevitch's herculean effort to acquire the new overcoat becomes the equivalent of an effort on his part to recover or secure his masculinity.[73] Similarly, Lovecraft conceded that a suit was to him an integral outgrowth of his

---

71. H. P. Lovecraft, MS. letter to Mrs. Lillian D. Clark, dated October 24–27, 1925, JHL.
72. Ibid.
73. Sigmund Freud, *The Interpretation of Dreams*, London: Hogarth Press, 1953, pp. 360–61.

personality and aesthetic sense. The right suit would impart to him a somber, quiet dignity, marking him at once as a successful person, a descendant of the master conquer or type. In short, a man.

But the right suit was hard to come by with Lovecraft's scanty resources.

> I descended to the depths, & took the subway for the 14th St.—7th Ave. colony. Pegāna, what a gauntlet to run! Indescribable scum pulling one into holes in the wall where flamboyant monstrosities ululate their impossibility beneath price cards of $4.95, $7.50, $10.00—puffy, rat eyed vermin hurling taunts when one does not buy & airing spleen in dialects so mercifully broken that white men can't understand them. Craziness in cloth hanging in fantastic attitudes & displaying unheard-of anomalies—before Heaven I vow that despite the horrors I've seen *on* people, I never saw the like of these fungous freaks *off* people! Perhaps the human form inside a suit fills it out to some semblance of Nature—certainly these empty nightmares swinging in the winds like gallows-birds had nothing of Nature in them! Once . . . I saw something in a "bargain basement" that caused my heart to flutter . . . but I found it was *second-hand* & fled![74]

Escape was the only solution. He had erred in attempting to compromise with his deepest feelings. New York was, and would always be to him, a place of clumsy, alien trappings or, nearer the truth, a trap. But how could he gracefully return to Providence?

On August 11, 1925, he wrote his short story "He." It is not the minor 2,500 word failure that Lovecraft later judged it. Defects can be found. If one expects a writer to show with each new story a consistent improvement in technique, in effectively shaping materials, then "He" must so signify a diminution of Lovecraft's powers. "He" does not add to his nascent mythology, nor does it plumb the atavistic theme. Stylistically it clenches into the stock adjective noun syntax to arouse horror: "In those greenish beams the candles paled, and a new

---

74. H. P. Lovecraft, MS. letter to Mrs. Lillian D. Clark, dated October 24–27, 1925, JHL.

IV. A Protracted Season in Hell

semblance of decay spread over the musk-reeking room with its wormy paneling, sagging floor, battered mantel, rickety furniture, and ragged draperies."[75] The minuscular plot line is suggestive of his earlier "The Festival" where a sinister man in Puritan dress led the narrator into the past. And here, as there, the conclusion is too abrupt; a black thing wriggles across the floor, engulfs and carries off the evil Puritan; the house collapses and the narrator wakes up injured the next day wondering what it was all about.

Granted these defects, what is left? One succinct though brilliant stretch of writing. The opening of "He" is an overt and specifically personal statement of Lovecraft's feeling. It is the "cry of a soul in torment."[76] Not only Lovecraft's soul but all souls that have found metropolitan life so juiceless.

> My coming to New York had been a mistake; for whereas I had looked or poignant wonder and inspiration in the teeming labyrinths of ancient streets that twist endlessly from forgotten courts and squares and waterfronts to courts and squares and waterfronts equally forgotten, and in the Cyclopean modern towers and pinnacles that rise blackly Babylonian under waning moons, I had found instead only a sense of horror and oppression which threatened to master, paralyze, and annihilate me . . . success and happiness were not to be. Garish daylight showed only squalor and alienage and the noxious elephantiasis of climbing, spreading stone where the moon had hinted of loveliness and elder magic; and the throngs of people that seethed through the flumelike streets were squat, swarthy strangers with hardened faces and narrow eyes, shrewd strangers without dreams and without kinship to the scenes about them, who could never mean aught to the blue-eyed man of the old folk, with the love of fair green lanes and white New England village steeples in his heart.
> . . . I gradually formed the habit of keeping off the streets by day and venturing abroad only at night, when darkness calls forth what little of the past still hovers wraithlike about, and old white doorways remember the stalwart forms that had once passed through them. With this mode

---

75. H. P. Lovecraft, "He," *The Outsider*, p. 97.
76. Cook, p. 15.

of relief I even wrote a few poems, and still refrained from going home to my people lest I seem to crawl back ignobly in defeat.[77]

Lovecraft believed that a city like New York killed the best in any creative person. He pictured Hart Crane, for example, as a child of the times, victimized and ruined by the "blessings" of twentieth century civilization. In point of time Crane, Lovecraft thought, would have been better off with him in the eighteenth century. "Hart Crane," he wrote to Aunt Lillian, "just back from the country & only about ¼ 'lit up' by his beloved booze. Poor Crane! A real poet & man of taste, descendant of an ancient Connecticut family & a gentleman to his fingertips, but the slave of dissipated habits which will soon ruin both his constitution & still striking handsomeness!"[78]

Two and a half years later Crane exited Manhattan for promised joy only to uncover another brand of ennui. "The nearest thing to reality," he wrote, "is the greasepaint and the vulgarity of the boulevard that runs through Hollywood. Broadway around Times Square at any time of the day is better."[79] If the task of the American writer is to come imaginatively to terms with American experience, what does he do with a scene of "expensive cars by the legion and frizzed poodles and parading vampires"?[80] Crane saw California as "a great pink vacuum filled with machinery and chewing gum and millions of 'up-to-date' little stucco pseudo-Spanish villas. Thank God the sea is near," he cried in dreadful anticipation, "that's all I can be grateful for."[81] Motion to Crane equaled hope. To stay in motion is to deal with anxiety.

---

77. H. P. Lovecraft, "He," *The Outsider,* p. 92.
78. H. P. Lovecraft, MS. letter to Mrs. Lillian D. Clark, dated October 14–15, 1925, JHL.
79. Hart Crane, letter to Gorham B. Munson, dated April 17, 1928. Microfilm: *123 Original Letters of Hart Crane to Gorham B. Munson, from 1919–1928.* Columbus, Ohio: Ohio State University Libraries.
80. Ibid.
81. Ibid.

IV. A Protracted Season in Hell

Things will be better beyond the horror zone. That which piqued him in one place would not—he hoped—infuriate him elsewhere. He was conquering space and trying to come to terms with his experience. We have heard the stale joke that every young American writer aspires to write *the* great American novel or epic. In that one single work he will swallow up hell in his American *Aeneid* or *King Lear*. Crane failed as the palpitating shadows drew close and, on April 27, 1932, at noon, aboard the *S. S. Orizaba*, bound for America, Crane saw and took the night, while others returned each morning, yawning.

Back in 1925, Lovecraft in Brooklyn temporarily suspended his own somnambulistic act to operate a writer's revisionist service by mail. A few advertisements in the New York papers elicited a book-length manuscript that was all but unreadable. Lovecraft felt it would be cheap to encourage this tyro who was painfully devoid of any writing promise. He returned the manuscript and stopped any further ads.[82]

There was occasional revision work for Bush and a few others. To the Amateur journals he still contributed verse and fiction. His next short story "In the Vault" was published in *Tryout* in November, 1925, probably after it had been rejected by *Weird Tales* on the first submission.[83] Like "He," this story is a minor effort having little relationship with his earlier tales of extraterrestrial horror. It has all the stock accessories of a New England Gothic tale: the receiving vault, the callous grave digger who is locked in the vault at night. Outside, the horse neighing; within, the grave digger working to free himself. (Vaults and massy tombs appear quite often in Lovecraft's stories. They were familiar to him from his youth since St. John's and Swan Point Cemetery are studded with those commodious, solid tombs that remind one of German pillboxes.) The imprisoned grave digger, Birch, places several

---

82. In private conversation with George Kirk on March 12, 1961.
83. [HPL sent "In the Vault" to the *Tryout* before sending it to *Weird Tales*, because an anecdote by C. W. Smith had inspired the story. *Weird Tales* did in fact reject the story later but later accepted it; it appeared in the April 1932 issue.]

coffins in a stair-like arrangement and standing on the top one begins chiseling around a transom. The flimsy coffin beneath him splinters and he falls into Sawyer's rotting corpse:

> In another moment he knew fear for the first time that night; for struggle as he would, he could not shake clear of the unknown grasp which held his feet in relentless captivity. Horrible pains, as of savage wounds, shot through his calves; and in his mind was a vortex of fright mixed with unquenchable materialism that suggested splinters, loose nails, or some other attribute of a breaking wooden box.[84]

Finally he crawls out of the transom. His ankles are so badly torn that he is left permanently lamed, "but I think the greatest lameness was in his soul," says the narrator.[85] Later the doctor who dressed Birch's wounds discovers that Birch had cut off the feet of Asaph Sawyer in order to fit him into a smaller, cheaper casket. Birch had appropriated Sawyer's elaborate coffin for a friend who had died at the same time. Birch's punishment is thus an example of pat justice. This story may remind one of Ambrose Bierce's "The Boarded Window" where a dead woman twitches to life to fight some kind of wild animal which had invaded her open coffin. The story ends with a memorable sentence, "Between the teeth was a fragment of the animal's ear."[86] Writers, like Civil War historians, are free to interpret the same dramatic situations. "In the Vault" is an absorbing tale, not a great one, but one which is surprisingly restrained and effective despite its sensational subject matter.[87]

---

84. H. P. Lovecraft, "In The Vault," *The Outsider*, p. 167.
85. Ibid., p. 168.
86. Ambrose Bierce, "The Boarded Window," *Tales of Terror* ed. Herbert A. Wise and Phyllis Fraser, New York, Random House, p. 61.
87. Some of the strangest graveyard stories appear in the newspapers. I unroll the Camden, New Jersey *Courier-Post* (September 29, 1961) and read on the front page that "Police Chief Neale today assigned a special team to investigate a series of mysteries at Evergreen Cemetery. The mysteries included: A woman who has disrobed in the cemetery twice within the past three months, leaving her dress and

IV. A Protracted Season in Hell   125

Lovecraft considered "In the Vault" a trifle, "one of my worst."[88] Yet some earlier mediocre stories had at least been saleable. While 1925–1926 did not see a sustained horror story leave his pen, the germ concepts for future stories which he recorded in his notebooks show that his imagination was busily drawing from his readings and his vivid dreams. This repository of germinal ideas is a treasure house for writers in the weird tradition. Most of the ideas consist of a few lines: "Castaways on island eat unknown vegetation & becomes strangely transformed," "Insect hypnotizes man & leads him to his death," "Evil wizard employs metempsychosis to survive in animal forms and carrying out revenge," while other jottings remind Lovecraft to recheck certain articles in books and newspapers. Some entries are place names or quotations which have a hideous ring to them, viz., "Azathoth," Kaman-thoh-del."[89] Lovecraft began the notebook habit quite early in his writing career, probably 1914.[90] Its suggestions were incorporated into every story from that date. Only a fraction of the ideas were used—necessarily, since the list was copious and varied. Those accepted were mulled over, held in abeyance, fermenting as in 1925–1926 when no heady mixture was released. It was not yet time. His letters to his aunts made it abundantly clear that Brooklyn was not a suitable

---

undergarments on a tombstone. Vandalism of at least one vault, including missing contents from coffins. Dice games late at night . . . The metal ladder extending 25 feet down to the entrance of the crypt is believed to be nearly 70 years old. A section of a newspaper, the June 30, 1906 edition of the *Morning Public Ledger* was nearby . . . Lt. Howard Clayton said a boy accidentally hanged himself from a tree while playing in the cemetery last year. He said children often play in the cemetery."

88. From a letter to August Derleth. Cited in reportorial notes of Winfield Townley Scott, deposited in the John Hay Library.

89. H. P. Lovecraft, "Commonplace Book," *The Shuttered Room*, pp. 97–123. [The text properly reads "Sinister names—Nasht—Kaman-Thah." The "del" refers to the fact that the entry was deleted, but this appears in R. H. Barlow's typescript, not the original ms.]

90. [The commonplace book was probably begun in late 1919 or early 1920.]

place for a writer. The tawdry scenes siphoned his vitality. He wanted to return to Providence, but to save face the invitation had to come from them. Meanwhile, every topic of mutual interest was tumbled around by Lovecraft in his blunt, well-meaning way to show his exquisite nostalgia.

> Jamaica retains some sunset spark of its old American village life, & as I entered the peaceful portals of the old gambrel-roofer, I felt a something in common with the old places of New England with their mellow ancestral memories—of being in touch with a holy & venerable Sacrament kept alive amidst chaos & decay, & standing at one with the soul of Providence, & Newport, Boston & Concord, Salem & Marblehead, Portsmouth & Newburyport. It was a breath of life from the sources that inspire my being![91]

While he waited for deliverance, he hoped to keep his nerves in a detached state, independent of time, space, or environment. Virtually the only tender concern he manifested during the Autumn and Winter of 1925 was directed toward unhuman objects, like colonial buildings and cats:

> I found a mother-cat with two of the finest imaginable black & white kittens—irresistibly lovely little rascals—& this time the temptation was too strong to resist. I put one of them in my [old blue] coat pocket, with his head out, & carried him around with me for nearly an hour. I saw many other small kittens during my jaunt—this must be the Fall harvest, bless their little hearts![92]

In his study of the Outsider, Colin Wilson has listed as one of the Outsider's traits his lack of identification with the world around him.[93]

---

91. H. P. Lovecraft, MS. letter lo Mrs. Lillian D. Clark, dated November 14–15, 1925, JHL.
92. H. P. Lovecraft, MS. letter to Mrs. Lillian D. Clark, dated November 22, 1925, JHL.
93. Wilson's book is, admittedly, an overrated work, contradictory at times, an unscientific eclecticism tenuously linking the most unlikely bedfellows—Nijinsky, Fox, Sartre, Blake, Shaw, etcetera—to membership in the Outsider Club. I never-

IV. A Protracted Season in Hell

"The Outsider is never alive in what he does."[94] This does not apply to the Outsider with mystic visions: a man like Blake, for example, was wide awake, attuned to the social and political cataclysms of his era; he was alive in a way that Stoyte had never thought of being, alive in a way that few have ever been. Mysticism, communion with God, as a solution to the Outsider's growing spirit of isolation, were never seriously considered by Lovecraft. In his essay "Idealism and Materialism: A Reflection" (1919), he expatiated that the universe was a purposeless, automatic chaos, a "Godhead dying downwards,"[95] though he censured the rabid atheist whose own brand of religion led him on to a destructive course, pulling down what he could not replace.[96]

He was an archetype of the Dreamer, but in his daylight hour she was Lovecraft the cold rationalist or scientific skeptic, as he preferred to think of himself, who had dismissed God, along with Santa Claus, at the tender age of nine. The almost Buddhistic spirit of resignation growing from his belief that "all worlds and epochs are alike of no importance," criss-crossed his letters with streaks of sardonic humor, although the effect desired was to be one of supreme objectivity. We have his account of what is basically a telling experience—the forced eviction of a middle-aged woman:

> An added feature introduced itself when, at Sheridan Square, we were witnesses to a rather picaresque eviction—a dumpy-looking woman (whether peasant or pseudo-artist we could not decide) having been

---

theless mention the book here because it has been to date the most popular treatment of a perennial theme in life and literature; with the breakup of family, caste, title, and religion, man has been feeling this loneliness to a greater degree in this century than in the past. See Henry Miller's *The Time of the Assassins* (New Directions) for a brilliant discussion of this dilemma.

94. Colin Wilson, *The Outsider,* Boston, Houghton Mifflin Co., 1956, p. 73.
95. Thomas Hardy, "Nature's Questioning," *Poems for Study,* ed. Leonard Unger and William Van O'Connor, New York, Rinehart Co., 1957, p. 569.
96. H. P. Lovecraft, "Idealism and Materialism: A Reflection," *The Shuttered Room,* pp. 90–91.

turned out on the sidewalk with all her domestick furniture, whilst an aesthetic-looking youth with wavy brown hair, dreamy eyes, a black-&-red checked flannel shirt & a crimson silk sash supporting flaring trousers, brought her a pail of coffee from a neighboring cafeteria to dilute the saline streams from her unhappy eyes. A curious crowd supplied the requisite background for this infelicitous idyll.[97]

If the Outsider is "not himself" it follows that if he is to save himself from a life of maddening greyness, it is his proper concern "to find a course of action in which he is *most himself*, that is, in which he achieves the maximum self-expression."[98] To the artist, as an Outsider, this ideally would mean freedom to paint, play music, dance, or write.

Fortunately it was obvious that writing was Lovecraft's natural mode of expression. "If the ability or opportunity for that goes, I have no further reason—or mind to endure—the joke of existence,"[99] he had pronounced gravely. Writing sustained and nourished his spirit. His essays for the numerous Amateur publications permitted him to be an authoritarian on topics of literature and history. In his continuous chain of epistles to his aunts he could rave and spew at the trivialities that plagued him. And, of course, there were his short stories which offered a retreat into the realm of fantasy.

> I must slough off for a space the real & practical world, & isolate myself behind the opera-glasses of glamour & fantasy, so that I may see again the unreal world of wonder, which being seen, at once animates my pen & stamps itself on paper! My nervous poise & aesthetick articulateness are to be attained only by telling the world to go to the deuce, and proceeding to set down the transformations which a naturally fantastic imagination makes in the visual images set before it. These visual images I shall choose with care; making solitary pilgrimages to picaresque rural spots, outlying villages, Colonial city neighborhoods, & vistas of gro-

---

97. H. P. Lovecraft, MS. letter to Mrs. Lillian D. Clark, dated December 3, 1925, JHL.
98. Wilson, p. 73.
99. H. P. Lovecraft, MS. letter to Mrs. Lillian D. Clark, dated November 17, 1924, JHL.

IV. A Protracted Season in Hell

tesque or beautiful skyline, in order to fill my mind with that which most powerfully affects it & moves it to artistic utterance.[100]

The most ambitious and artistically satisfying project which Lovecraft accomplished during this New York period came in the early part of 1926 when W. Paul Cook, the owner-printer of the Recluse Press in Athol, Massachusetts suggested that he write a lengthy essay on the supernatural element in English fiction for the first issue of his new Amateur magazine, *The Recluse*. Lovecraft accepted this formidable assignment. From his childhood days, Lovecraft's reading of horror literature had been extensive and perceptive to an astonishing degree. He went about the article with all the ebullience of a young boy. In the morning he arose, ate a light breakfast, and caught the subway for downtown Manhattan where he went to the Fifth Avenue Public Library. (He told Loveman that he had found a way of reaching the Library in twelve steps from the subway exit, thus sparing himself the sight of New York's populace.)[101] At the Library he took copious notes. At home in the evening he would continue reading. After supper, he went either to a movie or took a nocturnal stroll. Home again, he would read Machen to achieve a reposeful mood before lucubrating into the early dawn. The article gave him a legitimate excuse for absenting himself from the time-consuming Kalem Club meetings. It also sharpened his literary technique and restored his mind to its natural habitat of bookish seclusion.

In writing "Supernatural Horror Literature," Lovecraft had as his precedent two surveys in the field. One was Dorothy Scarborough's bulky *The Supernatural in Modern English Fiction* (1917)[102] and the other, *The Tale of Terror* (1921) by Edith Birkhead. Miss Birkhead, after skim-

---

100. H. P. Lovecraft, MS. letter to Mrs. Lillian D. Clark, dated December 10, 1925, JHL.
101. Samuel Loveman, "Howard Phillips Lovecraft," *Something About Cats,* p. 231.
102. [HPL did not read this treatise until 1932.]

ming over some pre-eighteenth century tales of terror, traced the Gothic Romance from *The Castle of Otranto* through the novels of Mrs. Ann Radcliffe, "Monk" Lewis, Beckford, Godwin, Jane Austen, and Scott. The penultimate chapter was given over to Hawthorne and Poe. Miss Birkhead ventured only briefly beyond the 1850s for after that date the Gothic Romance "lost its individuality, and was merged into other forms. To follow every trail of its influence would lead us far afield."[103] Brander Matthews praised *The Tale of Terror* as "a contribution to knowledge; and if it had been prepared for an American university it would have justified the bestowal of the Ph. D. degree."[104]

Four years earlier *The Supernatural in Modern English Fiction* had earned for Dorothy Scarborough a doctorate at Columbia University—which fact, to judge from critical reviews of the work, must have raised doubt in some minds over the practice of moulding America's graduate education in the humanities along German lines. Miss Scarborough's display of industry exceeded Miss Birkhead's and Lovecraft's. Unquestionably. She had looked at three thousand short stories, plays, and novels in the horror genre in the period roughly from 1800 to 1917. (Slightly less than a third of these titles were mentioned in her study.) But this scholarship got in her way. She read, summarized, and card indexed ghost scenes from Hamlet to O. Henry and Frank Stockton. Page after page of condensed ghostplots followed with little, often no commentary. As a sampler the book had its uses, but in place of a systematic history she classified spirits according to whether they were dismembered, crippled, maimed, decapitated; ghosts who wore clothes or appeared nude; ghosts who were naughty or well-mannered, serious or frivolous. She went out of her way to be witty and missed the point when she said "Perhaps the most valuable contribution that the Gothic school made to English literature is Jane

---

103. Edith Birkhead, *The Tale of Terror*, London: Constable & Co. Ltd., 1921, p. 221.
104. "The Cabinet of Gothic Tales of Terror," rev. Brander Matthews, *The New York Times Book Review* 2 (September 25, 1925).

IV. A Protracted Season in Hell 131

Austen's inimitable satire of it, *Northanger Abbey*."[105] After unleashing legions of titles, a thousand or so, she drew this weak summation from her thesis: "In conclusion, it might be said that fiction offers the most popular present vehicle for expression of the undoubtedly reviving supernaturalism in English literature. And fiction is likewise the best form, that which affords the more varied chances for effectiveness."[106] "It must be a relief to have the thing off her mind," one contemporary critic wrote of Miss Scarborough's study.[107]

Prior to writing his "Supernatural Horror in Literature" Lovecraft studied both of these ladies' books with attention before deciding which of their divergent approaches to follow. He chose Miss Birkhead's, but as an Anglophile conversant with modern horror literature he was naturally eager to include such modern masters as Arthur Machen, Algernon Blackwood, Lord Dunsany, and M. R. James.

He unveils his study with these words:

> The oldest and strongest emotion of mankind is fear, and the oldest and strongest kind of fear is fear of the unknown. These facts few psychologists will dispute, and their admitted truth must establish for all time the genuineness and dignity of the weirdly horrible tales as a literary form. Against it are discharged all the shafts of a materialistic sophistication which clings to frequently felt emotions and external events, and of a naively inspired idealism which deprecates the aesthetic motive and calls for a didactic literature to "uplift" the reader toward a suitable degree of smirking optimism. But in spite of all this opposition the weird tale has survived, developed, and attained remarkable heights of perfection; founded as it is on a profound and elementary principle whose appeal, if not always universal, must necessarily be poignant and permanent to minds of the requisite sensitiveness.[108]

---

105. Dorothy Scarborough, *The Supernatural in Modern English Fiction*, New York: G. P. Putnam & Sons, 1917, p. 47.

106. Ibid., p. 309.

107. "The Supernatural in Horror Literature," anon. rev. *Dial* 63 (December 6, 1917): 590–91.

108. H. P. Lovecraft, *Supernatural Horror in Literature*, New York, Ben Abramson,

It is probable that Lovecraft had Edmund Burke in mind when he wrote the opening passages of "Supernatural Horror in Literature." Burke's *On the Sublime and Beautiful* (1757) had a penetrating influence in washing away some of the rigid neo-classical ideals by suggesting that the sublime or the majestic in literature was achieved through scenes dealing with darkness, terror, obscurity, power, irregularity, and magnitude. Without sanction of Lovecraft's acknowledgement to Burke it still seems to me that the preceding quotation is a coupling of what Burke wrote in Section II, on Terror: "No passion so effectually robs the mind of all its powers of acting and reasoning as fear. For fear being an apprehension of pain or death, it operates in a manner that resembles actual pain."[109] Immediately after, in discussing Obscurity, Edmund Burke wrote: "To make anything very terrible, obscurity seems in general to be necessary. When we know the full extent of any danger, when we can accustom our eyes to it, a great deal of the apprehension vanishes. Everyone will be sensible of this . . ."[110]

Neither Burke nor Lovecraft hazard a guess why fear, if it is so disagreeable, should find perennial form in literature. Freud believed that fear of the supernatural had two sources: survival of animistic beliefs and repressed infantile complexes.[111] Others, literary critics in particular, would submit more simply that horror and mystery stories are told for their own sake and are appreciated best by those most secure from peril. These stories satisfy that *sehnsucht* to experience new thrills without actual danger.

After noting the antiquity of the horror story, Lovecraft attends Miss Birkhead's study closely in the rise of the Gothic novel *The Castle*

1954, p. 12.

109. Edmund Burke, "On the Sublime and Beautiful," *Works*, Boston: Little, Brown & Co., 1901, I.130.

110. Ibid., p. 132.

111. *Das Unheimliche*. Sigmund Freud's Gesammelte Werke, vol. 12. Cited by Penzoldt in *The Supernatural in Fiction*, p. 5.

IV. A Protracted Season in Hell   133

of Otranto and the host of fifth-rate novels which it spawned. Mrs. Radcliffe's novels had greater subtilization but her ghostly visions were ruined with natural explanations. *The Monk*, albeit a masterpiece of terror, drags on the whole. "It is too long and too diffuse, and much of its potency is marred by flippancy and by an awkwardly excessive reaction against those canons of decorum which Lewis at first despised as prudish."[112]

If Lovecraft tends to share Miss Birkhead's reactions it does not mean that he was devoid of critical imagination. He knew that her response was the best one to these works. It has been only within recent years that literary discoveries and scholarship have seen Walpole's seminal novel, for example, in a new light, i.e. Devendra Varma's *The Gothic Flame* (1957) which presents a sympathetic though not completely convincing claim that *The Castle of Otranto* is the first surrealistic novel, a term which might have meant nothing to Lovecraft since the 1920 experiments of Philippe Souplaut's writing under hypnosis had been largely ignored.[113]

Contained among unpublished Lovecraft letters possessed by August Derleth are occasional references to Professor Birkhead's and Scarborough's works; the former praised, the other regarded somewhat critically.[114] In "Supernatural Horror in Literature" Lovecraft does not flay Miss Scarborough's book (what gentleman would!), tempting as the assault may be. One may, even without benefit of those letters, see where they cleaved. Where Lovecraft's tone is impersonal and the documentary style clipped and to the point, Miss Scarborough is willing to be cozy and cute. For all her erudition she deals with her subject impressionistically. "I don't know much about them,"

---

112. *Supernatural Horror in Literature*, p. 31.
113. See Devendra Varma's *The Gothic Flame*, Arthur Baker, Ltd., London, 1957, especially pages 42–73.
114. August Derleth, MS. letter to Arthur Koki, dated April 5, 1961, AK.

she says meaning ghosts and devils, "I have no learned theories of causation. I only love them."[115] She sees were-wolfs in chauffeurs, hippogriffs instead of aeroplanes, and demons disguised as dumb waiters.[116] She considers Lord Dunsany more as a creator of persiflage, writing "joyously of fantastic creatures with a happy grace, sometimes like a lilting laugh, sometimes a lyric rhapsody. His evoked beings are sportive or awesome but never unclean."[117] Lovecraft, on the other hand, characterized Dunsany's work as a curious mixture of beauty and spectral terror.[118] There is room for both opinions of course in the corpus of Dunsany's short stories and plays.

There is no easy meshing of their attitudes on Arthur Machen. Out of a decorous, delicately feminine sensibility, Professor Scarborough considers his stories obscene. They "leave a smear on the mind,"[119] and, moreover, he "deals with strange, sinister aspects of supernaturalism unlike the wholesome folklore that other writers reveal to us … one feels one should rinse his mind out after reading Arthur Machen's stories, particularly the collection called *The Three Impostors.*"[120] This is not at all how Lovecraft judges the Welsh author for "of living creators of cosmic fear raised to its most artistic pitch, few if any can hope to equal the versatile Arthur Machen [in whose stories] the elements of hidden horror and brooding fright attain an almost incomparable substance and realistic acuteness."[121] Edmund Wilson, to drop a name in partial defense for all concerned, while praising Lovecraft's "Supernatural Horror in Literature" as a "really able piece of work," thought that the enthusiastic praise for Machen and Dunsany showed "lack of

---

115. Scarborough, p. 4.
116. Ibid., p. 3.
117. Ibid., p. 249.
118. *Supernatural Horror in Literature*, pp. 99–100.
119. Scarborough, p. 271.
120. Ibid., p. 247.
121. *Supernatural Horror in Literature*, p. 88.

IV. A Protracted Season in Hell

sound literary taste," though clearly, "he [Lovecraft] had read comprehensively in this special field—he was strong on the Gothic novelists—and writes about it with much intelligence."[122] Lovecraft's esteem for Machen was, nevertheless, justified because he was recommending to his readers an exquisitely lyrical stylist who had been too long neglected since the rise of the proletarian novel with its concern for the heroic laborer and unemployed masses. Lovecraft supplied one of the most up-to-date appraisals of Machen's horror stories. It is, naturally enough, a one-sided commentary on his techniques, a rather specialized view which forgoes Machen's translations and non-fiction.

From his letters to Aunt Lillian Clark it is clear that writing "Supernatural Horror Literature" was an agreeable program for rereading as well as reading at first-hand stories which he had known previously only as names in Miss Scarborough's pages.

> My latest discovery is a pair of French writers (19th Cent.) who collaborated under the hyphenated designation of Erckmann-Chatrian. Their "Man Wolf" is a marvellously effective tale of a Gothick castle & a transmitted curse, whilst some of their short stories are of ineffable power. However, they must all bow before my new idol of idols, the erudite Montague Rhodes James, Litt. D., erudite antiquary student of old cathedral lore & architecture, & a provost of Eton College. I shall give James a very prominent mention in my article.[123]

When he turned to early American literature, Lovecraft's discussion of Charles Brockden Brown was spotty and conventional. Brown "stands the closest in spirit and method [to Mrs. Radcliffe]. Like her, he injured his creations by natural explanations; but also like her, he had an uncanny atmospheric power."[124] But Lovecraft shows imagina-

---

122. Edmund Wilson, "Tales of the Marvellous and the Ridiculous," *Classics and Commercials*. New York: Farrar, Straus & Co., 1950, p. 289.
123. H. P. Lovecraft, MS. letter to Mrs. Lillian D. Clark, dated January 26, 1916, JHL.
124. *Supernatural Horror in Literature,* pp. 218–19.

tion in his chapter devoted to Edgar Allan Poe. It is a balanced eight page account in which he deftly puts his finger on Poe's innovations, genius, and literary absurdities. He waived the *artiste maudit* recital. (The French had done that with all the rhetorical skill at their disposal until Poe became a domesticated beast over there.) In discussing "The Fall the House of Usher" Lovecraft was the first writer to suggest the correct relationship between Roderick, Madelina, and the house;

> "Usher," whose superiority in detail and proportion is very marked, hints shudderingly of obscure life in inorganic things, and displays an abnormally linked trinity of entities at the end of a long and isolated family history—a brother, his twin sister, and their incredibly ancient house all sharing a single soul and meeting one common dissolution at the same moment.[125]

Subsequent research by Poe scholars proved the validity of Lovecraft's explanation. Professor Thomas Ollive Mabbott, currently editing the definitive edition of Poe's works, wrote that "H. P. Lovecraft must always be remembered as a Poe student of highest rank," in part, at least, for his imaginative grasp of "Usher" which "enables us to throw away several unhappy interpretations—which range from an incestuous relation to autobiography—that have been offered by less perceptive critics."[126]

It is regrettable that no financial mogul came into Lovecraft's life to underwrite a book on Poe. Unfortunate, since Lovecraft had the scholar's questing mind: plus two things more—a distinct empathy with the subject and the advantage of being a writer in the horror genre aware of its problems even when he could not always successfully resolve them himself. But he apparently did not entertain more ambitious aims for his essay. As it was, he accomplished what he set out to

---

125. Ibid., p. 58.
126. Thomas Ollive Mabbott, "Lovecraft as a Student of Poe," *Fresco*, 8, No. 37 (Spring 1958).

IV. A Protracted Season in Hell

write. "Supernatural Horror in Literature" is an excellent one hundred page introduction to a vast, fascinating subject.

Lovecraft's health during the writing of the essay in 1926 seemed good, the only complaint being an itchy scalp and loss of hair:

> The big thinning of my hair—a worse thinning than any which has come since—occurred during the first month of 1922. I can still recall the bewildering way I felt of my hair at first, wondering what had happened! Instead of resistance, I met only flatness! But now all my brushing methods are accomodated to the new technique, so that I don't realise the loss any more. And in a decade, if I be still alive, I suppose I will be polishing with equal complacency a perfectly egg-bald crown![127]

Aside from this, there was little to disturb him. His prejudices and his hopes of returning to Providence were not forgotten but were pushed in the background.

At this time Sonia returned from Cleveland. Her arrival for Lovecraft meant bigger and better meals, though he would write to his aunts in shocked disgust and horror at the prospect of gaining weight. He would now be treated to occasional nights out to restaurants, movies, plays, and pocket money, and other sundry items he might desire.

> SH became impressed with the fact that all the $1.25 specimens are uncertain & mediocre, (mine worked only fairly) & that to obtain real satisfaction since she said she does not care for a pen—she proposed, with character is tick generosity, the exchange of both her pen & mine for one good Waterman—the difference to be paid in cash! There was no stopping this Quixotically philanthropick resolve, & I did not escape from the emporium till a *$6.25* Waterman reposed in my pocket.[128]

Lovecraft may have discarded Santa Claus and turned his back on the idea of a benevolent deity in the universe, but he freely accepted all the gifts his wife lavished on him. Mrs. Lovecraft had looked upon her role as wife in a somewhat loftier context. "I saw in Howard," she

---

127. H. P. Lovecraft, MS. letter to Mrs. Lillian D. Clark, dated January 11, 1926, JHL.
128. H. P. Lovecraft, MS. letter to Mrs. Lillian D. Clark, dated January 30, 1926, JHL.

wrote, "a Socratic wisdom and genius. I had hoped in time to humanize him further, to lift him out of his abysmal depths of loneliness and psychic complexes by a true, wedded love ... I had hoped, in other words, that my embrace would make of him not only a great genius but also a lover and husband."[129] It is difficult from this distance to know whether Mrs. Lovecraft was exaggerating her own importance in the above manifesto. One feels that a very real cleavage existed between them; although she may have glimpsed his peculiar genius, she never shared the same aesthetic point of view nor fully understood his solitary intelligence. Rarely did he refer to his wife and himself as "we"; rather, it was "SH & I." A sense of alienation was there. They were good "pals" who occasionally shared the same apartment but more often slept apart. Her positions in New Jersey and Cleveland may have been prompted by the unsatisfactory nature of their marriage. Her hopes of making a lover of Lovecraft were ironic, assuredly, since he was very reserved; even in his stories he eschewed sex-sensation completely, seldom including women and then only briefly and without warmth. The words "breast" or prosaic "bosom" hardly ever escaped his chaste pen. Adultery and seduction were alike foreign to his fictional realm. In real life, Mrs. Lovecraft later said that "when it came to performing the [sexual] act, Mr. Lovecraft was adequate—but little else."[130] Apparently he had given her to understand that her erotic desires were an imposition on his solitude. The Wife of Bath and the Clerk of Oxenford could not have been more improperly paired.

If he was something less than the perfect lover, the reasons are not difficult to discover. Mrs. Lovecraft's love, however sterling and expansive, could not absorb the pressures and anxieties from which Lovecraft suffered. An ordinary man would have found a real source

---

129. Davis, p. 243.
130. The offhand statement was made to a relative of a close mutual friend of Mr. and Mrs. Lovecraft.

IV. A Protracted Season in Hell

of comfort and a sense of security in a woman's love, but Lovecraft was not an ordinary person. "In the last resort," stated Freud, "we must begin to love in order that we may not fall ill, and must fall ill if, in consequence of frustration, we cannot love."[131] The inner turbulences can, however, be worked out in the act of creation:

> Krankheit ist wohl der letzte Grund
> Des ganzen Schopferdranos gewesen;
> Erschaffend konnte ich genesen,
> Erschaffend wurde ich gesund.[132]
>
> Disease at bottom brought about
> Creative urgence, for, creating,
> I soon could feel the pain abating,
> Creating, I could work it out.

We are again cognizant that writing served a therapeutic function in Lovecraft's life. But this does not tell us why he chose writing instead of love, that of Mrs. Lovecraft. The reason was Mrs. Lovecraft herself. She was all that he was not. She was resourceful and talented in the business world; she had a zest for life and a happy facility for making the best of any situation. Her literary abilities were inconsequential; her one or two short stories in the horror vein were extensively revised, ghost written actually, by Lovecraft and appeared in one of the obscure Amateur publications. Her affinities for fantasy and the eighteenth century were not conspicuous, nor did they blossom after marriage. There were more practical considerations to think about. Since Lovecraft had remained dormant, Mrs. Lovecraft had assumed the dominant role. To create a semblance of normalcy, she had, in her own words, "effaced my own interests and deferred to him upon all matters and domestic problems regardless of what they were. Even to the spending of money I not only consulted him but tried to make him

---

131. Sigmund Freud, *Collected Papers*, New York: Basic Books, Inc., 1959, 4.12.
132. Ibid., Heine, quoted by Freud.

feel that he was the head of the house."[133] Although she did not mention it, she had, naturally enough, urged him to intensify his efforts in securing employment. Later, in retrospect, he considered that she had "driven him" and he resented it.[134]

There was also the disparity in their background. Here again he had compromised with one of his deepest, traditional beliefs—his mistrust of the "foreigner"—by marrying a non-Anglo-Saxon. When his marriage failed to achieve true happiness, he conveniently overlooked his own ineptitude and submitted the notion that ethnic backgrounds and finances were responsible. He had always been convinced that each racial group had distinct traits which mixed as badly as water and turpentine. This point was evident from his abhorrence of missionaries:

> As I have always said, missionaries are infernal nuisances who ought to be kept at home—dull, solemn asses without scientific acumen or historical perspectives; & cursed with the eternal blindness to the obvious fact that different lands, races, & conditions naturally develop & demand different cultural standards & usages & different ethical & social codes.[135]

Whenever he spoke of New York's "mongrel population" in his wife's presence, she reminded him that she too was of the "alien hordes"—to which replied he, "You are now Mrs. H. P. Lovecraft of 598 Angell Street, Providence, Rhode Island."[136]

Mrs. Lovecraft's tenderness toward her husband degenerated into a gift-giving proposition, though their relation continued to all appearances on an amiable level: the "best of pals." Someone coming upon the Lovecraft correspondence, unless told that "SH" meant Mrs. Lovecraft, would most likely mistake her for one of Lovecraft's friends in the Kalem Club.

---

133. Davis, p. 241.
134. Mrs. Muriel E. Eddy, MS. letter to Arthur Koki, dated June 25, 1959, AK.
135. H. P. Lovecraft, MS. letter to Mrs. Lillian D. Clark, dated September 12–13, 1925, JHL.
136. Davis, p. 142.

IV. A Protracted Season in Hell

It was fortunate for Lovecraft that many women, particularly women in America, aware of their own cultural deficiencies, have readily married and pampered ne'er-do-wells who could string together words, paint, or read. Their choice may be considered as foolish, perhaps, but, actually, they have been courageous and idealistic.

In February, Mrs. Lovecraft left for Cleveland. Lovecraft was now close to finishing his article for Cook and, with nothing else to preoccupy him, he began to look about once more and brood. A curious feeling of ennui and irritation clawed at him. Even the presence of some of the Kalem Club members was irksome:

> In nations, as in society, *Congeniality* is the important principle. As for me, I'm sick of Bohemians, odds & ends, freaks, & plebeians . . . & satellites & miscellany &c. They amuse for awhile, but begin after a time to get frightfully on one's nerves. People get on one's nerves when they harbour different kinds of memories & live by different kinds of standards & cherish different kinds of goals & ideals. The only company for a regular conservative American is that formed by regular conservative Americans—well-born & comfortably nurtured in the old tradition. That's why Belknap is about the only one of the gang who doesn't irritate me at times. He is *regular*—he connects up with innate memories & Providence experience to such an extent as to seem a real person instead of a two-dimensional shadow in a dream, as most Bohemian personalities do . . . And if one cannot find a niche in congenial society, one can at least be *alone*, & that is enough for me. To be clear of irritant & hostile social fabrics is the thing—for otherwise, faced by a life of exile in hateful chaos, a bullet through the brain is the only solution.[137]

Frank B. Long, Jr. wisely perceived that Lovecraft was becoming dreadfully depressed and, fearing a nervous collapse or suicide imminent, he wrote an urgent appeal to Lovecraft's aunts, begging them to take their nephew back to Providence, even for one month's visit. They promptly asked Lovecraft to return. He replied ecstatically:

> Well!!! All your epistles arrived & received a grateful welcome, but the

---

137. H. P. Lovecraft, MS. letter to Mrs. Lillian D. Clark, dated February 20, 1926, JHL.

third one was the climax that relegates everything else to the distance! Whoop! Bang! I had to go on a celebration forthwith . . . & have now returned to gloat & reply.

And now about your invitation. Hooray!! Long live the State of Rhode-Island & Providence Plantations!!! But I'm past the *visiting* point. Even if my physique is flourishing, my nerves are a mess—& *I could never board train away from Providence toward York again* . . . I'm not eager for ignominious returns via the small orifice of the trumpet; but if you & AEPG think it's perfectly dignified for me to slip unobtrusively back toward civilization & Waterman St., I'm sure I couldn't think of anything else logical for one who is an integral part of Rhode Island earth. Only last night I dreamed of Foster. If I ever use my brain, I guess it'll have to be in R.I.—though I might stand the Boston area if any imperative business fixed me there. But as to details—I'm all in favour of letting you & AEPG do *all* the planning, if you don't mind, & of sending my things ahead of me. When I land in person, I want my address to be *115 Waterman St.* Your plan for the little apartment is so ideal that I can't do anything but blister my palms applauding—& once I'm in it, I'll certainly hustle like the devil with writing to see if I can make enough to assure its permanence.

I trust you to do all the arranging—you know how big the room at 169 is, & exactly what's in it; & can easily see that the new quarters come up to space requirements. There's no hurry—just wait till all is well, then hire your space & *let me know!* Packing will be a deuce of a job—but with a new lease on life at stake I shall have the energy of a daemon! . . . Had I better wait till some Providence moving-man has his van in N. Y. before arranging for any large shipments? All this can be extended over weeks if necessary—I shall be perfectly content to camp out here amidst diminishing possessions. Only one thing I must have *new* & that is a *couch.* I will not have a *bed* in my room, for it must be primarily a pleasant study as now. I am now used to sleeping on a narrow couch, (I never open the one here when alone) & wish a cheap specimen of the same.[138]

Mrs. Lovecraft stated that her husband had wanted to return to Providence almost from the very day of their marriage. Only the idea of inconveniencing her had deterred him.[139] But in the profuse correspondence to his aunts mention of his wife is rare. She had already

---

138. H. P. Lovecraft, MS. letter to Mrs. Lillian D. Clark, dated March 27, 1926, JHL, "AEPG" is Mrs. Annie E. P. Gamwell.
139. Davis, MS. "The Private Life . . . Lovecraft," p. 16, JHL.

IV. A Protracted Season in Hell

spent considerable time away from him and he evidently saw no reason why she could not continue to work in Cleveland or elsewhere while he waited for her in quarters more congenial than New York.

His two aunts were disturbed by the high spirits which their nephew displayed in accepting their proposal. True, Providence was superior to New York, but still . . . He calmed his tone.

> Now about migrations—there is no question of disillusion involved. I don't expect to live in a seventh heaven of happiness anywhere, & only want to drag out my last days in some quiet backwater where the general environment isn't too obtrusively offensive. There is no question of illusion or disillusion about Providence—I know what it is, & I have never mentally dwelt anywhere else. When I look up from my work it is Angell St. I see outside the windows, & when I think of going out to buy anything it is Westminster St. that comes to my eyes until objective realism painstakingly corrects the image, I have no emotional as apart from intellectual conviction that I am not in Providence this very moment—indeed, psychologically speaking, I *am* & always will be there. Whenever I hear a whistle in the night I always think it is some boat in the bay, or some train down at the Bristol Depot.[140]

To add still further to his joy, his aunts found on Barnes Street a suitable apartment and made tentative arrangements to lease it.

> Whooppee!! Bang!! Rah!! For God's sake jump at that room without a second's delay. I can't believe it—too good to be true! Bet it'll evaporate like that one we picked out in Garden Place a year ago. Somebody wake me up before the dream becomes so poignant I can't bear to be waked up!!
>
> Take it? Well, I should say so!! I can't write coherently, but proceed to do at once what I can about packing. Barnes near Brown! What deep breaths I can take after this infernal squalor her!!! I'll wait & finish my article at home! I can't write connectedly now—too excited—but merely dash off an ecstatic affirmation & appreciation! Hope you can get a room for yourself in the same place—hurrah for the corners & characters of Providence![141]

---

140. H. P. Lovecraft, MS. letter to Mrs. Lillian D. Clark, dated March 29, 1926, JHL.
141. H. P. Lovecraft, MS. letter to Mrs. Lillian D. Clark, dated April 1, 1926, JHL.

Mrs. Lovecraft, working in Cleveland, was informed of his deliverance from bondage. There was some concern on Lovecraft's part that she would take it "in too melancholy a light or as something to be criticised from the standpoint of loyalty & good taste."[142] She was sensible enough to see where his real happiness lay. On April 8th she came to New York and "helped valiantly"[143] with the packing and shipping arrangements. To get the bad taste of New York out of his mouth, she sported her husband to a round of gormandizing.[144]

At last all was in readiness. He bid his few friends goodbye. With them he would still correspond. There would also be occasional stop-over trips to New York to see the old gang. But now Providence was upper most in his mind.

> I was drawn back to ancestral sources more vividly than at any other time I can recall; and have since thought about little else! I am infus'd and saturated with the vital forces of my inherited being, & re-baptised in the mood, atmosphere, & personality of sturdy New England forbearers. A pox on thy towns & decadent modern notions—one sight of the mossy walls & white gables of true agrestick America, & pure heredity can flout 'em all! And health to His Majesty's Providence of Rhode-Island & Providence-Plantations! GOD SAVE THE KING![145]

The wayward son who had compromised with himself had at last returned home.

---

142. H. P. Lovecraft, MS. letter to Mrs. Lillian D. Clark, dated April 6, 1926, JHL.
143. H. P. Lovecraft, MS. letter to Mrs. Lillian D. Clark, dated April 12, 1926, JHL.
144. H. P. Lovecraft, MS. letter to Mrs. Lillian D. Clark, dated April 12–13, 1926, JHL.
145. H. P. Lovecraft, MS. letter to Mrs. Lillian D. Clark, dated April 16, 1926, JHL. [This letter is in fact addressed to Frank Belknap Long, October 26, 2926]

V.

Home

> Slightly soured by exile, perhaps, but the same tough nut at heart, & ready for writing.[1]

Once more at home in Providence, H. P. Lovecraft settled into his favored mode of existence, sleeping by day and writing into the night and approaching dawn innumerable letters to his Amateur correspondents and occasional stories for *Weird Tales*. No longer would robbers break into his apartment or mice contaminate his daily bread.

I would like to be persuaded by Mr. Cook that Lovecraft emerged from his New York experience "pure gold"[2]—whatever that means. But the evidence is not entirely amicable to Mr. Cook's belief. There are letters (some to be cited) and there are the stories. Lovecraft never lost the opportunity to warn younger correspondents who might be tempted to go to New York, and on one occasion he commended a friend for having left New York City to return to the Middle West.

> A wise move, in my opinion, since the cheap ego-tickling atmosphere of Greenwich Village was rapidly making a poseur & whiskey-sponge out of him. Whatever may be said in favour of New York's more solid phases, I can't see that Greenwich Village's "arty" bohemianism has any justifica-

---

1. H. P. Lovecraft, MS. letter to Mrs. Lillian D. Clark, dated March 27, 1926.
2. Cook, p. 14.

tion for existence. Its net effect is to dry genius & sidetrack potential talent into cheapness, triviality, & waste.³

After his New York experience Lovecraft was a freer spirit because the irritants of metropolitan life had been removed.

With his two aunts he moved to 10 Barnes Street,⁴ a gabled Victorian house where, mercifully, every lodger was descended "from the best Rhode Island colonial stock."⁵ Mrs. Gamwell had an apartment of her own, while Mrs. Lillian Clark, a partial invalid unable to keep house, had a large sunny room upstairs. Lovecraft's downstairs room was so shadowed by a porch and other buildings as to be virtually lightless, but he simply "cut loose from the external world, pulled down the shades, & burned 135 watts of current night & day . . . *with the landlady's permission.*"⁶ When he did roll up the shade and blink out, he could catch "an exquisite glimpse of fresh village scenery; an old, decaying mansion with a wooded yard in picaresque wilderness, a trim little yellow cottage, & a well-kept Georgian garden with white fence & urn-topped posts."⁷ He did not linger. There were promises he meant to fulfill.

"I certainly intend to have the leisure residue *purely & simply for myself*—my own personal reading & literary composition,"⁸ he said seven weeks before leaving New York. Earlier, in July, he wrote Aunt Lillie that "Very shortly I shall start some businesslike writing—copying

---

3. H. P. Lovecraft, MS. letter to Margaret Ronan, n.d., circa 1936. Collection of Margaret Ronan. Hereafter abbreviated to MR.
4. [Only Lillian D. Clark moved to 10 Barnes Street with HPL, living in an apartment on the second floor while he lived in a separate apartment on the first floor. Annie E. P. Gamwell lived elsewhere.]
5. H. P. Lovecraft, MS. letter to Samuel Loveman, dated July 6, 1927. Collection of Samuel Loveman. Hereafter, SL.
6. H. P. Lovecraft, MS. letter to Margaret Ronan, n.d., circa February, 1937, MR.
7. H. P. Lovecraft, MS. letter to Samuel Loveman, dated July 6, 1927, SL.
8. H. P. Lovecraft, MS. letter to Mrs. Lillian D. Clark, dated March 4, 1926, JHL.

V. Home

more stories for *Weird Tales* & beginning some new ones whose ideas are clamoring for expression."[9] Such remarks are frequent in Lovecraft's pre-exodus correspondence. They were heavy-laden hints that he was on the verge of writing some powerful, aesthetically-satisfying stories if only he could calm his mind or place himself in a milieu more suitable than Brooklyn. The opportunity came in April, 1926, and Lovecraft seized it. He rolled down the shade and set to work. The year 1926 must stand as one of the most important in his writing career.

Weird Tales published "The Tomb" (see Chapter II) in January, 1926. It had first appeared in the Amateur journal, *The Vagrant*, in March, 1922. Although Professor T. O. Mabbott considered "The Tomb" a good Poesque variation,[10] Lovecraft, with typical severity, criticized the story, saying, "As for 'The Tomb'—I'm not especially fond of that, for to my mind it's distinctly stiff & crude. It was the first tale I wrote after an hiatus of 9 years—1908 to 1917—& shows a distinct cumbrousness & rustiness."[11] But fond of them or not, he enjoyed copying out for publication Amateur stories which he had originally written with no expectation of money.

The next issue of *Weird Tales* in February, 1926, included "The Cats of Ulthar," the Dunsanian fantasy which had first appeared in *Tryout*, November, 1920.

Written in 1921, but not previously published elsewhere, "The Outsider" was printed in the April *Weird Tales*. It is a first-person narrative of imprisonment, escape, and ironic recognition. He, the Outsider, had been cut off from companionship, the sound of a human voice, or the simple consolation of a mirror. The only living creatures he knew were "noiseless rats, and bats and spiders, while around him

---

9. H. P. Lovecraft, MS. letter to Mrs. Lillian D. Clark, dated July 27, 1927, JHL.
10. T. O. Mabbott, rev. *The Outsider and Others, American Literature* (March 1940), p. 136.
11. H. P. Lovecraft, MS. letter to Mrs. Lillian D. Clark, dated December 2, 1925, JHL.

bones and skeletons lay strewn. Self-taught through moldy books, he would "longingly picture [himself] amidst gay crowds in the sunny world beyond the endless forest."[12] He escapes after arduously crawling up the slimy sides of the dark prison. When he pushes open the overhead trap door and crawls out, exhausted, he is stunned to discover himself at ground level in a graveyard. He flees into the woods and after a few hours arrives at an ivied castle "maddeningly familiar, yet full of perplexing strangeness to me,"[13] where a merry party attracts him into the brightly lit ballroom. Hysteria coincides with his arrival. "Flight was universal, and in the clamor and panic several fell in a swoon and were dragged away by their madly fleeing companions. Many covered their eyes with their hands, and plunged blindly and awkwardly in their race to escape, overturning furniture and stumbling against the walls before they managed to reach one of the many doors."[14] The Outsider stalks around the room, looking for the cause of this disturbance. He glances into an adjoining room and sees the thing, an incredibly old and putrid creation. "God knows it was not of this world—or no longer of this world—yet to my horror I saw in its eaten-away and bone-revealing outlines a leering, abhorrent travesty on the human shape."[15] Hypnotised by the glassy stare confronting him, the Outsider approaches the monster. He yet finds enough strength to ward off the "fetid apparition" by throwing out a hand . . . but his outstretched fingers *"touched a cold and unyielding surface of polished glass."*[16]

It has been said of "The Outsider" that if the manuscript had been submitted as an unpublished tale by Poe no one would have challenged it.[17] The story's early development does echo "Berenice," for

---

12. H. P. Lovecraft, "The Outsider," *The Outsider*, p. 63.
13. Ibid., p. 65.
14. Ibid., p. 64.
15. Ibid., p. 66.
16. Ibid.
17. *The Best Supernatural Stories of H. P. Lovecraft*, p. 8.

V. Home

example, where the narrator's isolation is stressed and the suspicion of madness confirmed as his tortured mind seeks to distinguish reality from the fantasy in his memory—"a memory like a shadow—vague, variable, indefinite, unsteady."[18] Yet Egaeus, to continue the "Berenice" comparison, is insane, unquestionably, but still human. He would gaze "for long unwearied hours . . . on the margin or in the typography of a book; to become absorbed for the better part of a summer's day, in a quaint shadow falling aslant upon the tapestry or upon the floor."[19] Unlike any of Poe's characters, the Outsider is a ghoul. A few hints would indicate that prior to his transformation, the Outsider was once a human being since he retains dim memories of a previous human existence before his underground confinement, and he is shocked speechless upon first looking into the mirror; with ghoulish pluck he accepts his heritage and rides out "with the mocking and friendly ghouls on the night wind [to] play by day amongst the catacombs of Nephren-Ka in the sealed and unknown valley of Hadath by the Nile."[20] Since the Outsider is an *outré* being, the description of his imprisonment in the crypt and of himself tends toward the overly bizarre. It is, in other words, brushed on too thick in spots: "I cannot even hint what it was like, for it was a compound of all that is unclean, uncanny, unwelcome, abnormal and detestable. It was the ghoulish shade of decay, antiquity and dissolution; the putrid, dripping eidolon of unwholesome revelation . . ."[21] This could have come from Poe's hand, but it would have been Poe at his weakest. It would have been Poe overwriting "Ligeia." Dark thoughts in a dark chamber with rats scurrying among the skeletons may convince some readers that Lovecraft has

---

18. Edgar Allan Poe, "Berenice," *Edgar Allan Poe: Tales of Mystery and Imagination,* New York, Heritage Press, 1941, p. 142.
19. Ibid., p. 143.
20. "The Outsider," p. 66.
21. Ibid.

hoisted a tableaux from a Gothic novel. A much better scene is the one where the ghoul enters the castle. It is as unforgettable as the Red Death's violation of Prince Prospero's majestic apartments. There is the vivid contrast between the gaiety and airy babble in the castle and the pandemonium which erupts when the Outsider appears and shatters their polite world.

The surprise ending story is rare in Lovecraft when the canon of his work is examined. He distrusted tales dependent on trick conclusions. "Best horror dwells in atmosphere, even in language itself," he wrote, "and not in obvious stage-managed documents and literary cap-pistol shots."[22]

Poe is the apparent stylistic influence in "The Outsider," but quite probably the source for the story is Nathaniel Hawthorne specifically a plot idea he jotted in "The Journal of Solitary Man":

> I dreamed one bright forenoon I was walking through Broadway, and seeking to cheer myself I entered the warm and busy life of that famed promenade ... I found myself in this animated scene, with a dim and misty idea that it was not my proper place, or that I had ventured into the crowd with some singularity of dress or aspect which made me ridiculous ... Every face grew pale; the laugh was hushed ... and the passengers on all sides fled as from an embodied pestilence ... I passed not one step farther, but threw my eyes on a looking-glass which stood deep within the nearest shop. At first glimpse of my own figure I awoke, with a horrible sensation of self-terror and self-loathing ... I had been promenading Broadway in my shroud![23]

There is elsewhere in Hawthorne, in *The American Notebooks*, a briefer note—"To make one's own reflection in a mirror the subject of a story."[24] In his own Commonplace Book, Lovecraft scribbled out in 1919

---

22. H. P. Lovecraft, MS. letter to Robert H. Barlow, dated October 22, 1934, JHL.
23. Quoted by George Wetzel in "The Cthulhu Mythos: A Study," *Howard Phillips Lovecraft: Memoirs, Critiques, & Bibliographies*, p. 24.
24. *The Portable Hawthorne*, ed. Malcolm Cowley, New York, Viking Press, 1948, p. 549.

V. Home

an idea which suggests The Outsider: "Fear of mirrors—memory of dream in which scene is altered & climax is hideous surprise at seeing oneself in the water or mirror (Identity?)."[25] There is also another entry which may also have been a germ idea: "Dried-up man living for centuries in cataleptic state in ancienttomb."[26]

The editor of *Weird Tales* in fulsome praise of "The Outsider" asked, "Where in the whole realm of literature will you find a more original conception, or more consummate artistry in the workmanship, than in this story? Its every sentence bears the mark of the master literary craftsman... Not even Poe in his wildest flights of fancy has surpassed the winged beauty of this imaginative weird tale."[27]

Equally laudatory, though less suspect, was Ray Cummings, the science-fiction author ("Tarrano the Conqueror" and "Shadow Girl") who, in a letter to the editor of *Weird Tales,* demanded to know "Who in blazes is H. P. Lovecraft? I never heard the name before. If he is a present-day writer—which I cannot imagine him to be—he deserves to be world famous ... Never have I encountered any purer, more beautiful diction."[28] Cummings' letter was printed in June, 1926, the same issue of *Weird Tales* which contained yet another early Lovecraft story, "The Moon-Bog," written in 1921. It is a brief, conventional story which neither enriches nor appreciably diminishes the corpus of Lovecraft's fiction. Set in Ireland, "The Moon-Bog" tells what happens when a wealthy American, come back to the sod, orders the drainage of a peat bog on his estate. This against the better advice of the superstitious peasants. The disturbance of a Greek moon-goddess temple submerged in the bog heralds disaster. In the night an eerie piping sound floats through the air and white-clad naiads lead the workmen

---

25. H. P. Lovecraft, "Commonplace Book," *The Shuttered Room,* p. 102.
26. Ibid., p. 107.
27. "The Eyrie," *Weird Tales* (April 1926), p. 566.
28. Quoted by Moskowitz, p. 42.

and servants into the marshland. "The line of followers, never checking their speed, splashed awkwardly after them and vanished amidst a tiny vortex of unwholesome bubbles."[29] The Irish-American is shanghaied, twisted down into "a vague contorted shadow struggling as if drawn by unseen demons."[30]

The story was written in March, 1921, for a special occasion. Lovecraft had been invited to an Amateur gathering in Boston, the meeting coinciding with St. Patrick's Day. Placing the manuscript in his overnight grip, he took care before leaving Providence *not* to wear a conspicuous green necktie in honor of the late Celtic saint.[31] At the home of one Amateur, he read "The Moon-Bog" aloud and felt pleased by the other members' appreciative responses. The pleasure was sweetened by the contrasting mediocrity of some of the other stories read. There was, for example, Mrs. Ellis, the chairman herself:

> ... and she read an original story which was absolutely the worst I have ever encountered in Amateur journalism. It was hardly more than a collection of later Victorian stock phrases & situations, & for a long time I fancied the intent was satirical—on the order of Leacock's Nonsense Novels in Harper's. But it was all meant seriously, as I finally saw. The next day it was the standing joke of the household, & laughter was evoked merely by quoting a sentence or two from it.[32]

If he was cruel on Mrs. Ellis, his later judgement of "The Moon-Bog" was equally pointed. "Pretty bad" was his verdict.[33]

This was also his opinion of "The Terrible Old Man," written on January 28, 1920, published first in *Tryout*, July, 1921, and professional-

---

29. H. P. Lovecraft, "The Moon-Bog," *Beyond the Wall of Sleep*, p. 53.
30. Ibid., p. 54.
31. H. P. Lovecraft, MS. letter to Mrs. W. S. Lovecraft, dated March 17, 1921, JHL.
32. Ibid.
33. From a letter to August Derleth. Cited in the reportorial notes of Winfield Townley Scott, deposited in the John Hay Library.

V. Home

ly in *Weird Tales,* August, 1926. The four characters in the story are three thugs and an old sea captain who lives in virtual seclusion in Kingston.[34] The palsied captain, by secret means, disposes of the intruders who had come to rob him, and their bodies are later washed up on the seashore "horribly slashed as with many cutlasses, and horribly mangled as by the tread of many cruel boot-heels."[35] The loss is not great for we were told that Messrs. Ricci, Czanek, and Silva were not of Kingston blood, but were instead "of that new and heterogeneous alien stock which lies outside the charmed circle of New England life and traditions."[36] It may be asked whether Lovecraft changed the Amateur stories he later submitted to *Weird Tales.* There probably was little, if any, alteration. A comparison of the original manuscript of "The Terrible Old Man," now in my possession, and the version printed in *Weird Tales,* reveals that the two versions are one and the same, without a variation in word or punctuation.

The next Lovecraft story which *Weird Tales* published was "He" (quoted in Chapter III) in September of 1926. Like most of his brief efforts, it was completed in one day. Without benefit of the original manuscript, but from a letter to one of his aunts, the date of composition of "He" can be pinned down to a day in August, 1925, when Lovecraft was living in Brooklyn:

> At a small shop I bought a dime composition book; & having a pencil & pencil sharpener (in a case, which SH gave me) in my pocket, proceeded to select a site for literary creation. Scott Park . . . was the place I chose; & there, pleasantly intoxicated by the wealth of delicate unmetropolitan greenery & the yellow & white Colonialism of the gambrel-roofed Scott house, I settled myself for work. Ideas welled up unbidden, as never before for years, & the sunny actual scene soon blended into the purple & red of a hellish midnight tale—a tale of cryptical horrors among

---

34. [Koki means Kingsport, although the town was not yet identified with Marblehead, MA.]
35. H. P. Lovecraft, "The Terrible Old Man," *The Outsider,* p. 139.
36. Ibid., p. 138.

tangles of antediluvian alleys in Greenwich Village—wherein I wrote not a little poetick description, & the abiding terror of him who comes to New York as to a faery flower of stone & marble, yet finds only a verminous corpse—a dead city of squinting alienage with nothing in common either with its own pastor with the background of America in general. I named it "He" & had it nearly done by three, when . . . my engagement called me back to Babylon. Finishing the tale en route . . .[37]

"He," "The Terrible Old Man," "Moon-Bog," "The Outsider," "The Cats of Ulthar," and "The Tomb" comprised Lovecraft's work in *Weird Tales* for 1926. The stories stood up well against other macabre [tales] in the magazine, but generally suffer [in] comparison with his later work. A beachhead had been established at any rate. Of greater significance than the stories sold were those that he wrote in 1926–1927, but which, through Lovecraft's peculiar work habits or the added vagaries of the editors, were not to be published until later, in one case—*The Case of Charles Dexter Ward*—fourteen years later. Four types of stories were to be developed: (1) the ghoul or ghoul-changeling stories, already seen in "The Picture in the House," "Rats in the Walls," and "The Outsider"; (2) the stories of psychic possession (an early example of this was "The Tomb"); (3) the dream phantasies of Randolph Carter; and (4) the Cthulhu Mythos. This latter must be considered Lovecraft's greatest achievement. One may go so far as to call it "the most stirring, consciously created single myth in scientific fiction."[38] The Cthulhu mythology, replete with gods, minor deities, battles of light and dark powers, sacred texts, and incantations, explains the origin of the cosmos, pre-human races, and man's extinction. The suggestion of categories for Lovecraft's fiction does not insist that his stories easily fall into place. Most of them are actually mixed types, variations on a grand theme.

---

37. H. P. Lovecraft, MS. letter to Mrs. Lillian D, Clark, dated August 13, 1925, JHL.

38. J. O. Bailey, *Pilgrims Through Space and Time*, New York: Argus Books, Inc., 1947, p. 318.

V. Home

The concept of beings from other worlds is deftly treated in "The Strange High House the Mist," a short story which recalls the early Lovecraft with his Dunsanian taste for strange homes, enveloped in mist, set high by the sea. An almost inaccessible cottage is visited by a professor during his vacation. Its occupant, an old man, "whose eyes were phosphorescent with the imprint of unheard-of sights,"[39] invites him inside and holds him spellbound with stories "of the dim first age of chaos before the gods or even the Elder Gods were born, and when *the other gods* came to dance on the peak of Hatheg-Kla in the stony desert near Ulthar, beyond the River Skai."[40] At night, Neptune and the minions of his court take the professor and the old man on a trip. The professor returns to his family the next day, safe though sad in spirit. One discerns touches of humor placed here and there by Lovecraft's attitude toward man and his institutions. Professor Olney in the story is described as one who "taught ponderous things in a college by Narragansett Bay ... his eyes were weary with seeing the same things for many years, and thinking the same well-disciplined thoughts."[41] His mate is drawn with less charity as a "stout wife [who] prayed to the bland proper god of Baptists, and hoped that the traveller [Olney] would borrow an umbrella and rubbers unless the rain stopped by morning."[42]

Successive readings of "Pickman's Model" (1926) persuade me to feel that it, too, despite its horror, has humor—indeed, it comes close to satirizing the ghoul theme.

Briefly, the story is about Richard Pickman, a Boston artist whose pictures of ghoulish horror are so realistic-looking that his friends repudiate him. All except one—Thurber, the narrator, who is invited to a clandestine visit to Pickman's secret studio in Boston's North End,

---

39. H. P. Lovecraft, "The Strange High House in the Mist," *The Outsider*, p. 25.
40. Ibid.
41. Ibid., p. 23.
42. Ibid., p. 26.

that area which is steeped in tradition and atmosphere "overflowing with wonder and terror and escapes from the commonplace," as Pickman says.[43] Inside the dingy cellar studio, Thurber is appalled by the paintings which Pickman has executed with scientific realism. "Nothing was blurred, distorted or conventionalised; outlines were sharp and lifelike, and details were almost painfully defined. And the faces!"[44] Thurber lets out a scream which echoes through the nitrous cellar. A clawing, squealing noise responds outside the studio and Pickman nervously steps out to chase the thing away. He fires his revolver into the air and returns to apologize for the rats which infest the subterranean tunnels under the North End. By this time, Thurber, whose nerves are near the breaking point, leaves. The next morning he notices in his coat a curled-up photograph which he had unconsciously pulled off and pocketed when he screamed in Pickman's studio. The photograph had been tacked to an especially terrifying canvas. He imagines it at first to be a photograph of some familiar Boston landmark which Pickman planned to use as a background to his pictures. But he sees to his horror that the photograph is not a background at all. It is a snapshot of the ghoul in the painting, taken from life.

A clever denouement, this is one of the most original ideas in the history of the weird tale.[45] It is as ingenious as Lord Dunsany's "Two Bottles of Relish," and it is this cleverness only which one remembers. "Pickman's Model" is one of Lovecraft's few stories that can be reduced to a cartoon: the large unfurnished studio, here the artist with his Rollei and there, across the room, poses "the dog face with its pointed ears, bloodshot eyes, flat nose, and drooling lips ... scale claws ... mould-caked body. . . half-hooved feet,"[46] its eyes cast down

---

43. H. P. Lovecraft, "Pickman's Model," *The Outsider*, p.172.
44. Ibid., p. 175.
45. Penzoldt, p. 167.
46. "Pickman's Model," p. 176.

V. Home

with the refined coquetry of a modest ghoul.

When "Pickman's Model" was published in *Weird Tales* (October, 1927), a young admirer of Lovecraft's named Robert Bloch sent him ten crayon drawings on cardboard, one of which showed Pickman's ghouls gleefully tearing a man apart under an archway marked "Dine & Dance."[47] Lovecraft took the joke in good spirits and kept the drawings. He encouraged young Bloch when the latter turned his hand toward macabre fiction and went so far as to predict that the boy would one day achieve success in that genre.[48] Bloch, in "The Strange Island of Dr. Nork," written with his characteristic drollery-amid-horror, may originally have had "Pickman's Model" in mind, although "Dr. Nork" has wider application as a satire against comic books and mad scientists. In its effort to achieve realism, the largest publisher of "funny" books hires Dr. Nork "a broken-down old Nobel Prize winner," to create living monsters which will serve as models for its artists. He obliges with an asylum of oddities: zombies, the Frog-man, Fire-bug (who eructs living flame), a talking gorilla, and a perfect super-criminal called the Faceless Fiend, who runs amuck.[49]

Lovecraft left the anthropophagous ghouls harboured in Boston's bowels and elsewhere to embark for *terra incognita* in the time-space travels and the dream phantasies of Randolph Carter. This Lovecraftian hero appears in four works: "The Statement of Randolph Carter," "The Silver Key," a novelette titled *The Dream-Quest of Unknown Kadath*, and "Through the Gates of the Silver Key," which was written in collaboration with E. Hoffmann Price. The stories are loosely connective, though it is preferable to read them together and in their chronological

---

47. [This must have happened sometime after Bloch first came in touch with HPL in the spring of 1933. Bloch (b. 1917) was only ten years old when "Pickman's Model" was first published.]
48. In private conversation with Frank B. Long, Jr., on January 25, 1961.
49. Robert Bloch, "The Strange Island of Dr. Nork," *The Unexpected*, ed. Leo Margulies, Pyramid Books, 1961, pp. 42–60.

sequence since references and summaries of the early stories occur in the latter two. The French published this quartet under the title *Démons et Merveilles* as one novel, with each story considered a section.

It was earlier noted in Chapter II that "The Statement of Randolph Carter" (1919) was the result of a particularly vivid dream Lovecraft had experienced in which he was Randolph Carter while Samuel Loveman was the unfortunate Harley Warren. Between Lovecraft and Carter there are undeniable similarities of temperament which tend to suggest that the fictional persona, to some degree, is Lovecraft. With Olympian detachment, Lovecraft in most stories sacrificed characterization for atmosphere. When we find him devoting more than half of "The Silver Key" to Carter's philosophy, it is plain that a certain fascination has developed. It may be pushing too hard, however, to say, as Jacques Bergier did, that "The Silver Key" "est la seule autobiographie spirituelle de Lovecraft qui nous soit parvenue. Elle nous fait suivre le chemin qui mène hors de notre univers, dans les continus de l'inconnu."[50] If Monsieur Bergier had read certain of Lovecraft's articles in the now dead, forgotten Amateur Press magazines, he would have seen how similar Randolph Carter's pensees are to "Idealism and Materialism: A Reflection" (1919), "A Confession of Unfaith" (1922), "Nietzscheism and Realism" (1921), and "Some Causes of Self-Immolation." There has been, in sum, no evolution of Lovecraft's thought. No spiritual crisis. Only a reaffirmation of former beliefs.

In "The Silver Key," Randolph Carter is visited in a dream by his grandfather who reminds him of a key capable of opening the lost gate of dreams. Carter finds the huge key, tarnished and covered with cryptical arabesques, hidden in the attic of his Boston home. He then visits the deserted family birthplace in witch-haunted Arkham. There, key in

---

50. H. P. Lovecraft, *Démons et Merveilles,* Paris: Deux Rives, 1955, p. 9. ["The Silver Key" "is the only spiritual autobiography by Lovecraft that has come down to us. It makes us follow the path that leads out of our universe, into the continuum of the unknown."]

V. Home

pocket, he walks into the woods and disappears. Lovecraft's indifference to the claims of organized religion echo when we learn that "It wearied Carter to see how solemnly people tried to make earthly reality out of old myths which every step of their boasted science refuted, and this misplaced seriousness killed the attachment he might have kept for the ancient creeds had they been content to offer the sonorous rites and emotional outlets in their true guise of ethereal fantasy."[51] In his essay "Idealism and Materialism: A Reflection," Lovecraft stated that the vociferous atheist "should be censured when hostility to religion leads him on to a destructive course. He should not pull down what he cannot replace."[52] Between the Scylla of childlike faith and the Charybdis of crass materialism, Carter "tried to live as befitted a man of keen thought and good heritage . . . under the ridicule of the age he could not believe in anything, but the love of harmony kept him close to the ways of his race and station."[53] Randolph Carter was for Lovecraft a wish-fulfillment—the sort of man he might have been if only Mother had snapped up a suitor of noble lineage and ample purse; if only his own health had been stronger then he too, like Carter, might have fought with the French Foreign Legion instead of being rejected as 4-F by the Rhode Island National Guard. With his inheritance, Carter lived "on a rarer plane, and furnished his Boston home to suit his changing moods; one room for each, hung in appropriate colours, furnished with befitting books and objects, and provided with sources of the proper sensations of light, heat, sound, taste, and odour,"[54] Lovecraft came closest to his hero when he attributed his own dreams to him. For an hour he too played the epicurean. Living atop College Hill, locked in the rich gloom of his tiny apartment, he lapsed into reverie.

---

51. H. P. Lovecraft, "The Silver Key," *The Outsider*, p. 33.
52. H. P. Lovecraft, "Idealism and Materialism: A Reflection," *The Shuttered Room*, p. 90.
53. "The Silver Key," p. 34.
54. Ibid., 34–35.

Which brings us by a commodious vicus of recirculation back to Lovecraft's Dunsanian period and *The Dream-Quest of Unknown Kadath*, his first short novel and his last dream phantasy. It was written either in late 1926, or early the following year, but remained in manuscript until 1943. Reading *The Dream-Quest of Unknown Kadath* for the first time is apt to be an infuriating experience—the same sort of violent reaction that Sterne, Richardson, or Henry James calls forth from the unprepared.

Randolph Carter travels through dreamland in quest of unknown Kadath in order to see its rooftops burnished gold in the sunset. Wise men had warned him that Kadath was a forbidden place. It was jealously guarded by its *genii loci*. Few men had even dared to go there. Carter, nevertheless, "descended the seven hundred steps to the Gate of Deeper Slumber and set out through the Enchanted Wood."[55] After several adventures along the way he reaches Kadath only to be told by Nyarlathotep, messenger to the Mindless Chaos, Azathoth, to return to Boston. "For know you," says Nyarlathotep, "that your gold and marble city of wonder is only the sum of what you have seen and loved in youth ... the glory of Boston's hillside roofs and western windows aflame with suns ... you need only to turn back to the thoughts and visions of your wistful boyhood."[56] Such is *The Dream-Quest of Unknown Kadath* in its briefest outline. It is a surrealistic novel. Surrealism is an attempt to transcend the limitations of reality and to utilize dreams, automatic association, and the unconscious for literary effect. The work is organized in apparent disorder to simulate the unconscious. Surrealism has been called "a *reductio ad absurdum* of romanticism."[57] At any rate, one expects to find an active play of the imagination as well as a

---

55. H. P. Lovecraft, *The Dream-Quest of Unknown Kadath, Beyond the Wall of Sleep*, p. 77.
56. Ibid., p. 133.
57. *The Dictionary of World Literature*, ed. Joseph T. Shipley, New York, Philosophical Library, p. 403.

V. Home

preoccupation with the bizarre. In *The Dream-Quest* we do find this gamy spirit, particularly in stylistic matters. Although words are not employed with new, varying, or unusual significations, there is a self-conscious artistry; thus:

> Two mornings after that there loomed far ahead and to the east a line of grey peaks whose tops were lost in the changeless clouds of that twilight world. And at the sight of them the sailors sang glad songs, and some knelt down on the deck to pray; so that Carter knew they were come to the land of the Inquanok and would soon be moored to the basalt quays of the great town bearing the land's name.[58]

The preponderance of monosyllables build to a drumming, hypnotic effect, relieved only rarely by tingling "ing" present participle endings. A strained loftiness is achieved by placing the most important word at the end of the sentence. Lovecraft retains his interest in exotic proper names. This may prove more a pain to a reader relatively unacquainted with Lovecraft's stories than to one who has encountered them in earlier stories. Randolph Carter, the cats of Ulthar, Azathoth, Nyarlathotep, and Richard Pickman (now a ghoul) reappear, though no prior knowledge of them is expected. What is most impressive in *The Dream-Quest* is Lovecraft's descriptions. They are sharp and concrete, and do not dissolve into sheer mistiness. A group of creatures are described as "greyish-white slippery things which could expand and contract at will, and whose principal shape—though it often changed—was that of a sort of toad without any eyes, but with a curious vibrating mass of short pink tentacles on the end of its blunt, vague snout."[59] There is also a sense for the tactile: "When the galley landed at the greasy-looking quay of spongy rock a nightmare horde of toad-things wriggled out of the hatches."[60]

---

58. *The Dream-Quest of Unknown Kadath*, p. 106.
59. Ibid., p. 84.
60. Ibid.

Another accomplishment is Lovecraft's feeling for the vastness of space and time. The eternal silence of infinite space (Pascal acknowledged) at once awed and stirred Lovecraft's imagination to populate other worlds with fantastic forms of life: menacing monsters, some as large as a mountain, who possess an intelligence superior to man's; gigantic birds, covered with reptilic, glimmering scales, who serve as flying steeds. (The weird profusion and precise details make one wish that a Dulac or Hannes Bok had been available to illustrate this novel. *The Dream-Quest of Unknown Kadath* demands fine art work, typography, and a sumptuous binding.) Surrealism has as its aim to stretch the mind beyond the limits of understanding. Herbert Read said that the "distance beyond may be spiritual, or transcendental, or perhaps, merely fantastical."[61] *The Dream-Quest* belongs to the third category. Like most dream literature, it takes the form of an odyssey, or one may reject this analogy and call it a ragout, where it appears that the leftovers from the writer's notebook are scraped into the kettle. In its love for Oriental textures and colors, its gratuitous cruelty, sly humor, *The Dream-Quest* suggests *Vathek*. Yet unlike *Vathek*, and most dream literature for that matter, it is deficient in love interest. Mr. Vane pined for Lona, and Walpole's Manfred loved his daughter-in-law in a sinful way, but Randolph Carter wants only to be ravished by a beautiful sunset. He is the scholar bachelor, faithful to his vision. His compassion is reserved for felines—"He loved nothing on earth more than small black kittens."[62]

There is enough to indicate that Randolph Carter was an extension of Lovecraft's personality, though it is more. In its conception and breadth, *The Dream-Quest of Unknown Kadath* is one of the latest successful dream novels in a line that runs through *Castle of Otranto*, George MacDonald's *Lilith* and *Phantastes*, to Julian Gracq's *Castle of Argol*.

---

61. Herbert Read, *The Meaning of Art*, cited by Varma in *The Gothic Flame*, p. 69.
62. *The Dream-Quest of Unknown Kadath*, p. 80.

V. Home

(Ayn Rand's *Atlas Shrugged* was called a "Non-Stop Daydream," [*Saturday Review,* October 12, 1957], though I believe something else was meant by it.) W. H. Auden holds that the *sine qua non* for a writer of dream literature is the gift of mythopoeic imagination.[63] Lovecraft had this genius for mythology.

Few writers do. "L'originalite de Lovecraft n'est pas due à son incontestable talent de conteur: elle est celle d'un créateur de mythes. Ce qui est tout autre chose. Forger une mythologie n'est pas un exercice à la portée du premier venu," noted a French literary critic, who immediately asked, "Qui aurait eu l'audace (ou l'inconscience . . .) de croire qu'une mythologie fût possible de nos jours? De croire, à fortiori, en l'efficacité de pareille entreprise?"[64]

Never were Lovecraft's mythopoeic powers better expended than in the Cthulhu Mythos—the collective name posthumously given to fourteen of his stories. The earlier "The Nameless City" (1921) and "The Festival" (1923) belong, but only incidentally, to the Mythos. It remained for "The Call of Cthulhu," written in 1926, to enlarge the then meagre mythology and make it tangential if not central to subsequent stories.

The paragraph which opens "The Call of Cthulhu" is an abstract of Lovecraft's fictional world and it should be understood as one of the keys to his work.

> The most merciful thing in the world, I think, is the inability of the human mind to correlate all its contents. We live on a placid island of ig-

---

63. George Macdonald, *The Visionary Novels of George Macdonald: Lilith and Phantastes,* New York, Noonday Press, 1954, p. v.
64. Michel Deutsch, "Lovecraft ou la Mythologie," *Esprit,* September, 1957, p. 257. ["Lovecraft's originality is not due to his undeniable talent as a storyteller: it is that of a creator of myths. This is an altogether different thing. To fashion a mythology is not an exercise within anyone's capacity. . . . Who has the audacity (or the obliviousness) to believe that a mythology is possible in our time? To believe, *à fortiori,* in the efficacy of such an enterprise?"]

norance in the midst of black seas of infinity, and it was not meant that we should voyage far. The sciences, each straining in its own direction, have hitherto harmed us little; but some day the piecing together of dissociated knowledge will open up such terrifying vistas of reality, and of our frightful position therein, that we shall either go mad from the revelation or flee from the deadly light into the peace and safety of a new dark age.[65]

Eons ago, before men evolved, a race called the Great Old Ones descended from a distant star to our planet. They eventually left, some taking refuge inside the earth; others, beneath the sea. They yet communicated to certain men in their dreams. Cults to the Old Ones were established in scattered regions. These cults, yielding to animal fury and orgiastic license, practiced a hideous ritual which included human sacrifice and a liturgy from the pre-human *R'lyeh Text*[66]—*"Ph'nglui mglw'nafh Cthulhu R'lyeh wgah'nagl fhtagn"*—a key response, which, when translated reads: "In his house at R'lyeh dead Cthulhu waits dreaming."[67] Cthulhu, god of the waters and a messenger to the Old Ones, lay imprisoned in the submerged stone city of R'lyeh, once their earthly metropolis. His eventual release was predicted by a couplet in the *Necronomicon*:

> That is not dead which can eternal lie,
> And with strange eons even death may die.[68]

Cthulhu escaped. At the proper time, when the stars are in the desired conjunction, he will rouse the Old Ones from slumber and they will reclaim the earth. Large as a hummock, gelatinous and gaseous in substance, great Cthulhu is indestructible.

This much of the Cthulhu mythology may be learned from "The

---

65. H. P. Lovecraft, "The Call of Cthulhu," *The Outsider*, p. 255.
66. [The *R'lyeh Text* is an imaginary book invented by August Derleth after HPL's death. The line in question is not stated as being part of any text.]
67. Ibid., p. 261.
68. Ibid., p. 265. [The couplet first appeared in "The Nameless City."]

V. Home

Call of Cthulhu." The "piecing together of dissociated knowledge" is achieved by Lovecraft with no little skill. In its suspense, restrained tone, and patient accumulation of evidence, "The Call of Cthulhu" is closest to "The Shunned House" (1924), one of his successful earlier stories. As in that story, Lovecraft here draws on College Hill for his setting. The narrator's granduncle, Dr. George Gammell Angell, is "Professor Emeritus of Semitic Languages at Brown University." As with Dr. Elihu Whipple in "The Shunned House," he is killed during the course of investigation.

Lovecraft tends to be most effective when he draws upon his rich New England background for setting. And his deficiency at characterization is less noticeable when he casts something of himself in the role of the reserved and scholarly narrator. "The Call of Cthulhu" is assembled from the notes of the narrator's late uncle, from a newspaper cutting, and a sea captain's logbook. This posits an order on the narration and curbs Lovecraft's tendency toward bombast. When he comes to describe a statuette of Cthulhu, he does so with all the exactitude of an archeologist noting some unearthed potsherd.

> The figure ... was between seven and eight inches in height, and of exquisitely artistic workmanship. It represented a monster of vaguely anthropoid outline, but with an octopuslike head whose face was a mass of feelers, a scaly, rubbery-looking body, prodigious claws on hind and fore feet, and long narrow wings behind. This thing, which seemed instinct with a fearsome and unnatural malignancy, was of a somewhat bloated corpulence, and squatted evilly on a rectangular block or pedestal covered with undecipherable characters. The tips of the wings touched the back edge of the block, the seat occupied the center, whilst the long, curved claws of the doubled-up, crouching hind legs gripped the front edge and extended a quarter of the way down toward the bottom of the pedestal. The cephalopod head was bent forward, so that the ends of the facial feelers brushed the backs of the huge forepaws which clasped the croucher's elevated knees.[69]

---

69. Ibid., p. 260.

Reaction to this fidelity has been sharply divided. To Edmund Wilson, Lovecraft's monsters merit polite laughter. "Such creatures would look very well on the covers of the pulp magazines," he feels, "but they do not make good adult reading."[70] With equal aplomb, another writer suggests that "Lovecraft's monsters are usually ridiculous compounds of elephant feet and trunks, human faces, tentacles, gleaming eyes and bat wings . . . The reader is often amused rather than frightened by the author's extraordinary surgical talents. Wells' Dr. Moreau could hardly have done better."[71] On the other hand, there are critics who see these demonic creatures as something more than soggy animal crackers which have become stuck together. "Le valeur intrinsèque de la représentation n'existe qu'en fonction de la foi qui habite l'artiste et qui seule est capable de conférer sa vérité à l'image symbolique"[72] To Lovecraft's mind the universe is sprawled in hostile indifference to mankind. This reality which Lovecraft perceives is so out of proportion with our cherished self-esteem as to be, almost literally, unimaginable. Only a mythology with its horrific symbols is capable of even suggesting this reality. In this way the description of Cthulhu—with all his disorder, so loathsome to behold—is Lovecraft's way of ordering and accepting the shocking facts of life.

The symbol hunters of Lovecraft's stories will be comforted to know that he was looking out for them. "Something in the basic mental & imaginative makeup of the human animal seems to call for tangible symbolism—or audible incantation—in approaching or invoking the imagined powers of the cosmos—when I write a story I try . . . to be reasonably unhackneyed in choosing a symbol for such purposes."[73]

---

70. Wilson, p. 288.

71. Penzoldt, pp. 170–71.

72. Deutsch, p. 260. ["The intrinsic value of the depiction exists only in terms of the faith that dwells in the artist and is alone able to confer its truth to the symbolic image."]

73. H. P. Lovecraft, MS. letter to Kenneth Sterling, dated August 3, 1935, KS.

V. Home

Is a monster, like Cthulhu, capable of raising dreadful feelings, or is he so patently absurd that the story evaporates under a loud guffaw? Generally, though not always, Lovecraft is convincing. His artistry is such that he suspends disbelief and checks the natural tendency to laugh when one is presented with an accumulation of horror. "Lovecraft ne nous font jamais rire. Ni même sourire, en dépit des naïvetés qu'on peut parfois relever."[74] It was an acknowledged rule with Lovecraft in his stories to avoid humor "something which utterly kills all weird emotional appeal as far as I am concerned."[75]

While humor, as such, is lacking, there are private jokes and idiosyncrasies which will be recognized by Lovecraft's friends or by the Lovecraft specialist; these allusions need not concern the general reader. Flicked into his work are his own reactions to such unhappy modern phenomena as functional architecture, jazz, and T. S. Eliot. Occasionally he plucks character names from his family tree or from acquaintances. In "The Call of Cthulhu" a member of Cthulhu's fifth column is named Castro, probably after Adolphe Danziger de Castro, a New York bookseller who had literary aspirations.[76] He had tried to persuade Lovecraft to ghostwrite a book on Ambrose Bierce for him.[77] Lovecraft regarded de Castro with humorous contempt, privately referring to him as "an innocuous and engaging old charlatan."[78]

Two stories were written in 1927, the following year. Both belong to the Cthulhu Mythos. The first was *The Case of Charles Dexter Ward.* Some

---

74. Deutsch, p. 266. ["Lovecraft never makes us laugh. Not even smile, in spite of the naïvetés that can sometimes be pointed out."]

75. H. P. Lovecraft, MS. letter to Richard Ely Morse, dated August 9, 1932, NYPL.

76. [HPL only encountered Adolphe de Castro a year after writing "The Call of Cthulhu."]

77. H. P. Lovecraft, MS. letter to Maurice W. Moe, dated "Thanksgiving Day," 1934, AK.

78. H. P. Lovecraft, MS. letter to Richard Ely Morse, dated November 8, 1936, NYPL.

forty thousand words in length,[79] it was, up to that point, Lovecraft's most ambitious work in the horror field. It remains his best plotted story.

Ward, who mysteriously vanished from a mental hospital, was in the grip of "a madness which held no affinity to any sort recorded in even the latest and most exhaustive of treatises, and was conjoined to a mental force which would have made him a genius or a leader had it not been twisted into strange and grotesque forms."[80] The story moves back into time. Charles Dexter Ward of Providence, Rhode Island, was a reserved, intelligent young man with antiquarian interests. Also, he was a bit of a dreamer, quite like Lovecraft, in fact: "Tall, slim, and bland, with a slight stoop."[81] One day Ward learned that he once had an eighteenth century ancestor who was reputed to have been a wizard. What follows is actually a recapitulation of the macabre activities of this evil forebear, Joseph Curwen. To the disgust of his neighbors, this Curwen lived to a fantastic age, but never showed it. He had acquired strange powers through research, and corresponded with others who had mastered the black arts. While on Curwen's trail, Ward uncovered the necromancer's books of incantations and busily set to work deciphering them. Ward turned secret. In order fully to understand Curwen's practices, he became an overwrought scholar of the occult. He traveled abroad extensively. Three years later the young man, on the brink of insanity, returned home to Providence and his indulgent parents. Thundering incantations and disgusting odors came from his locked door, until, at last, Joseph Curwen, summoned by Ward from the grave, annihilated the young experimenter and assumed his identity—an easy matter since their appearance was similar. Before Curwen is found out and destroyed (by magical means, of course) many of the classical "properties" of the horror tale are used: black

---

79. [The novel is 51,000 words.]
80. H. P. Lovecraft, *The Case of Charles Dexter Ward, Beyond the Wall of Sleep*, p. 135.
81. Ibid., p. 138.

V. Home

magic, demonic possession, vampirism, rifling of graves, raising of the dead, the chemical manufacture of monsters, exploration of underground labyrinths, lights going out in same, moanings, incantations, and things that go "bump" in the dark. This catalogue may give the impression that *The Case of Charles Dexter Ward* is a confusing amalgam of cabalistic nonsense.

In point of fact the iniquities of Joseph Curwen are not dribbled out in ludicrous haste, but are instead slowly disclosed and then only after sufficient preparation. Lovecraft applies to *The Case of Charles Dexter Ward* a power of logic, compelling the reader's conviction in the incredible against his will. He raises into this story a claustrophobic quality which confines the reader into a temporarily believable world. The mellow calm of Providence sets the scene—a treacherous serenity for the villainy which breaks through the surface.

Lovecraft's particularization of eighteenth century Providence is vividly circumstantial in its mention of actual prominent citizens, homes, and streets. One wonders whether there may not have been an original for Joseph Curwen living back there in the 1770s. Sooner or later, it was expected that Lovecraft would utilize his extensive knowledge of Rhode Island history as he did here. Indeed, Lovecraft may have erred slightly on the side of richness with his proclivity at times to "overload the canvas."[82] It is effective none the less. *The Observer* summed up the power of *The Case of Charles Dexter Ward* in a one sentence review: "Thaumaturgical terror in Providence, R.I., written with convincing discretion."[83]

My own quibble with this novel is its rather unimaginative title. When the Portuguese translated and published it in 1958, they changed it to *Os Mortos Podern Voltar*—The Dead Can Return.

---

82. "The Case of Charles Dexter Ward," anon. rev. *Times Literary Supplement*, February 22, 1952.
83. "The Case of Charles Dexter Ward," anon. rev. *The Observer*, February 10, 1952.

Lovecraft's gift for the macabre was fully demonstrated in this impelling fantasy. It is therefore surprising to learn that he did not submit the manuscript for publication. He had spent months writing the novel, but the chore of typing what would amount to one hundred seventy pages of typescript was just too much. When one of his young fans, Donald Wandrei, visited him in the summer of 1927, Lovecraft showed him the Ward manuscript. Wandrei, with boyish generosity, offered to type it, and Lovecraft agreed. Imagine Wandrei's surprise when he returned home to St. Paul and carefully looked at the manuscript. It was a typical word-defying Lovecraftian affair. Using the backside of letters, advertising circulars, and hotel stationery, it was written in a cramped hand with no margins at the sides, top, or bottom. Into this sea were wedged islands of interpolated sentences with arrows shooting off to indicate their proper locations. There were strange proper names, exorcisms written in his own language, and spelling peculiarities to swear over. Working part time, Wandrei completed the typing in four months. It was filled, not unexpectedly, with errors. When Lovecraft received it, he may have decided that it would take as much time to correct it as to retype it. There is no evidence that he did anything except to put it aside and go on to other stories. In 1940, the original manuscript was located and this time an accurate transcript was prepared and meticulously proofread—a painstaking two months task.[84]

His second story in 1927 had an easier time. "The Colour of Space" appeared in the September issue of *Amazing Stories* after it had been turned down by Farnsworth Wright of *Weird Tales*.[85] "The Colour out of Space" is included in the Cthulhu Mythos although no gods are

---

84. "The Eyrie," *Weird Tales* (May 1941), pp. 120–21. [This letter—written by Derleth and Wandrei—mentions Wandrei's preparation of a typescript. If he actually did so, it does not survive.]

85. [The story was submitted directly to *Amazing Stories* and was never submitted to *Weird Tales*.]

V. Home

introduced and nothing further is learned concerning the Old Ones, or the earth's history. It may be included in the Mythos because it takes place in Arkham, as do most of the other Cthulhu tales, and it deals with an invasion of sorts by a force beyond our earth.

The story begins by describing Arkham's blasted hath—"five acres of grey desolation"—which was once a thriving farm.[86] The narrator, a surveyor, curious as to how the land acquired this scorched appearance, learns that forty-four years earlier a "meteorite" had crashed near a farmer's well. Its arrival was announced by explosions and a white column of smoke rising up from the valley. Three professors from Miskatonic University came and gouged out samples of the oddly soft stone, but the rapidly evaporating specimens defied analysis. Soon the vegetation on the farm began to change its colors and shape monstrously. "The bloodroots grew insolent in their chromatic perversion ... the fruit was coming out grey and dwarfed and tasteless ... the roses ... in the front yard were such blasphemous-looking things."[87] Then, too, there was the disturbing way the trees twitched and swayed in the calm. By degrees fatigue and insanity came to the farmer's family. And death, at last, a slow-burning death that may best be described, in our times, as radiation poisoning. It left their corpses grey, brittle shells. One night, after the last member of the family died, a luminescent object rose from the well "malignly bubbling in its cosmic and unrecognizable chromaticism," and shot up toward the sky with a crackling eruption.[88] The blight had left—or had it?

When read slowly in its entirety this story of rotting organic matter has a terribly familiar ring. The familiarity, one realizes on reflection, is from reading descriptions of Hiroshima's destruction in 1945. Edmund Wilson, among others, noted that "The Colour out of Space"

---

86. H. P. Lovecraft, "The Colour Out of Space," *The Outsider*, p. 275.
87. Ibid., p. 280.
88. Ibid., p. 289.

"more or less predicts the effects of the atomic bomb."[89] Wilson gave a quiet nod of approval to this story for showing "some traces of his [Lovecraft's] more serious emotions and interests."[90] And Jacques Papy, Lovecraft's able French translator, considers it as one of Lovecraft's two masterpieces because of its brilliantly created atmosphere and power of suggestion.[91] Whether "The Colour out of Space" is, as one writer holds, "a pure, unadulterated science fiction tale,"[92] I do not know. Certainly it has two of the normal requirements for a science-fiction tale, i.e. science, and a serious attitude toward science. Perhaps Kingsley Amis was a bit hasty when he suggested that "The Colour out of Space" "occasionally finds its way into science-fiction collections, chiefly I imagine on account of its title."[93]

"The Colour out of Space" deserved the Roll of Honor award which it won in O'Brien's Best Short Stories of 1928. For the "Biographical Notices" in the book, Lovecraft wrote an ironic personal sketch which read in part:

> LOVECRAFT, HOWARD PHILLIPS. Was born of old Yankee-English stock ... Serious literary efforts now confined to tales of dream-life, strange shadow, and cosmic "outsideness" notwithstanding sceptical rationalism of outlook and keen regard for the sciences ... Lives quietly and eventlessly with classical and antiquarian tastes. Especially fond of atmosphere of Colonial New England. Occupation—literary hack work including revision and special editorial jobs ... Conservative in general perspective and method so far as compatible with phantasy in art and mechanistic materialism in philosophy.[94]

---

89. Wilson, p. 290.
90. Ibid.
91. Jacques Papy, MS. letter to Arthur Koki, dated September 28, 1961, AK.
92. Moskowitz, p. 46.
93. Kingsley Amis, *New Maps of Hell,* New York: Ballantine Books, 1960, p. 36.
94. *The Best Short Stories of 1928,* ed. Edward J. O'Brien, New York, Dodd, Mead, & Co., 1928, p. 324.

V. Home

There is a self-conscious note to this profile. It is, I believe, the effusion of a bittersweet realization that he was, after all, merely a pulp writer, appearing in the only market open to a fantasy-horror writer.

It was sometime in 1927 that Mrs. Lovecraft, long absent from the scene, left Cleveland and came to Providence to investigate the possibility of opening a women's fashion store there. Her plan was to purchase a large house, hire a maid, and turn one portion of the house over to the business while she, her husband, and his two aunts lived in on the other side. But the aunts gently yet firmly pointed out to her that the name of Lovecraft could not be associated with any mercantilistic enterprise, nor was a Mrs. Lovecraft in Providence ever to work for a living. There was the tradition, heritage, and pride of the family to be considered.[95] It was better by far to dwindle into genteel poverty than to enter the babbling arena of business. Mrs. Lovecraft took it stoically; "That was that," she said, "I knew then where we all stood."[96] *Ainsi soit-il!*

She went to Brooklyn, set up housekeeping, and opened a millinery shop in the neighborhood under her maiden name of S. H. Greene to save her husband any embarrassment should he return to live with her. When Lovecraft visited her in April, 1928, he wrote back to his aunts that "I sincerely hope the millinery venture will prove a success. I advised against such enterprises by letter when the plan was outlined, but upon viewing the location, I cannot help feeling that it will survive and prosper after all."[97] He tried justifying his living at her expense. "I shall make SH accept what I think the price of my food is—& I can assure you that I don't add any difficulty to the household work. I've even washed the dishes two or three times!"[98] In a self-

---

95. Davis, pp. 243–44. [There is no evidence that this incident took place in 1927. It is not clear when the incident occurred.]
96. Ibid., p. 244.
97. H. P. Lovecraft, MS. letter to Mrs. Lillian D. Clark, dated April 29, 1928, JHL.
98. H. P. Lovecraft, MS. letter to Mrs. Lillian D. Clark, dated May 3, 1928, JHL.

pitying tone he concluded, "I'm a poor man & the ordeal of paying out good hard cash is a terrific strain upon a sensitive nervous system!" His visit lasted through the summer. He saw his wife in the morning before she left for work, but Mrs. Lovecraft was happy since "even his nearness was better than nothing."[99]

Lovecraft visited with his old friends—"as loquacious & argumentative as ever"[100] and, most especially, with Frank Belknap Long, Jr. and his family. He recorded with delicacy and affection a trip taken with the Longs to Somers, New York to a place where Mr. Long, Sr., as a boy, had visited to build up his health.

> At many turns of the road he indulged in bursts of reminiscent admiration unusual in one whose daily mood is so prosaic; recalling here & there a brook he had fished in, a pool he had swam in, an apple-orchard he had sampled, & a slope on which he had lounged through the long summer afternoons of the bygone 'seventies. Once, when the car topped a rise beside a reservoir sunken valley, he waxed almost lyrical about a day when he had first driven there in a jolting carry-all by his uncle—a day in spring when the magic of scented fields & delicately leaved trees blended with the song of robins & the charm of apple-blossoms. Good soul—had to grope & fumble for the words in order to stammer out the picture & sensations he wished to convey; yet behind the rough ineptitude there lurked a genuine & unmistakable aesthetic feeling which might, under other circumstances, have made him an artist or poet.[101]

The New York vacation was a welcome change from his recent hibernation. That preceding winter had been spoiled for him. In his hack chores he had revised de Castro's novelette, "The Last Test." Lovecraft's fee: $16.00. De Castro sold the story to *Weird Tales* for $175.00. "I hope," said Lovecraft, "that I can banish revision sufficiently this summer to write a few things of my own—it would really be financially

---

99. Davis, p. 2.44.
100. H. P. Lovecraft, MS. letter to Mrs. Lillian D. Clark, dated May 3, 1928, JHL.
101. H. P. Lovecraft, MS. letter to Mrs. Lillian D. Clark, dated May 3–5, 1928, JHL.

V. Home

profitable as well as aesthetically preferable."[102]

Summer over, he rejoined his aunts and resumed his marriage by letters again. His wife was not content with this correspondence school arrangement and urged a divorce. He replied "a gentleman does not divorce his wife unless he has cause."[103] Were there not cases of prominent figures in the eighteenth century who lived apart from their wives while holding them in the highest regard? He himself knew of a happy couple whose marriage was conducted via the postal service, the wife living with her parents, and the husband, ill and confined, elsewhere. Mrs. Lovecraft was not impressed and repeated her declaration of togetherness or permanent separation. "No, my dear," Lovecraft replied, "if you leave me I shall never marry again. You do not realize how much I appreciate you!"[104] But Mrs. Lovecraft was not to be humored, and the divorce came in 1929.[105]

Or so we are told by Mrs. Lovecraft. A search through the divorce court records of Providence Superior Court yielded evidence at variance with her version. On January 24, 1929, a subpoena from the Providence court was issued to be served to Mrs. Lovecraft in Brooklyn. She was to appear at the Providence Superior Court on March first. On February sixth, Lovecraft, his aunt Mrs. Annie E. P. Gamwell, and a Providence friend, Clifford M. Eddy, walked into attorney Greenlaw's office in the Turk's Head Building. They presented testimony on Mrs. Lovecraft's wilful desertion. First, Lovecraft was questioned:

---

102. H. P. Lovecraft, MS. letter to Mrs. Lillian D. Clark, dated May 23, 1928, JHL.
103. Davis, p. 244.
104. Ibid., p. 245.
105. [In his account of the divorce, Koki does not clarify that it was pursued in Rhode Island—on the charade that Sonia had deserted HPL rather than the reverse—because divorce laws in New York State were very restrictive, whereas those in Rhode Island were more liberal.]

1Q (By Mr. Greenlaw) Your full name?

A   Howard Phillips Lovecraft.

2Q You have resided in Providence for more than two years prior to the 24th day of January, 1929?

A   Since April 17, 1926.

3Q And you are now a domiciled inhabitant of the City of Providence, State of Rhode Island?

A   Yes.

4Q And you were married to Sonia H. Lovecraft?

A   Yes.

5Q When?

A   March 3, 1924.

6Q Have you a certified copy of your marriage certificate?

A   I have.
    (Same received in evidence and marked by the
    Magistrate Petitioner as Exhibit A.)

7Q Now have you demeaned yourself as a faithful husband since your marriage?

A   Yes.

8Q And performed all the obligations of the marriage covenant?

A   Yes.

9C Now, has the respondent, Sonia H. Lovecraft, deserted you?

A   Since the 31st of December, 1924.

10C You gave her no cause for deserting you?

A   None whatever.

11C There were no children born of this marriage?

A   No.

V. Home

The testimony of Mrs. Gamwell and Mr. Eddy corroborated Lovecraft's assertion that his wife had deserted him, and that he was not to blame.[106]

The subpoena for Mrs. Lovecraft was issued, the testimony gathered up, and the Citation for Deposition placed before the judge. But the judge never signed the Final Decree which would have dissolved the marriage. The Lovecrafts remained legally husband and wife, although both considered themselves divorced. Why, after taking the necessary steps, did Lovecraft neglect to ask for the annulment? That he forgot to do so, can hardly be believed. I would imagine that he changed his mind at the last moment because of a slight hope that they might be reconciled. "Separation" sounds so casual, while "divorce" rings with cold finality. Today, the Lovecraft vs. Greene case is still open in the court under Petitions—Pending.

According to Lovecraft, financial difficulties were 99% responsible for the "divorce."[107] In that quaint and slightly absurd manner he often employed to conceal his true feelings, he wrote to a friend in 1931, that, aside from financial problems, his marriage had suffered from "divergences in aspirations and environmental needs."[108] One is more inclined to agree with Mrs. Lovecraft that, "marvelous person though he was, it was probably to 'save face' that Howard, having to give a reason, offered one that might be most easily believed."[109] Perhaps more than one face was saved.

The young man who had grown up in a dark house with a neurotic mother and two coddling aunts, the boy who had built altars to the

---

106. H. P. Lovecraft vs. Sonia Haft Greene, No. 23118 Petition for Divorce, including Citation for Deposition and Final Decree. March, 1929. Superior Court, Providence, R. I.
107. Derleth, *H. P. L.: A Memoir*, pp. 15–16. [Derleth is quoting a letter by HPL to himself (16 January 1931). In the letter HPL gives the figure as "98%."]
108. Ibid., p. 16. [From a letter to J. Vernon Shea (19 June 1931).]
109. Davis, p. 245.

classic gods and goddesses, was kindly advised by Mrs. Lovecraft to marry some lady of similar background and culture.

There was no indication that he intended to or that their separation was an especially poignant event for him. He was now in New England where gentle, kindly people led a different and more wholesome life. New Englanders spoke in "homely accents of Puritan speech." In the autumnal evenings there was the simple pleasure of walking by colonial homes frosted in the moonlight. This New England, founded on other concepts, seemed far different from his former drab ways with Mrs. Greene. No, she was not missed.

He was not soured on marriage, but as time went on, he tended to speak of it in impersonal terms:

> I do not regard marriage as a social superfluity, but believe it has extreme stabilizing value in the organization of a state. Its advantages are numerous & varied—& are indeed so apparent to the unbiased anthropologist that even Soviet Russia (where no traditional institution is kept up for tradition's sake alone) is beginning to urge its systematic maintenance & more faithful & universal practice.[110]

Three weeks after the divorce fuss, Lovecraft left on a one-month sojourn to the South. As usual, he stopped by the Longs' home on West 94th Street and availed himself of their hospitality. Familiar cries of mock distress came back to his aunts. "I have stark tragedy to report! ... *I have gained 8 pounds* since encountering the Siren-like enticements of the sumptuous Long table ... Here's Roodmas only 2 days away, & I'm 8 pounds above decent weight! My motto is now 140 by St. John's Eve."[111] New York behind, the opportunity to meet kindred souls and the prevalence of fine examples of Colonial architecture sent him singing the praises of Richmond and Fredericksburg.

---

110. H. P. Lovecraft, MS. letter to Margaret Ronan, n.d., circa January, 1937, MR.
111. H. P. Lovecraft, MS. letter to Mrs. Lillian D. Clark, dated April 28–29, 1929, JHL.

V. Home

There are very few foreigners—a mere handful of Greeks & Jews, & no Italians or Poles—& a very few people of any kind whose ancestors have not dwelt there for centuries. Niggers are not numerous—indeed, they are by no means a conspicuous feature of the Northern Virginia landscape. I was very fortunate in encountering a kindly, talkative, well-bred & scholarly old man who noticed my contemplative mien & frequent guide-book glances & who volunteered to guide me to the best Colonial reliquiae. He was a connoisseur of Georgian architecture, inhabiting a Colonial house himself & being something of a student of furniture, decorative detail, & early brick construction. Under his tutelage—& he tirelessly walked me through street after street, lean & alert despite his years—I absorbed dozens of sights & atmospheric touches which I would otherwise have missed . . . This good man is quite typical of nearly everyone I have encountered in the South—including the genial 'bus driver. Without question I find Southern people more congenial than any other type I have so far met—despite my devotion to New England's landscapes, architecture, & quiet ways. The Southerner reflects a civilisation of riper mellowness & higher graces than any other on this continent, &t I wish this civilisation had a greater chance of spreading & leaving its impress on the culture of the nation as a whole. After a week in the South it will seem like wading in mud putrescence to traverse the Manhattan region again, but thank heaven it will be a brief passing. . . . I dread coarse New York voices in subways & on the sidewalk.[112]

On the way back to Providence he stopped at Kingston, New York and lost his black enamel cloth case containing his spyglass, writing materials, and diary. "I had left it for the merest moment in the idyllic lane where I sat reading & writing, & when I returned from that moment's uphill climb it was gone!"[113] The previous day he had been so rapt in his sightseeing of Albany that he missed his bus connection for Kingston. Resourceful through necessity, he had stepped out of his prim posture "and hailed a driver of a passing Standard Oil truck. He proved to be a good fellow, & to be bound all the way to Kingston—

---

112. H. P. Lovecraft, MS. letter to Mrs. Lillian D. Clark, dated May 6, 1929, JHL.
113. H. P. Lovecraft, MS. letter to Mrs. Lillian D. Clark, dated May 13–15, 1929, JHL.

thus making my first attempt at 'hitch-hiking' a 100% success!"[114]

Waiting for him when he returned home was an accumulated pile of *Weird Tales* fan mail, Amateur Journal publications, and letters from Amateur members. Such a correspondent was Miss Elizabeth Toldridge of Washington, D. C. One of America's lesser known minor poets, her poems were once praised as "full of color and clear vision."[115] Her best remembered sonnet is "Expectancy," which opens:

> And lifted eyes discern etchings made
> Upon grey skies, of chimney-pot and spire,
> And slim beseeching boughs with fingers laid
> Together as for prayer, and straining higher.[116]

Miss Toldridge submitted all her poetry after 1928 to Lovecraft's criticism. To one of her earliest series he wrote, "They are indeed delightful & meritorious productions; not one touched with crudity or awkwardness & many of them possessing really exceptional excellence."[117] The quick, easy praise was always waiting for her. There is no evidence in Lovecraft's letters that he was paid for his services. The very volume of their correspondence would suggest a social relationship that was blandly intellectual. The topics ran from poetry to politics, history, science, and back to poetry. The difference in sex and intellect suited Lovecraft. Miss Toldridge was, let us be frank, a mediocre talent, but Lovecraft could play his favorite role of the learned gentleman, amused, though not caught, by the absurd fabric of life.

At first his major concern was with her poetry. He advised his poetess to shun cryptical adumbrations and to deal in crystal clear images. Occasionally he revised her poetry. When she worried over the propriety of incorporating his corrections as her own, Lovecraft assured her

---

114. Ibid.
115. Spencer, p. 122.
116. Ibid.
117. H. P. Lovecraft, MS. letter to Elizabeth Toldridge, dated November 20, 1928, JHL.

V. Home

that it was not only proper, but that Pope, as an example, had supplied a notable passage in Thomson's "Autumn," while some of the most striking lines in Goldsmith's "Deserted Village" were interpolated by Dr. Johnson.[118] One wonders if Miss Toldridge saw the humorous barb concealed in this modest self-image. He was helpful to Miss Toldridge in the way that anyone who teaches creative writing may be of some value because he serves as a task-master and an audience. Lovecraft was not himself an outstanding teacher. His prejudices cut him off from much that was new and exciting in poetry. Whitman and Eliot were anathema to him, especially Eliot, at the mention of whose name, Lovecraft would clasp his hands, roll his eyes, nod his head, while intoning all the while *"Shantih! Shantih!"*[119]

Poetry had been Lovecraft's literary preoccupation in his late teens and twenties. His mother had talked to the neighbors in a febrile manner concerning her only child, whom she called "a poet of the highest order."[120] In those days he could, without hesitation, write Alexandrian couplets on the death of a relative or the receipt of a picture postcard. His best poetry dealt with natural scenes, most of it is worthy of the Georgic poetasters. At his best he recalls James Thomson—which is to say that one page may be read with pleasure; more than that at one sitting and the effect is like swallowing a Nembutal. Several poems have sociological and biographical interest. With a monotonous sameness they bemoan the passing of those golden years before Mother Liberty was scuffed underfoot by the humble masses, yearning. Such a poem is "On a New England Village Seen by Moonlight":

> The squalid noisome village lies asleep;
> The dusk and quiet hide the monstrous mill:
> The bats their melancholy watches keep,

---

118. H. P. Lovecraft, MS. letter to Elizabeth Toldridge, dated February 21, 1929, JHL.
119. In private conversation with Samuel Loveman on August 9, 1961.
120. Scott, p. 319.

> Whilst all the rabbles' daytime cries are still.
> The alien serfs escape our sorrowing view;
> The tortur'd mind is lighten'd of its pain;
> Our own ancestral spirits reign anew,
> And old New England seems to live again.[121]

He repeatedly counseled Miss Toldridge (with grace and tact) not to whore after false gods. "Whether anyone else ever sees the product or not, is a wholly secondary matter."[122] The important thing in poetry was the creative process—the crystallization of what was before an elusive vision. He went further when he said "the prime essential of aesthetic effort is to repudiate mankind & the world, & stand alone in the cosmos, face to face with the revelation of beauty."[123] There is nothing to indicate if Miss Toldridge chafed under this credo, but at least one of Lovecraft's pupils, bent on crashing the fictional market, felt that his anti-commercial attitude was unsatisfactory.[124]

Aside from corresponding with Miss Toldridge, Lovecraft was involved in other poetical tasks in 1929. In July he revised a book, *Doorways to Poetry*, for an old Amateur friend, Maurice W. Moe.[125] Later that year he arranged and edited the poems of John Ravenor Bullen of Canada at the request of that late poet's family. In August, 1925, Bullen's mother had written to Lovecraft, then in New York, asking him for a loan of one hundred eighty-five dollars to finance publication of her late son's poems. Lovecraft had previously written a "tedious critique" (his words) on the late poet's work for one of the Amateur journals.[126]

---

121. H. P. Lovecraft, "On a New England Village Seen by Moonlight," *Beyond the Wall of Sleep*, p. 369.
122. H. P. Lovecraft, MS. letter to Elizabeth Toldridge, dated October 24, 1930, JHL.
123. H. P. Lovecraft, MS. letter to Elizabeth Toldridge, dated July 1, 1929, JHL.
124. Zealia Bishop, "H. P. Lovecraft: A Pupil's View," *The Curse of Yig*, Sauk City, Wis.: Arkham House, 1953, p. 150.
125. H. P. Lovecraft, MS. letter to Elizabeth Toldridge, dated July 31, 1929, JHL. [Moe's book was never published; the ms. is apparently nonextant.]
126. H. P. Lovecraft, MS. letter to Mrs. Lillian D. Clark, dated August 7, 1925,

V. Home

Thus Mrs. Bullen hoped he would be receptive to her proposition. It was a slightly pathetic situation. For security, Mrs. Bullen had sent him some shares of admittedly worthless stock (which her friends advised her to keep) with the plea "*Please* grant my request!"[127] Lovecraft, also financially embarrassed, turned her down. Now, in September, 1929 he conceded to the Bullens' request for literary aid. The task was made difficult by Bullen's tame and unoriginal verses. In writing the preface, Lovecraft fell back "on friendly memory more than on aesthetic enthusiasm as a stimulus—for Bullen was an admirable person."[128]

This involvement in the poems of others may have induced Lovecraft earnestly to resume writing poetry himself. A spate burst toward the close of 1929. From December 27 to January 4, 1930, he wrote thirty-six sonnets,[129] which he grouped under the title *Fungi from Yuggoth*. These sonnets are linked to the general theme of wonderment and horror. The fictional narrator is not named, but he could well be Randolph Carter. He steals an old book whose blasphemous knowledge permits entry into other worlds. Some of the sonnets are vignettes in themselves while in others Lovecraft seems to speak directly:

> I never can be tied to raw, new things,
> For I first saw the light in an old town.
> Where from my window huddled roofs sloped down
> To a quaint harbour rich with visionings.
> Streets with carved doorways where the sunset beams
> Flooded old fanlights and small window panes,
> And Georgian steeples topped with gilded vanes—
> These were the sights that shaped my childhood dreams.

JHL. [The critique was "The Poetry of John Ravenor Bullen" (*United Amateur*, September 1925), reworked as the preface to Bullen's *White Fire*, published in 1927 (not 1929 as Koki states).]

127. Ibid.

128. H. P. Lovecraft, MS. letter to Elizabeth Toldridge, dated September 16, 1929, JHL.

129. [Only 35 sonnets were written at this time; "Recapture" (later included as no. XXXIV) had been written earlier in December.]

> Such treasures, left from times of cautious leaven,
> Cannot but loose the hold of flimsier wraiths
> That flit with shifting ways and muddled faiths
> Across the changeless walls of earth and heaven.
> They cut the moment's thongs and leave me free
> To stand alone before eternity.[130]

In *Fungi from Yuggoth* Lovecraft escaped from the artificialities and the thersitical outbursts in his earlier effusions to write poetry that was mature, clear, and direct. The literary raconteur and poet Winfield Townley Scott believes that Edwin Arlington Robinson may have been the new influence here. There is nothing to date to show that Lovecraft was an admirer of Robinson. That he read him seems, however, probable. If an influence must be found, Robinson is a good candidate. His work does have some modernistic tendencies though he uses traditional forms, the sonnet, ode, and ballad. His flat diction, love of irony, understatement, wry humor, scientific materialism, and self-study that often turns to self-pity would have won a sympathetic response from Lovecraft. Working from what he chooses to call "internal evidence," Scott quotes ten lines of poetry from Lovecraft and nine from Robinson and suggests that in phrasing, tone, and general approach, the *Fungi* sonnets are "repeatedly Robinsonian."[131] *Fungi from Yuggoth* does have Robinson's prosody but, according to Scott, Lovecraft did not touch the depths of human significance.[132] Scott believes that Robinson did, but that is by the way, and therefore I need speak no further of it.

As the year 1929 came to a close, did Lovecraft pause a moment from his writing and draw his lips into a thin, sardonic smile over a year so pregnant with human folly and shattered hopes for Americans?

---

130. H. P. Lovecraft, "Background," *Beyond the Wall of Sleep*, p. 405.
131. Winfield Townley Scott, *Exiles and Fabrications*, New York, Doubleday, 1961, p. 76.
132. Ibid.

V. Home

It had opened auspiciously enough on a note of scientific interest with Admiral Byrd addressing the United States from Little America after he had gotten up from a New Year's dinner of pork and beans, bread, peanut butter, and applesauce.[133] In Chicago, mobsters had "bumped off" one another in rapid tempo, climaxing with the brutal, though efficient, St. Valentine's Day Massacre.[134] Bootlegging was flourishing with some 1,565 deaths—more than the *Titanic* disaster—attributed to alcohol poisoning. In their quest for sweet oblivion and surcease from cares, Americans were guzzling such toxic liquids as rubbing alcohol, antifreeze mixtures, and a distilled alcohol containing nitric and sulfuric acids that corroded the kidneys.[135] A steady improvement was seen in automobiles, roads, planes, and radio. President Hoover spoke confidently of a growing economy, while ex-President Coolidge thoughtfully penned his memoirs for *Cosmopolitan,* offering many observations ("When more and more people are thrown out of work, unemployment results.") drawn from his political savvy. The libido for riches was best seen in the widespread stock market speculations engaged in by people from all levels of life. Stocks spiraled upward to plunge in late October and November. Millions of dumbstruck Americans picked up the shattered pieces of their illusory lives and discarded them to begin anew. John Galbraith later analysed the 1929 speculative fever: "The mass escape into make-believe, so much a part of the true speculative orgy, started in earnest . . . Men sought not to be persuaded of the reality of things but to find excuses for escaping into the new world of fantasy."[136]

In one way or another the mass of Americans were seeking an escape from the present. Many sought it through the flesh, through

---

133. Joe Alex Morris, *What A Year!* New York, Harper & Bros., 1956, pp. 12–13.
134. Ibid., pp. 30–31.
135. Ibid., pp. 32–38.
136. Ibid., p. 300.

drink, or gambling. A few sensitive souls, articulate individuals such as Lovecraft, turned to their dreams.

The year of 1929 was a fitting climax to a decade variously called the Jazz Age, the Emancipation of Women, Flaming Youth, the Golden Era of Sports, Marathon Dances, the Era of Wonderful Nonsense. It was as well an era of tedious foolishness, for as F. Scott Fitzgerald recalled: "This was the generation that corrupted its elders and eventually overreached itself less through lack of morals than through lack of taste. May one offer in exhibit the year 1922! That was the peak of the younger generation, for though the Jazz Age continued, it became less and less an affair of youth. The sequel was like a children's party taken over by the elders . . . By 1923 their elders, tired of watching the carnival with ill-concealed envy, had discovered that young liquor will take the place of young blood, and with a whoop the orgy began . . . A whole race going hedonistic, deciding on pleasure."[137]

I pause over this raucous echo for this reason. For several weeks I had been reading through Lovecraft's letters and miscellaneous writings in the 1920–1930 period when I came across the phrase *"Certe, nullas bananas hodie habemus,"* which he had scribbled at the bottom of a letter.[138] At that moment I was finally jolted into realizing that here was a man who had lived through the Roaring Twenties (two of those years in New York) and yet his times are, at most, peripheral to his work and to his correspondence. The horseplay is absent, contemporary references are rare, and the slang of the time is used sparingly for comic effect.

Rather than risk losing his sanity and debasing his art, Lovecraft had striven to keep himself intact. In his high-button shoes he had treaded on tip-toe and with eyes cast down past the New American Female who had cut her hair, shortened her skirt, and had begun to

---

137. Ibid., p. 98.
138. H. P. Lovecraft, MS. letter to Mrs. Lillian D. Clark, dated February 23, 1924, JHL.

V. Home

smoke and drink in public, bidding a spectacular good-bye to her former domestic life. Abstemious, he had gingerly made his way through speak-easy neighborhoods, past college girls all moulded "smooth, hot, and snappy,"[139] away from jazz blaring the dubious pleasures of "Makin' Whoopee," and "Boogie Woogie." He had exited unscathed: a figure dressed in black, clutching a small valise; face smooth and pale out of which peered the tired eyes of a man who had accepted the role of Outsider.

During the 1929–1930 winter Lovecraft settled into his annual seclusion. Ghostwriting, the minor duties of Amateur Journalism, and a heavy correspondence kept him pleasantly occupied. Although *Weird Tales* occasionally reprinted an earlier story of his, it had been over a year since a new story had been submitted. Lovecraft seemed not to mind. When Miss Toldridge asked him in April if he had abandoned the field, he replied in the negative. "I shan't give up writing phantasy, although I think I shall have fewer & fewer readers as time passes. Fortunately I don't give a hang whether or not anybody reads what I write."[140]

So saying, he boarded a Greyhound the next day for a trip South. He stopped by to see the Longs, as he had done the year before, and then resumed speed. First stop was Columbia, South Carolina.

> In reply to all questions concerning the location of Paradise, I now have one answer ready—it is the more southerly part of His Majesty's Province of South-Carolina, which I this morning enter'd for the first time . . . What can I say of such a region as it glows under a June-like sun, & with such a vivid luxuriance of fresh verdure as I never before beheld? What a place! *A real civilisation,* with pure American people, a sense of leisure & repose, (a vast amount of very opulent (tho' not antiquarian) beauty. Why in Heaven's name does *anybody* live in the North—except from compulsion or from sentimental attachment? What a day! The song of the birds alone is worth the price of admission! Columbia, the capital

---

139. George Harmon Knoles, *The Jazz Age Revisited*, Stanford, California, Stanford University Press, 1955, p. 76.
140. H. P. Lovecraft, MS. letter to Elizabeth Toldridge, dated April 24, 1930, JHL.

of the state, is a fine, mellow town with broad, sleepy streets & not enough modernity to spoil it. Niggers are numerous, but they never get in the way; & there appear to be no foreigners whatsoever. The accent of the population charms me—I shall be using it myself if I do not keep on guard! . . . What trees! What parks! *What gardens!* In short—what a region! No—there is no mystery about Paradise. It is South Carolina![141]

After Columbia, he was exploring the colonial byways of Charleston with his customary thoroughness. The minor ills of the previous winter dissolved under the sun's salubrious warmth. He was proud of his appearance. "Some of my new coat of tan is peeling off, but a very fair residue remains, so that the gang will probably note a healthy-looking change when I hit N. Y."[142] Such a remark (and there are others) contradicts W. Paul Cook's statement that Lovecraft "never liked to tan, and a trace of color on his cheeks seemed to be a source of annoyance. He was the only person I ever met to be ashamed of a coat of tan."[143] This error was repeated by Edmund Wilson[144] and, more recently, by Winfield Townley Scott.[145] Of course it does seem more in character to have a horror writer with a pasty white complexion, like some charnel worm, yet the prosaic facts are against it.

On a trip such as this, one of Lovecraft's biggest expenses was for postage and postcards. It was surprising how much he spent. He made up the cash on meals, by staying at the Y.M.C.A., cutting his own hair with a patented barbering device, rinsing his own collars in the Y's washbowls, and pressing them over the radiators in his room. He resorted to these aids with good humor. It was part of his instinctive generosity to share his travel experiences with his friends. His letters grew to travelogues with sketches of street maps and Colonial homes.

---

141. H. P. Lovecraft, MS. letter to Mrs. Lillian D. Clark, dated April 28, 1930, JHL.
142. H. P. Lovecraft, MS. letter to Mrs. Lillian D. Clark, dated May 6, 1930, JHL.
143. Cook, p. 9.
144. Wilson, p. 290.
145. *Exiles and Fabrications,* p. 50.

V. Home

On the return trip to Providence he stopped in New York for an evening's chat with Samuel Loveman. Lovecraft had not been talking long when . . .

> About 8 o'clock the bell rang, & there appeared that tragically drink-riddled but now eminent friend of Loveman's whom I met in Cleveland in 1922, & once or twice later in New York—the poet Hart Crane, whose new book, "The Bridge", has made him one of the most celebrated & talked-of figures of contemporary American letters. He had been scheduled to speak over the radio during the evening; but a shipwreck off the coast (demanding the use of the ether for important messages) had cut off all local radio programmes & left him free. When he entered, his discourse was of alcoholics in various phases—& of the correct amount of whiskey one ought to drink in order to speak well in public—but as soon as a bit of poetic & philosophic discussion sprang up, this sordid side of his strange dual personality slipped off like a cloak, & left him as a man of great scholarship, intelligence, & aesthetic taste, who can argue as interestingly & profoundly as anyone I have ever seen. Poor devil—he has "arrived" at last as a standard American poet seriously regarded by all reviewers & critics; yet at the very crest of his fame he is on the verge of psychological, physical, & financial disintegration & with no certainty of ever having the inspiration to write a major work of literature again. After about three hours of acute & intelligent argument poor Crane left—to hunt up a new supply of whiskey & banish reality for the rest of the night! He gets to be a nuisance now & then, dropping in on Loveman for sympathy & encouragement, but Loveman is too conscious of his tragic importance & genuine genius as a man of letters to be harsh or brusque toward him. His case is surely a sad one—all the more so because of his great attainments & of the new fame which he is so ill-fitted to carry for any considerable time. He looks more weather-beaten & drink-puffed than he did in the past, though the shaving off of his moustache has somewhat improved him. He is only 33, yet his hair is nearly white. Altogether his case is almost like that of Baudelaire on a vastly smaller scale.[146]

From New York, Lovecraft followed a circuitous route home, stopping by Athol, Massachusetts to see an Amateur friend, W. Paul

---

146. H. P. Lovecraft, MS. letter to Mrs. Lillian D. Clark, dated May 24–25, 1930, JHL.

Cook. Lovecraft's strolls over the neighboring countryside stirred his imagination. To enter these old landscapes was "almost like walking at will through time & space, or climbing bodily into some strange picture on the wall."[147] He felt an odd, sinister undercurrent in the twisted trees and the small farmhouses. He had also felt it in those textile towns to the north, grim places like Lowell, Fall River, and Lynn, birthplace of Lydia Pinkham and one-time home of Mary Baker Eddy. Lovecraft was conscious of what he termed "a belt of decadence" which swept through central Massachusetts. In 1928 he had visited northeastern Springfield, Monson, and Wilbraham, and exaggerated their "grotesque idiosyncracies" into his story "The Dunwich Horror."[148] He had that same year visited Vermont and engrafted its rural speech ("caow," "daown") and its idiom into the Arkham setting of "The Dunwich Horror."

In 1930 he successfully used a Vermont setting for "The Whisperer in Darkness." The story is a variation on one of his repeated themes of the isolated individual whose curiosity leads him to destruction. In this case a recluse discovers that creatures from another planet are inside some Vermont hills, quarrying for a stone unobtainable on their own planet. Hideous winged things, the Outer Ones, these age-old cosmonauts, were on our earth long before man, and they are capable of dealing with him in ruthless fashion. "The Whisperer in Darkness" was written shortly after the discovery of the planet Pluto by C. W. Tombaugh in 1930. Lovecraft, to add a touch of immediacy to the story, had the Outer Ones using Pluto (called Yuggoth) as their outpost in our galaxy.

Any number of contemporary incidents may have sparked Lovecraft into writing his forty-five thousand word novelette *At the Moun-*

---

147. H. P. Lovecraft, MS. letter to Mrs. Lillian D. Clark, dated June 12, 1930, JHL.

148. H. P. Lovecraft, MS. letter to Richard Ely Morse, dated July 28, 1933, NYPL.

tains of Madness in 1931.[149] He had entertained for some time the idea of writing a horror story with a polar locale. As he said: "The idea of the great white antarctic—an alien world of death, and the last great *Terra Incognita* on this planet—has haunted me ever since I was ten years old; and in this yarn I tried to express, after a fashion, the feeling of mystery it inspires in me . . ."[150] Growing from the earlier expeditions of Scott, Amundsen, and now Byrd, public curiosity in the antarctic was keen in the 1930s.

That he decided to write a novelette indicates a confidence in his artistry and, possibly, a livelier eye on the commercial market. The previous year when Lovecraft had been on his southern junket, Clifton Fadiman of Simon and Schuster had sent him a letter. "If you are contemplating any longer work of fiction," wrote Fadiman, "please let me know."[151] Fadiman's note was a form letter which was sent to all whose names had appeared on the O'Brien rosters. Lovecraft took it seriously and wrote Fadiman that he hoped to submit a novel some day and that in the meantime he was sending a collection of his short stories.[152]

At the Mountains of Madness was written between February 24 and March 22, 1931.[153] From extant jottings and sketches on memo pads and on the back of a torn envelope, one may see how Lovecraft's imagination swiftly yet surely outlined his projected book. His physical conception of the mountains of madness was dramatically suggested by the paintings of Nicholas Roerich, whose studio on West 103 Street in New York Lovecraft had visited. He admired Roerich's fantastic

---

149. [The work is 41,500 words.]
150. H. P. Lovecraft, letter to Jim Blish and William Miller, Jr., dated May 13, 1936, reprinted in *Phantastique—Science-Fiction Critic* 2 (March 1938).
151. H. P. Lovecraft, MS. letter to Robert H. Barlow, dated May 24–25, 1930, JHL.
152. Ibid.
153. H. P. Lovecraft, MS. notes for *At the Mountains of Madness*, JHL.

Asian landscapes. "There is something in his handling of perspective & atmosphere," wrote Lovecraft, "which to me suggests other dimensions & alien orders of being or at least the gateways leading to such ... those curious cubical edifices clinging to precipitous slopes edging upward to forbidden needle-like peaks!"[154] And he acknowledged Roerich's imaginative aid by referring to him six times in the story. Poe's *The Narrative of A. Gordon Pym* was a stimulus here also as the piping cry of *"Tekeli-li! Tekeli-li!"* is heard; and a character in the story astutely observes that Mt. Erebus is quite likely the Yaanek of Poe's "Ulalume."[155] I do not, however, believe that Lovecraft's story is a "modernized sequel" to Poe's *Pym*.[156] Pym did not require a sequel.

At the Mountains of Madness is narrated by a scientist from Miskatonic University who is trying to dissuade further expeditions to the South Pole region which he and his party had previously explored. "It is absolutely necessary for the peace and safety of mankind," he warns at the conclusion of his story, "that some of earth's dark, dead corners ... be left alone; lest sleeping abnormalities wake to resurgent life."[157] The Miskatonic expedition had separated into two exploring parties. Under Professor Lake, one group was boring through an ice crust when they broke into a cavern. Inside were entombed fourteen lifeless animals. They were eight feet tall with grey membranous wings. Their bodies bulged like a barrel and their star-shaped heads were covered with multicolored cilia. Neither wholly animal or vegetable, the specimens had a tough, leathery surface. In place of blood was a greenish ichor. A hasty dissection by Lake deepened rather than cleared the mystery. When Lake's group failed to report, a party was sent out.

---

154. H. P. Lovecraft, MS. letter to Margaret Ronan, n.d., circa January, 1937, MR.
155. T. O. Mabbott, review of *The Outsider*, *American Literature* (March, 1940), p. 136. Also see *Fresco* (Spring 1958), pp. 37–39.
156. Moskowitz, p. 47.
157. H. P. Lovecraft, *At the Mountains of Madness*, *The Outsider*, p. 505.

V. Home

They found Lake and all of his men dead, save one who was missing. The dissected creature and five of his damaged kith had been carefully buried upright in nine-foot snow graves. Some of the equipment had disappeared, while much of what remained had been tampered with strangely. Later, the narrator and Danforth, a graduate student, flying over the area, saw stretched out for a hundred miles the ruins of a prehistoric city. Landing to explore, they found a bas-relief which detailed the fate of its inhabitants.

Years ago when the earth was young and dead, the star-headed Old Ones winged their way here through space. They settled in the sea at first, there creating primal earth life.[158] Among their protoplasmic assemblages they jestingly concocted "a shambling primitive mammal, used sometimes for food and sometimes as an amusing buffoon by the land dwellers, whose vaguely simian and human foreshadowings were unmistakable."[159] To assist in their gigantic building program, they created the shoggoths, fifteen-foot viscous, black globules which continually changed their shape under mental suggestions from their masters. Civilizations are subject to challenge and response, we are told, and it was so with that of the Old Ones. Geological upheavals shattered their marine cities. On land, they were challenged by another race which had filtered down from cosmic infinity. After a colossal war, peace was secured, and the Old Ones were given the sea and the antarctic, the eventual center of their civilization. The land masses in the Pacific sank, destroying the Old Ones' foes. Supreme once more, they moved across the land. As time moved on, the shoggoths became intractable until a war of resubjugation became necessary. This happened one hundred and fifty million years ago. The Old Ones achieved victory using "curious weapons of molecular and atomic disturbance."[160] Dur-

---

158. Ibid., p. 480.
159. Ibid., pp. 480–81.
160. Ibid., p. 482.

ing the Jurassic Age, the Old Ones were successfully challenged by new adversaries from outer space—the half-fungous, half-crustacean Mi-Go, who eventually drove the Old Ones into the antarctic waters.[161]

Exploring further along a tunnel, the narrator and Danforth discovered the corpse of the missing man from Lake's camp. Further ahead they came upon the headless bodies of eight of the Old Ones, sucked dry and covered with a black slime. The mist in the tunnel cleared and the piping cries of *"Tekeli-li! Tekeli-li!"* were heard. As the two explorers retreated, Danforth cast a backward glance. What he saw snapped his mind and he began chanting "South Station Under—Washington Under—Park Street Under—Kendall—Central—Harvard"—the stops of the Boston–Cambridge subway line. The narrator knew of "the monstrous analogy that had suggested it."[162]

At the Mountains of Madness is more circumstantiated than *The Case of Charles Dexter Ward*. In this quasi-scientific novelette, unlike *Ward*, no black magic is used to call down or destroy entities from other dimensions. The manner is scientific in its lengthy exposition of the crew and its equipment, geological formations, the Old Ones' appearance, the cyclopean city, and the detailed saga of the Old Ones. Lovecraft's submerging of the fantastic in realism has been called "tediously expert."[163] Jacques Papy found this story the most tiresome of Lovecraft's works to translate because of its minutiae.[164] Yet Lovecraft's soberly detailed stories are to be favored over his earlier works where he began by yelling at the top of his voice and kept on howling. They inevitably failed to draw a shudder. One became, as it were, hardened to the "pitch."

When Lovecraft completed *At the Mountains of Madness*, he was faced with its typing, an undertaking made harder by the possibility

---

161. Ibid.
162. Ibid., p. 506.
163. Damon Knight, *In Search of Wonder*, Chicago: Advent, 1956, p. 117.
164. Jacques Papy, MS. letter to Arthur Koki, dated September 19, 1961, AK.

V. Home

that it would be rejected, although, despite its occasional prolixity, he considered it the best thing he had ever written.[165] Even at *Weird Tales'* penurious one-cent-a-word-rate, Lovecraft stood to earn four hundred and fifty dollars. The money meant being able to travel, and travel meant a more interesting life.

As his name spread among readers of supernatural fiction, so too other writers in the genre began corresponding with him, asking him to come visit. Reverend Henry St. Clair Whitehead of Dunedin, Florida was such a person. A contributor to *Weird Tales,* he invited Lovecraft in May, 1931, to spend a month with him and his father. Lovecraft accepted. There were no pressing duties at home. His aunts would forward his mail to him, his ghostwriting and revision jobs were out of the way for the time. He had mailed *At the Mountains of Madness* to *Weird Tales* reasonably confident that it would be accepted.

His health was good. The weather remained perfect that May and June. His host was a gracious man, generous to a fault.

> Yes—Whitehead is certainly a great guy, & I find him one of the rare few to whom I can talk at length without running out of topics. He is about as far from the stereotyped clergyman—even intellectually—as anyone could well be; & he recognizes that even his assumption of a deity is only a guess suggested by tradition. He seems to be the idol of everyone in Dunedin, & especially of the small boys . . . His spontaneous generosity is so vast that one has actually to be careful about admiring anything of his, lest he offer it as a present! When I leave in about a week I shall bear away as gifts a jar of West Indian cherry marmalade, a copy of Paul Morand's 'Black Magic', & a copy of Wakefield's weird collection, 'Others Who Returned'.[166]

After leaving Reverend Whitehead, Lovecraft visited St. Augustine. A slow rejuvenation had been effected. A nervous tugging in his left

---

165. H. P. Lovecraft, MS. letter to Richard Ely Morse, dated August 9, 1932, NYPL.
166. H. P. Lovecraft, MS. letter to Mrs. Lillian D. Clark, dated May 30, 1931, JHL.

eye vanished, though he wore rimless glasses at the cinema. He was enjoying "the only long period of really *unbroken physical comfort* which I can recall in my decaying span of 41 years!"[167] One probable sign of his increasing vitality was his appetite. With what nostalgic regret do we learn that Lovecraft, staying at St. Augustine's Rio Vista Hotel, sat down to a dinner of spaghetti with grated cheese, pork chops with French fried potatoes, and coffee. All for thirty cents.[168] After exploring St. Augustine he planned to visit Savannah and Charleston. He wanted to walk over their brick sidewalks and view their palmettoes, Greek colonnades, and parklike squares. From there, he would stop in New York, and then home to Providence "blest haven" of the journey's end. While he was in St. Augustine anticipating the delights of the homeward route, his happy world momentarily collapsed. Farnsworth Wright, the editor of *Weird Tales,* rejected *At the Mountains of Madness.* "Confound that wretch Wright for turning down the tale I half-killed myself typing!" he boomed, "The accursed cheap-skate!! . . . Did quite a bit on a new story yesterday—but am so disgusted over Wright's latest rejection that I can't do a thing in that line today."[169] He soothed himself that day by reading the *New York Times* and sightseeing.

The rejection slip had gradually lost its sting by the time he arrived home and he resumed writing his work in progress, a short story called "The Shadow over Innsmouth." There had been some speculation among *Weird Tales'* writers as to the type of stories Editor Wright preferred. Some of them believed that he was partial to those which dealt with the decay of human beings, individually or collectively (as in Lovecraft's "Arthur Jermyn," "The Lurking Fear," "The Rats in the Walls," and "The Dunwich Horror"), and, if this was so, Lovecraft

---

167. Ibid.
168. H. P. Lovecraft, MS. letter to Mrs. Lillian D. Clark, dated May 8, 1931.
169. H. P. Lovecraft, MS. letter to Mrs. Lillian D. Clark, dated May 13, 1931, JHL.

V. Home

was hopeful because "The Shadow over Innsmouth," as he wrote, "is decay & nothing else but!"[170] It was told with consummate skill after Lovecraft had fortified himself by carefully outlining the story and drawing up factitious genealogical charts and Innsmouth street maps.[171] His ear for New England dialect is sure. He uses in the central portion of the story the Maugham technique of having a native acquaintance narrate part of the tale. The creation of all important atmosphere and mounting suspense is superbly rendered and maintained up to the anticlimactic revelation of the narrator's progenitors.

A professional handling of a pet theme did not prevent Farnsworth Wright from also rejecting "The Shadow over Innsmouth."[172] Since 1924, Wright had seen and turned down "In the Vault," "Cool Air," "The Shunned House," "The Colour out of Space," and *At the Mountains of Madness*. The overall mediocrity of *Weird Tales* must give us pause to wonder what standards, if any, Wright upheld. Zealia Bishop has noted that Wright suffered painfully from Parkinson's Disease.[173] Is there an unspoken implication in this that his lapses in judgement and memory were somehow engendered by his ailment? Anecdotes also tell of writers who resubmitted to him previously rejected manuscripts with the notation that they had incorporated his salient suggestions in the "new" version; this time he accepted.[174] Wright was not an imaginative editor. He played the ulcer-lacerating game of trying to guess what he thought his readers thought they thought they wanted in the way of weird fiction. And to cater to these chimeras he was will-

---

170. H. P. Lovecraft, MS. letter to Margaret Ronan, n.d., circa 1936, MR.
171. H. P. Lovecraft, "Notes for Shadow over Innsmouth," *Something About Cats*, pp. 170–84.
172. [HPL never submitted "The Shadow over Innsmouth" to Wright. August Derleth, without HPL's knowledge or permission, did so on two occasions during HPL's lifetime; both times, Wright rejected the story.]
173. Bishop, pp. 148–49.
174. In private conversation with Frank B. Long, Jr., on January 25, 1961.

ing to bypass intrinsically good writing. To be sure, Wright later accepted most of Lovecraft's previously rejected stories (some after Lovecraft's death), when he could no longer ignore the fact that Lovecraft was a major figure in the fantasy world with a faithful and vocal following.

The rejection in the same year of *At the Mountains of Madness* and "The Shadow over Innsmouth"—stories which he quite rightly considered among his best—so embittered Lovecraft that in the next five years (1932–1936) he submitted only five new stories to *Weird Tales*. It was not that he could brook no censure. If anything he was his own most severe critic, but clearly these two lengthy works were above the level of *Weird Tales'* acceptances. He was dissatisfied with *Weird Tales* for other reasons as well. The shabby payment would be withheld until publication. Physically, the magazine's make up offended his sensibility. Cover paintings which showed Nameless Horrors leering at seductive nudes so incensed him that he would either tear off the cover or fold it over.[175] In the back pages advertisements captioned "Are You Afraid to Love?" "Throw Away That Truss!" "What Strange Powers Did the Ancients Possess?" were flanked by smaller ads for the lonely hearted, and for various nostrums, of which an alarming number were for women with troublesome periods. *Weird Tales* was aimed at the purses of indiscriminate readers—unfortunately, because, like many publications, it underestimated the intelligence of its readers.

Lovecraft remained active in the weird writing field even if he was no longer a prolific contributor. He kept in touch with other writers, offered encouragement to beginners, and corrected or ghostwrote for the less talented. He preferred this revision work, which assured him a steady, though meagre, income; it released him from what was to him

---

175. In private conversation with Douglass Dana on January 28, 1959. [In fact, HPL's own copies of *Weird Tales*—now at the John Hay Library—have the covers intact. HPL frequently remarked that he was indifferent about the cover designs.]

V. Home

the supreme humiliation of visiting employment bureaus and prospective employers.

His letters to Amateur members showed no curtailment despite his repeated threats to drop the duller correspondents. Miss Elizabeth Toldridge was not an Ellen Terry or a Bluestocking, yet Lovecraft wrote a quarter of a million words to her. Clues from her side of the correspondence point to a woman of advancing age, a person of low vitality to judge from the brevity of her barely legible pencil scrawls. Always she is "charmed" and "delighted" by Lovecraft's lengthy epistles. There is something touchingly absurd in her sending best wishes to the kittens in Lovecraft's neighborhood, and a lace handkerchief gentility in the closing of her letters—"All fair fortune attend you, good Sir Knight."[176] It was precisely this childlike quality which Lovecraft sought. He needed someone who would listen and be awed by what he had to say, one, for instance, who would not laugh at his Tory posturing.

> There is a deifying Washington myth just as there is a cognate Lincoln myth. Actually, the general was a man of good ability, entire honesty, & the luck to be the head of the winning side of an illegal venture which happened to gain spectacular success. Without indulging in any idolatry, I have a sincere respect for Genl. W. as an honourable Virginia gentleman of steady competence, aristocratic sincerity, truly English determination, & general good taste. What I deplore is his choice of sides in the unfortunate business of 1775–83—a mere accident of circumstances; since if his mother had let him join the Royal Navy in youth, there is little doubt but that he would (being broadened by travel & the influence of the regular service) have remained loyal to his rightful King & served capably in Britain's sea forces under Lord Howe.[177]

More interesting than his Anglicisms were his scientific predictions

---

176. Miss Elizabeth Toldridge, MS. letter to H. P. Lovecraft, dated July 19, 1935, AK.

177. H. P. Lovecraft, MS. letter to Elizabeth Toldridge, dated April 20, 1932, JHL.

to Miss Toldridge. Considering that in his fiction Lovecraft daringly smashed our time-space continuum to smithereens, it is mildly surprising how guarded were his space age prognostications. He believed the moon would be reached by a rocket before many years, but he had doubts concerning living passengers making such a trip. Beyond the moon, prospects were doubtful, he felt, but he would not be surprised if "before the end of the existing civilisation some wholly new principle might enable men to reach the moon, & possibly Mars & Venus."[178] If from our vantage point of over thirty years Lovecraft seems conservative, it must be remembered that the common attitude toward rocketry thirty years ago was one of indifference or, worse, ridicule. Lovecraft watched Dr. Goddard's experiments with interest and sympathy.[179]

Lovecraft did some traveling himself in the spring of 1932, as he continued his now customary routine of visiting the South. As usual, he journeyed by bus. He could not understand why some complained of bus travel. To him the constant unfolding of new scenery fulfilled his idea of "adventurous expectancy." He did not indulge in impromptu quartets or chance acquaintants but he was never disturbed when younger and more gregarious passengers felt impelled to sing or crack jokes. To him the smoke-trailing Greyhound was near allied to the Boston Post Chaise of colonial New England.[180]

His antiquarian jaunt through Vicksburg, Natchez, and New Orleans was uneventful. On his stop-over in New York he received a telegram which extinguished his pleasant memories and sent him hastening home. It told of the sudden death of his semi-invalid aunt, Mrs. Lillian D. Clark. For traditional reasons the funeral service was

---

178. H. P. Lovecraft, MS. letter to Elizabeth Toldridge, dated July 1, 1929, JHL.
179. [Robert H. Goddard (1882–1945), American physicist who launched the first liquid-fueled rocket in 1926. He is mentioned in two of HPL's letters to Toldridge ([8 January 1930] and 27 March 1936).]
180. H. P. Lovecraft, MS. letter to Margaret Ronan, n.d., circa 1936, MR.

V. Home

held according to the Anglican rites, although, as Lovecraft wrote, "my aunt had no more belief in childish theology & immortality myths than I have."[181] Mrs. Clark was buried in the Clark plot in Swan Point Cemetery, among the graves of the Clark ancestors extending to 1711. When Miss Toldridge sent her sympathy Lovecraft replied that "The sense of vacancy resulting from the bereavement is of course very considerable, but one has to realise the inevitability of such events."[182]

Four months after his aunt's passing, another death occurred which made 1932 take its place along the black years in Lovecraft's memory. His gracious Floridian host Reverend Henry Whitehead died.

> Bad news. Whitehead died last Wednesday. I knew he was in rotten health, but had no idea it was as bad as all this. He wrote breezily & optimistically less than a fortnight ago. Really, this gives me a hell of a jolt. He was such a splendid chap in every way—brilliant, courageous, attractive, learned, & everything else admirable. It'll be a frightful blow to his father—now 84.[183]

There is something heroic in Lovecraft's bearing before Death. The refusal to mourn in public. The sentimental deception of himself or others is tucked out of sight. This tough mindedness at the "inevitability of such events" more clearly characterizes his later years than the beer garden or chemical analogies which seek to make him "mellow" or "pure gold."

His calm acceptance of reality embraced his writing as well. He had in 1932 submitted a collection of his short stories to Putnam.[184] They were rejected—the reason being that his tale "had an *over-explanatory* quality," a lack of subtlety undoubtedly caused by the pulp magazine standards. "On reflection," said Lovecraft, "I concurred in this objection—even though I have always (at least since 1925) sought

---

181. H. P. Lovecraft, MS. letter to Elizabeth Toldridge, dated July 30, 1932, JHL.
182. Ibid.
183. H. P. Lovecraft, MS. letter to Robert H. Barlow, dated November 5, 1932, JHL.
184. [This happened in 1931.]

to repudiate the popular commercial tradition."[185] But, since this is not the age of the enlightened patron, Lovecraft found it impossible to dismiss a magazine's slant.

An example of this is "The Thing the Doorstep." It is the story of Edward Pickman Derby and his *outré*-directed wife, Asenath, who exchanges her body for that of her husband. This *striga* extinguishes by degrees Derby's already feeble spirit and periodically usurps his body for her own vigorous activities, such as participating in unspeakable rites with subterranean creatures. Derby in a moment of strength kills Asenath and buries her body, but Asenath's superior will forces his spirit into her rotting corpse and she moves into his shell. Derby, however, claws his way out and shortly thereafter expires in a putrescent smear on the threshold of a friend's home. A note written by Derby to the narrator-friend explains his metamorphosis and pleads that Asenath be destroyed. Asenath's body is actually housing a non-human creature who had appropriated her body several years earlier. In sum, a story of metempsychosis, not quite *The Progresse of the Soule*,[186] to be sure, and so over-explanatory that when we read the final sentence "Some dental work positively identified the skull as Asenath's"[187]—we are not startled; nor is it a confirmation of our suspicions since there were numerous earlier references which prepared us for this climax. While I would not go so far as to call the conclusion of "The Thing the Doorstep," in which the dissolution of the putrescent corpse is detailed, as showing "Lovecraft at his worst,"[188] it is gratuitous and inferior to the first half of the story. It is there because Lovecraft could do these decaying scenes, and the *Weird Tales* readers had come to enjoy this sort of thing.

---

185. H. P. Lovecraft, MS. letter to Richard Ely Morse, dated August 9, 1932, NYPL.
186. [*The Progress of the Soul* (1601), also called *Metempsychosis,* an unfinished long poem that proposes the notion of the transmigration of souls.]
187. H. P. Lovecraft, "The Thing on the Doorstep," *The Outsider,* p. 233.
188. Penzoldt, p. 170.

V. Home

"The Thing on the Doorstep" is unique in having a main character who is a woman. Asenath's "crowning rage" was that she was not a man.[189] A woman of great energy, she dominated her shy, bookish husband, watching over him with "an almost predatory air."[190] One cannot avoid wondering whether Asenath is meant to be an exaggerated picture of Lovecraft's wife Sonia; and may there not be something of Lovecraft in the hapless Derby?

A more impressive example of his talent is "The Dreams in the Witch House," a story potently centered around a pre-Revolutionary dwelling, a house, in fact, similar in appearance to the one which allegedly inspired Hawthorne's *The House of the Seven Gables*—that brooding Pyncheon mansion which remains a memorable symbol of the outworn past. The protagonist in this story is Walter Gilman, a student of mathematics at Arkham's Miskatonic University. He is also a keen folklorist, as was Professor Wilmarth in "The Whisperer in the Darkness." Occasionally we see Lovecraft using as characters "ils seront curieux de folklore, de sociologie ou d'archéologie, disciplines où les frontieres entre le science et l'imagination sont assez imprécises."[191] Gilman moves into a decrepit house, once inhabited by a condemned "witch," old Keziah Mason. As a student of science, Gilman does not believe in witches, but he is anxious to learn what strange mathematical insights this seventeenth century hag had somehow acquired. For according to old court records, "She had told Judge Hathorne of lines and curves that could be made to point out directions leading through walls of space to other spaces beyond." And shortly after she was jailed, "she had drawn those devices on the walls of her cell and disap-

---

189. "The Thing on the Doorstep," p. 220.
190. Ibid.
191. Claude Ernoult, "Lovecraft ou le mythe revolution," *Les Lettres Nouvelles* 21 (November 1954), p. 668. ["They are curious about folklore, sociology, or archaeology, disciples where the borderlines between science and imagination are somewhat imprecise."]

peared."[192] Gilman resolutely moves into her old quarters, an irregular shaped chamber with slanting walls and ceiling. Nothing unusual occurred at first, but later Gilman began to have terrifying dreams in which he would plunge through abysses of colored twilight and "distorted sound."[193] The dreams acquired new violence and he would see a hag, in whose face were mixed "hideous malevolence and exultation," beckoning to him.[194] Close to her, a small furry creature flashed his yellowish-white fangs. Both were often seen with a tall Black Man. Gilman joined them in his dreams by approaching a corner of his room at a certain angle. He accompanied them on their evil haunts, which included the kidnapping of a child who was later sacrificed in a sealed chamber above Gilman's room. That these experiences were dreams was greatly doubted by the less sophisticated boarders of the house for Gilman would awaken with mud-caked night clothes or bloody, scratched hands. Once a strange object, defying all earthly geometrical patterns, was found in his room—a memento from some other plane of existence? Gilman's death was hideously real. The ratlike creature tunneled into Gilman's body and ate out his heart.

When the house was finally demolished, it revealed books of black lore, the skeletons of small children, the bent bones of an old woman, all stored in an attic chamber. To some people it grimly confirmed the real though insane "other world" into which the somnambulist Gilman had strayed.

It is curious what Lovecraft has wrought in "The Dreams in the Witch House." He has used the same horrors that stalk into a child's nightmare; the witch, puckered and ugly as one can imagine; the vicious rat, with his not quite human face, who will chew and tear you to bits; the bogey-man, huge, because he is seen from a child's perspec-

---

192. H P. Lovecraft "The Dreams in the Witch House," *The Outsider*, pp. 194–95.
193. Ibid., p. 196.
194. Ibid., p. 200.

tive; and the naked child defenseless beneath the enormous knife poised . . . the fantasies are here flagrantly apparent if we stop to separate and tally. We should then be insouciant and smile at Lovecraft's childish pranks. Nevertheless, the obvious is not always expected and certain subconscious feelings are disturbingly aroused within us. Our mature attitudes toward witches and supernatural horrors are lulled in the beginning as Lovecraft discreetly presents a reassuringly familiar world of mathematics and materialistic skepticism.[195] The bizarre is put down as a bad dream. The witch, Keziah Mason, is, so far as Gilman is concerned, "a mediocre old woman,"[196] who had stumbled across mathematical formulae. Gilman does not connect her with the crone he later encounters. The Black Man is symbolically approached rather than blatantly thrust before us as a child menacer. He reminds Gilman of Nyarlathotep, the swarthy demon who embodies chaos and darkness in the Cthulhu mythology.

It is a credit to Lovecraft's fictional powers that in "The Dreams in the Witch House" he can write of mathematics and magic in the same sentence without appearing laughable. Gilman as a student mathematician and folklorist is skeptical of black magic yet receptive to the fantastic mathematical concept that other worlds, other time-space continua touch our planet at various points. One has only to learn the place and direction of approach. Thus, argues Lovecraft for the purposes of fiction, science had its birth in magic, but when it left superstition behind, it lost some of its greatest truths—truths, paradoxically, that open vistas to new horrors and reveal man's incredible insignificance in the cosmos.

Gilman is a Lovecraftian character. A superior intellect, *per se,* isolates him from the ordinary human conventions. Gilman's isolation is amplified since most of the roomers in the Witch House are Polish immigrants. With near comic realism, Lovecraft portrays them as reli-

---

195. Ernoult, pp. 669–70.
196. "The Dreams in the Witch House," p. 195.

giously superstitious people, drinking and whining against the unholy presence which they intuitively feel lurking in the house. Their prayers, recited in feverish haste, echo in Gilman's room with the distant chant of the Sabbat, the rats scratching behind the walls, and other whimperings and demonic shrieks.

An eighteenth century gabled house was in Lovecraft's mind when he wrote "The Dreams in the Witch House."[197] The room itself with its slanted construction may have been suggested to him by an incident which happened some nine years earlier in July, 1925, when he and his wife went to Coney Island for an afternoon. They saw there a "House of Wonder" whose floor, walls, and ceiling distorted normal perspective, creating such optical illusions as a ball rolling up a steep floor. Lovecraft sketched a diagram and explained the riddle to Sonia, who was so proud that she told the gate-keeper. To Lovecraft's pleasure, "The gate-keeper . . . professed a respectful surprise upon seeing my pencil diagram. He admitted that I was right, inquired what my profession was, & stated that he had seldom seen solutions produced so completely on the spot."[198]

The houses which crop up in four Lovecraft titles—"The Picture in the House," "The Strange High House in the Mist," "The Shunned House," "The Dreams in the Witch House"—and the prominence of a house in such stories as "The Music of Erich Zann" and "The Rats in the Walls" are a sign of Lovecraft's sensitivity to their eerie suggestions. Only one who could think of a house as an organic body, which acquires its owner's personality, could have so happily analysed Poe's "The Fall of the House of Usher." It was not only a black gabled house with its diamond-shaped windows glaring in the light that affected him. Location also played a part. The real "shunned house" at

---

197. H. P. Lovecraft, MS. letter to Richard Ely Morse, dated October 17, 1933, NYPL.
198. H. P. Lovecraft, MS. letter to Mrs. Lillian D. Clark, dated July 27, 1925. JHL.

V. Home

135 Benefit Street had nothing of the sinister in its appearance or annals. It had belonged to friends of the Lovecraft family since its erection in 1760. Wrote Lovecraft: "The steep hill, the rustic, half-uncared-for yard stretching far behind it always gave it a factitiously sinister air in my eyes."[199] Unfortunately such dark spots of neglect are harder to find with each passing year. The existence of old homes and baronial mansions in England helps to explain why the tale of terror has so long subsisted there and, conversely, why it may not be expected to do so in America. It requires generations to have a ghost in the house, family legends, the accumulated presence of ancestors who have exhalated, sweated, and expired within those same walls. Time is required. But the bulldozer in the name of progress must break old ground for shopping centers and monolithic apartments—a modern antiseptic world which admits no mystery.

Lovecraft's night thoughts on dejected-looking homes and landscapes was eclipsed by his genuine appreciation for the beauties of Colonial architecture, and never did he sing those praises with such enthusiasm as when—after a lifetime of longing to live in a real Colonial house—he moved into a one-hundred fifteen year old dwelling. With his aunt, Mrs. Annie E. P. Gamwell, he moved from 10 Barnes to 66 College Street on May 14, 1933.[200] They rented the second floor and a monitor-crowned attic from Brown University. By a coincidence the house was located just in back of the John Hay Library, the library which one day would house an impressive collection of his correspondence and manuscripts. Steam heat to the home was piped in from the John Hay's heating plant. An unfailing source of warmth was crucial to him because of his susceptibility to cold weather. Let winter come now. What did he care? He would turn the radiators on all the

---

199. H. P. Lovecraft, MS. letter to Richard Ely Morse, dated February 9, 1936, Collection of Professor Thomas Ollive Mabbott. Hereafter, TOM.
200. H. P. Lovecraft, MS. letter to Robert H. Barlow, dated May 26, 1933, JHL.

way until his study was a comfortable 87°.

The white frame house gave the outward appearance of being rather tiny. Actually it was quite roomy inside. The upper flat had five rooms, bath, and kitchen, plus, upstairs, the attic with that monitor which permitted a magnificent view of the city.[201]

The new home atoned for all the work involved in moving. "There is a thrill to coming home & entering a Colonial doorway like that of my bookplate, in sitting beside a Colonial mantel, or gazing out of an ancient small-paned window."[202] Sixty-six College Street was so perfect in every way, down to the wide plank floors, that for the first month he often had the odd feeling of being in a museum from which he would be ushered out by the guard at five o'clock.[203]

Life resumed its normal turn for Lovecraft. The revision of an eighty-thousand word novel was brought to completion.[204] To his correspondents he apologized for neglecting them, but he had, as they could see, recently moved, et cetera, et cetera. He was back in print that year. The February, 1933, issue of *Weird Tales* had reprinted "The Cats of Ulthar." The July issue carried two stories by him. One was "The Dreams in the Witch House," and the other was "The Horror in the Museum," which he ghostwrote for Hazel Heald.[205] Some of his

---

201. This house was moved on September 21, 1959, to make way for a Brown University parking lot. The *Providence Journal* noted, with pictures and copy, the home's journey. "The late H. P. Lovecraft wrote many a tale of horror laid in an old New England house—but none of the houses moved two-and-a-half blocks as did one he used to live in early today. The historic old house at 66 College St. was trundled through a parking lot in the early hours, loaded on a low gear flat bed truck and hauled to 67 Prospect Street at the corner of Meeting Street. The moving was accomplished without incident on the steep hill as a crowd of about 200, many of them college students, watched the process . . ."
202. H. P. Lovecraft, MS. letter to Robert H. Barlow, dated May 26, 1933, JHL.
203. H. P. Lovecraft, MS. letter to Elizabeth Toldridge, dated June 7, 1933, JHL.
204. Ibid. [This work has never been identified.]
205. H. P. Lovecraft, MS. letter to Elizabeth Toldridge, dated July, 1933, JHL.

V. Home

earnings he set aside for a trip to Quebec in September. He had briefly visited this historic city three years earlier, and praised it generously.[206] This second weekend trip was also a success. Returning to Providence, he passed the remainder of the year uneventfully.

In what was for Lovecraft a rare action, he left his home after Christmas to visit his friends in New York. Trips to the museums, excursions, gab-fests, and Sunday dinner with the Longs were on his program.

> I saw the old year out at Samuel Loveman's—where one of the guests was the mother of the hapless poet Hart Crane, who committed suicide in 1932. Loveman quite overwhelmed me by giving me several objects for my collection of antiquities—a real Egyptian *ushabti* (small funerary statuette) 5,000 years old, a Mayan stone idol of almost equal antiquity, & a carved wooden monkey from the East Indian Island of Bali.[207]

Lovecraft no sooner returned home than he found an invitation to come South. The offer was extended by Robert Barlow of Cassia, Florida. Barlow was a boy of sixteen years, a member of the N.A.P.A., contributor to the *Fantasy Fan,* and an admirer of Lovecraft's stories. He had first written to Lovecraft in 1931 when he was thirteen years old. Preliminary chit-chat revolved around fantasy and weird literature. Lovecraft drew up a bibliography of his works, discussed some of his own stories, the market. Barlow, on his side, anxious to please, offered to type those Lovecraft stories which were in manuscript. When the boy sought advice on the most universal of writer's problems, the acquisition of style, Lovecraft replied: "The only way to *begin* to acquire a good style is to copy those who seem to be saying what you want to say. That's the way I did myself—copied Poe & Dunsany until their styles fused into something at least outwardly original."[208] This did not

---

206. H. P. Lovecraft, MS. letter to Richard Ely Morse, dated August 30, 1933, TOM.
207. H. P. Lovecraft, MS. letter to Elizabeth Toldridge, dated January 21, 1934, JHL.
208. H. P. Lovecraft, MS. letter to Robert H. Barlow, dated February 18, 1933, JHL.

hold for poetry, apparently, for he had earlier confessed to Miss Toldridge that "In verse I have cheated myself of a style by copying the styles of others."[209]

His letters to young Barlow acquired a tenor more personal, even melodramatic, at times. "When I was 18," he wrote, "I suffered such a breakdown that I had to forgo college. In those days I could hardly bear to see or speak to anyone, & liked to shut out the world by pulling down dark shades & using artificial light—acute kidney trouble—malfunction of nerves."[210] He grew reminiscent of his adolescence and spoke to Barlow in as intimate a tone as he had formerly used with his late aunt Lillie.

> There isn't a taste or interest in my whole psychology which didn't exist in some form or other before I was five years old. My style in both prose & verse was basically the same at 11 or 12 as it is now (although of course my handling of ideas & images was then ludicrously immature)—& my continuous memory of those far-off days is so keen that I can still enter into all the thoughts & feelings. It takes no effort at all—especially when I am out in certain woods & fields which have not changed a bit since my boyhood—for me to imagine that all the years since 1902 or 1903 are a dream . . . that I am still 12 years old, & that when I go home it will be through quieter, more village-like streets of those days—with horses & wagons, & little vari-colored street cars with open platforms, & with my old home at 454 Angell St. still waiting at the end of the vista—with my mother, grandfather, black cat, & other departed companions alive & unchanged.[211]

However much some people may contend that people change substantially as they go through life, a study of Lovecraft's voluminous correspondence would buttress, not destroy, the quotation cited. In Lovecraft's case the change was slight. A person is altered by the external circumstances which swirl about him, the active play of various

---

209. H. P. Lovecraft, MS. letter to Elizabeth Toldridge, dated March 8, 1929, JHL.
210. H. P. Lovecraft, MS. letter to Robert H. Barlow, dated April 10, 1934, JHL.
211. H. P. Lovecraft, MS. letter to Robert H. Barlow, dated August 8, 1933, JHL.

V. Home

minds against his, the places seen, the books read, etc. The greater the number and variety of these experiences, the more resilience and growth there is likely to be—a myth—one must never presume this with Lovecraft. There was a liberal change in his politics toward the end of his life, but generally speaking he limited his vision of life and ruthlessly clung to it, avoiding the new and the challenging. He passed up a trip to the World's Fair, saying, "The insufferable & freakish ugliness of those modernistic exposition buildings would give me nausea lasting the rest of my life. This damned modern faddism in architecture is to me as a red rag to a bull. Thank heaven we haven't any of it around Providence yet!"[212] In another letter he had spoken in a refrain similar to his autobiographical letter to Baird ten years earlier.

> I place so little value on life & its events, & regard man & his acts & feelings as so wholly a matter of deterministic mechanism—*that I have very little to be sad about,* no matter how much weak nerves might *invite* me to melancholy. All I want is peace, freedom to read & write, & cash enough to hang on to the books, pictures, furniture, & other objects which mean home to me—plus a bit extra to travel on once in a while. All *worry* with me is boiled down strictly to the *financial.* As to my health—I simply don't give a god damn about it; it is a matter of perfect indifference to me whether I shuffle off to oblivion tomorrow or live to be 100—provided in the latter case that I can have enough cash to keep my possessions around me. If I ever speed up the grim reaper it will be simply from lack of money to live decently.
>
> My last *laugh* was in 1928, at an incident which struck me with peculiar humorousness . . . when a fussy little man, to sustain his austere classical dislike of light music, hurried out of the room where a bunch of us were assembled because the radio was playing "The Mikado." He asked to be called back when it was all over![213]

Barlow became impatient to meet Lovecraft in person. So, early spring, 1934, the invitation was accepted. Something should be said concerning the prospective host. Robert Barlow was born into a mili-

---

212. H. P. Lovecraft, MS. letter to Robert H. Barlow, dated Ma y 26, 1933, JHL.
213. H. P. Lovecraft, MS. letter to Robert H. Barlow, dated April 10, 1934, JHL.

tary family in 1918, in Leavenworth, Kansas. His father, in line with his duties as a lieutenant colonel in the U.S. Army, frequently changed residence so that Robert managed to see most of the United States with his family, constantly and quickly learning here and there. Much later, one of Robert Barlow's colleagues was to write of him: "Tal vez este continuo ir y venir le haya dado esa amplitud de miras y de inter eses intelectuales. Esas educaciones algo caóticas y sin arraigo suelen producir frutos espléndidos en ciertos individuos."[214] Despite the unfortunate handicap of poor eyesight, he was exceedingly clever in drawing, painting, clay modeling, photography, and general craftsmanship.

During Lovecraft's visit, which lasted from May second to June twenty-first, Barlow kept a rough series of notes concerning his guest. The boy drove the old family Ford to the DeLand drugstore and waited tensely for the bus to swing in. It finally arrived and Lovecraft stepped out "a tall, stooped figure with grey-brown hair and a protruding jaw." He spoke in a pleasant yet somewhat high voice, and "he proved to be a smooth-skinned man of [a] face not unlike Dante's."[215]

Mrs. Bernice L. Barlow, Robert's mother, remembered that her son and Lovecraft were inseparable. They stayed up all night talking, and did not bother coming down to breakfast.[216] Their days were spent rowing on the lake, playing with Barlow's cats, Cyrus, Darius, and Alfred A. Knopf, the latter so baptized by Lovecraft. (Knopf had turned down a collection of Lovecraft's short stories.)[217] They strolled along the highway flanked by pines, cypresses, and live oak tangled with

---

214. Ignacio Bernal, "Necrologia: Robert H. Barlow," *Sobretiro del Torno XIII del Boletin Bibliografico de Antropologia Americana*, 1950, p. 1. ["Maybe this frequent coming and going has given him a wide variety of views and intellectual pursuits. In some individuals this type of education, chaotic and errant, sometimes yields splendid fruits" (translation by Ovidio Cartagena).]
215. "The Barlow Journal," *Some Notes on H. P. Lovecraft*, p. 25.
216. Mrs. Bernice L. Barlow, MS. letter to Arthur Koki, dated September 5, 1961, AK.
217. [This had occurred in 1933.]

Spanish moss. And always they conversed, with Lovecraft speaking volubly and incessantly on topics as unrelated as the Abyssinian War, chemistry, and Lord Dunsany. The Barlows had built a "backwoods" cabin between Eustis and DeLand. It was sometimes used as a retreat by Colonial Barlow, now retired, to improve his health. He had been in Walter Reed Hospital with a nervous breakdown.[218] Robert used it as a workshop. While Lovecraft talked, the boy bound books with the skins of snakes he had shot for that purpose. "They are masterpieces in their way," Lovecraft quietly observed.[219]

Often he would tell the Barlow family of the dreams he had had the night before, while at other times he was prevailed upon to read aloud his own stories. He read "with sinister tones and silences in the appropriate places. Especially he liked to read with an eighteenth century pronunciation, *sarvant* for 'servant' and *mi* for 'my.'"[220] Although he had a strong affinity for woodland scenes, he was definitely not at home in the unfamiliar terrain of Cassia, as was apparent by a berry-picking expedition he took with Barlow and two of his companions:

> We picked for over an hour, Lovecraft blundering about in the bushes, striving valiantly to keep up with us, though, being an amateur at berry-picking, he managed only half a basket by the time we had finished. So we helped him fill the basket, and started for home, H. P. L., by his own choice, bringing up the rear. When we came to the creek, I called out to him to point out where the board-bridge was; he replied that he saw it, so we went our way.
>
> When we reached home, he was no longer with us. He came in considerably later, soaked to the skin. He had not, after all, seen the plank on which he was to cross, but had plunged into the creek . . . bedraggled and woebegone, he was still first and foremost the gentleman—he apologized to my mother for losing the berries![221]

---

218. Ibid.
219. H. F. Lovecraft, MS. letter to Elizabeth Toldridge, dated December 29, 1934, JHL.
220. Robert H. Barlow, "The Wind That Is in the Grass," *Marginalia,* p. 314.
221. "The Barlow Journal," p. 31.

He did not have another suit with him, so he went to bed while Mrs. Barlow dried and pressed his clothes.[222] Almost magically one evening they saw a magnificent lunar rainbow—the brightest and loveliest that Mrs. Barlow ever recalls seeing. Lovecraft enjoyed the spectacle immensely and he speculated aloud about space and eternity.[223] In late June he left the Barlows with a promise to return the following year.

The dizzy breadth of his encyclopedic knowledge and his ever ready attitude for reading and criticizing the literary efforts of younger writers never flagged. One writer, August Derleth, wrote to him as "a youngster striving to be rational against a background of midwestern Catholicism, in rural Wisconsin,"[224] and continued a correspondence lasting from 1926 to 1937, in which time Derleth matured under Lovecraft's tutelage into a prolific and successful author. To this young man who was soon to see falangism in Franco Spain, dictatorships in Germany and Italy, and revolutions in Latin America, Lovecraft spoke of the necessity of respecting our past heritage.

> No individual or group, trying to break away from what blind hereditary tradition has bequeathed, ever achieves much real sense of harmony or repose in the new system. There is a feeling of something broken a lack of harmony with past and background which promotes a restlessness often expressed in further marks of aimlessness and incongruity; an unconscious aesthetic sense protests against a violation of a certain unity in the historic stream—and this whether or not the old code has any merely rational value. Of course, this disharmony and protest do not occur in cases of gradual modification extending over several generations. In a word—it is a fact that we cannot gain any *really satisfying* illusion of values and ends in life except through the engulfing effect of encountering this same illusion throughout the pages of ancestral history. When that illusion breaks, all illusions break—and a long reign of unstable equilibrium is ahead. Nor is it possible for one self-defined class to secede

---

222. Mrs. Bernice L. Barlow, MS. letter to Arthur Koki, dated September 5, 1961, AK.
223. Ibid.
224. August Derleth, "Lovecraft As Mentor," *The Shuttered Room,* p. 169.

V. Home

and pretend to establish new illusions of its own. Ties with the parent body are too well remembered. I don't think existing evidence sustains your theory that any group of 'intellectuals' has evolved a single definite code. There are groups and groups and groups within groups, and codes and codes, and fractions of codes. Drink, drugs, perversion, disintegration . . . madness, suicide, the emptiness of futility . . . some get by, some do not . . . but it is all very natural, and life goes.[225]

Lovecraft exerted a strange fascination on his more than one hundred correspondents, who ranged from precocious teenagers, to lonely spinsters, to jejune young men, and the artistically incompetent. He held them all by the sheer keenness, refinement, and power of his intellect, coupled with that touching nobility and magnanimity which reminds one of Cardinal Newman's definition of a gentleman: "He is tender towards the bashful, gentle towards the distant, and merciful towards the absurd . . . If he engages in controversy of any kind, his disciplined intellect preserves him from the blundering discourtesy of better, though less educated minds; who, like blunt weapons, tear and hack instead of cutting clean . . ."[226]

Lovecraft's generosity with his time and undeniable talents came from no other source than the need for love and human contacts. The steady arrival of letters to his door also stroked alive that feeling of "adventurous expectancy," which he had come to look for in life. Did he, one wonders, delay opening his mail to prolong the feeling of exquisite torture and pleasure? Winfield Townley Scott is persuaded that in Lovecraft's social affairs, "One can say that almost all his adult relationships were homosexual, if the word is intended in its blandest sense: there is no sign of strong sexual impulse of any kind."[227] The second locution of Mr. Scott's sentence confutes the first. What wondrous anomaly is a homosexual, bland to be sure, who shows "no sign

---

225. Ibid., pp. 168–69.
226. Cardinal John Henry Newman, *The Idea of a University*, New York: Doubleday, 1959, pp. 144–45.
227. Scott, *Exiles and Fabrications*, p. 71.

of strong sexual impulse of any kind"? When other critics can find sexual impulses behind the gentliest of human activities, from rubbing one's nose to overeating, it is regrettable that Mr. Scott shies away without enlightening us on this ambiguous sentence which so casually tosses in a charged word.

Lord Byron without his cape, Casanova confined to a Morris chair, Marvell without his coy mistress—under which picture do we find H. P. Lovecraft?

I demur at Scott's opinion that "there is no sign of strong sexual impulse of any kind," in Lovecraft's relationships. May we not consider that his correspondence, which bulked to well over five million words, is a protracted wooing of a highly sublimated and ethereal nature? This idea may seem repugnant at first blush, but consider for a moment the letters which have been cited. Lovecraft's avuncular pose is sometimes coy and kittenish; his wide scholarship is flaunted as a prowess. His self-aspersions are designed to attract denials, as with lovers in the "I'm-not-worthy-of-you" pattern. It is going much too far to interpret these letters literally as the enticements of a modern Socrates (though Lovecraft did call his wife Xantippe!) since there is nothing of sex in the epistolary attitude at all, in the usual sense, but the *sexual gesture* is there, nevertheless. It is not homosexual or heterosexual, because it is disembodied—a rare feat.

In his attempt to overwhelm the gentle sex, Lovecraft presumably showed all the liveliness of a gaily garbed, inimitably droll monkey. If we are to accept the word of one of his correspondents, Lovecraft reached a sophistication of great singularity when he began writing letters in no less than eight languages. For according to Mrs. Zealia Bishop, he wrote to her in Greek, Latin, and Spanish, as well as five exotic African tongues. Mr. Lovecraft was "well versed in the language of the Kaffirs, Damores, Swahili and the Chulu and Zani—who are extremely

V. Home

tenacious of their ancient religion."²²⁸ Disregarding that last *non-sequitur,* I cannot persuade myself that Lovecraft was a linguist, though he may have copied (not at all the same thing) Swahilian phrases or paragraphs. In jest? Why learn Zani or Damores? (Would, one wonders, Mrs. Bishop recognize these languages if she saw them?) Lovecraft had studied Greek and Latin at Hope High School and may have been able in his adult years to give brief disclosure of this knowledge. He never studied Spanish formally, though on May 27, 1911, he had purchased *Ollendorff's New Method of Learning to Read, Write, and Speak the Spanish Language.* It was a 558-page book designed for "young learners and persons who are their own instructors." What knowledge, if any, Lovecraft acquired from it, I cannot say. His copy is not annotated or underlined. Either from age or constant use, the back spine has come off completely.²²⁹

Doubts raised over his knowledge of foreign languages do not abrade his real accomplishments. Besides, to quote W. Somerset Maugham: ". . . it is of no spiritual advantage that I can see to know half-a-dozen languages. I have met polyglots; I have not noticed that they were wiser than the rest of us."²³⁰ His excellence as a correspondent was honed by his pursuance of many subjects. Astronomy, Colonial history and architecture, English history, poetic metrics, supernatural literature, classical mythology, daemonology, genealogy—his mind reminds one of nothing so much as the bulging pockets of a small boy. He did not lose the boy's indiscriminate enthusiasm for sundry bits of information. A university education had not shunted him into narrow labyrinths of study. He rove like Burton's ranging spaniel "that barks at every bird he sees, leaving his game."²³¹ As with many persons who are

---

228. Bishop, p. 141. [HPL did not know any African languages.]
229. Lovecraft's autographed and date inscribed copy in my possession.
230. W. Somerset Maugham, *The Summing Up,* p. 101.
231. [From Robert Burton's *Anatomy of Melancholy* (1621).]

largely self-educated, he could not resist parading his learning and incidental wisdom.

This partly explains why his female correspondents and revisionist clients did not achieve any success on their own. Sonia H. Greene, Zealia Bishop, Hazel Heald, Anne Tillery Renshaw, Elizabeth Toldridge. They do make a small claim for the attention of the Lovecraft student since what little they did publish was largely revised or ghostwritten by Lovecraft, the work of the first four ladies in especial. His erudition, his ruthlessly detailed corrections of their manuscripts must have subtly impressed upon them their own clumsiness. Although they were incapable of sustained serious writing, Lovecraft held up impossible goals to them. To Zealia Bishop, a student at Columbia's School of Journalism, he wrote, "Think of nothing but real people and what they actually think and feel and say and experience. That is the way to write *literature* as opposed to the wearisome pap and patent bourgeois-fodder of the best-selling popular novelists. Be a Dreiser or a Mrs. Wharton—not a Harold Bell Wright or Fanny Hurst—and you can be one of these."[232] But even being a Fanny Hurst, Mistress of the Expanded Cliché, is not within the grasp of everyone.

Lovecraft's own shortcoming as a teacher was his lack of sympathy with commercial considerations. He was chilly to Zealia Bishop's desire to write for the confession magazines. "Avoid anything savoring of the sentimental popular novel tradition," he reiterated. In retrospect, she felt that Lovecraft had undermined her self-confidence and natural ability.[233] Lovecraft could not always pick and choose which stories he would revise, but he tried to dissuade people from writing love stories with mechanically happy endings. When asked by a young man if he used a "plot genie," Lovecraft replied that he had tried and hated it. "I could *revise* crap but the attempt to construct such stuff was

---

232. Bishop, p. 144.
233. Ibid.

beyond me. I tried to put order, coherence, direction, and comprehensible language into something whose Neanderthaloid ineptitude was *already* mapped out."[234]

He fared better as a friend and mentor to many of the young men with whom he corresponded. To Donald Wandrei, August Derleth, Robert Bloch, Donald Wollheim, Robert E. Howard, Frank Belknap Long, Jr., Henry Kuttner, and Clark Ashton Smith, Lovecraft gave story germs, listened to gripes, and invited them to contribute to his Cthulhu mythology by inventing other gods and books of devilish lore in their own stories. Most of them had sold their first stories to *Weird Tales* when they were still in high school. All were concerned professionally with the genre and not with love stories of one kind or another. In this congenial setting, Lovecraft's stock of knowledge acted more as a stimulus than as a deterrent, which seemed to be its function for the distaff recipients of his letters. Miss Toldridge, who could only muster a weak reply to his missives, sent him newspaper clippings: her subterfuge for conversation. Men, on the other hand, were hungry for discussion. Some of them lived in lonely one-horse towns where one had to fight to meet any people of culture. August Derleth, living in Sauk City, Wisconsin, consoled himself by reading Emerson and Thoreau, and going for long walks through the countryside. Painter, sculptor, and writer, Clark Ashton Smith lived in a ramshackle house with his parents in wind-swept Auburn, California. In Cross Plains, Texas, Robert Howard, the only professional writer for miles around, imagined himself laughed and sneered at by the more practical citizens in town. There were some who were out to "get" him. He was sure of it.[235]

"Two-Gun Bob," as Lovecraft tagged Robert Ervin Howard, was one of *Weird Tales'* most popular writers. Howard began writing fiction

---

234. H. P. Lovecraft, MS. letter to Kenneth Sterling, dated December 14, 1935, KS.
235. E. Hoffmann Price, "A Memory of R. E. Howard," *Skull-Face and Others* by Robert E. Howard, Sauk City, Wis.: Arkham House, 1946, pp. xx–xxi.

when he was fifteen, and three years later, in 1925, he sold his first story, "Spear and Fang," to Farnsworth Wright. From then on he wrote and sold consistently. He was never forced to take a job on the side. He could evoke atmosphere and describe cyclopean ruins of prehistoric kingdoms as skillfully as a Lovecraft, but his forte lay in creating valorous warriors who slashed and hacked their way out of one sanguinary fracas into another. Commercially speaking, he was shrewder than Lovecraft. Unlike Lovecraft, who dealt with a specific type of horror, rooted in the same locale, Howard wrote about mythical empires, Celtic and Viking sagas of plunder, Westerns, and stories set in fog-laden London. He raised a crew of hirsute, intrepid heroes. Solomon Kane, King Kull of Valusia, King Conan, Bran Mak Morn, Sailor Steve Costigan. They are one and the same. They are what Howard thought he was. His stories lend themselves to an easy sarcasm. Unquestionably extravagant, bombastic, they nevertheless had flamboyance and a glorious lack of restraint to recommend themselves as adventure stories. Lovecraft wrote of their ultra-romantic creator: "He was, above everything else, a lover of the simpler, older world of barbarian and pioneer days, when courage and strength took the place of subtlety and stratagem, and when a hardy, fearless race battled and bled, and asked no quarter from hostile nature."[236]

Lovecraft and Howard never met though they had half-seriously considered doing so. It would be fun, they agreed, to take a motor trip through Mexico with E. Hoffmann Price, another writer. Price knew both writers personally. He had met Lovecraft in New Orleans in June, 1932. His impression of that meeting followed the by now familiar and predictable sequence of surprise at Lovecraft's (1) intense brown eyes, (2) long, thin face, (3) formal and academic diction, and (4) amazing knowledge of many topics. From there, unabashed admiration. "I nev-

---

236. H. P. Lovecraft, "Robert Ervin Howard: A Memoriam," *Skull-Face and Others*, p. xiv.

er before met the like, and I knew that not even a remotely similar personality existed."[237]

Lovecraft smacked his lips over a chile con carne repast which Price had prepared and spiced to a near-incendiary degree. With his stomach cheerily scorched, Lovecraft settled back to drink coffee, cup after cup, thick with sugar, while Price imbibed homemade (illegal) brew. In the course of their evening's conversation, Price had told his guest that "The Silver Key" was one of his favorite stories and, in rereading it, a sequel had suggested itself to him. Lovecraft, pleased by Price's interest, agreed to collaborate on a new Randolph Carter adventure.[238]

Some months later, Lovecraft, now in Providence, received a six-thousand-word first draft from Price. Lovecraft praised the effort, and then mailed him a fourteen thousand elaboration of his own. When the two manuscripts were compared, it was found that Lovecraft had retained only fifty of Price's words: a mere paragraph.[239] If the pride of E. Hoffmann Price was bruised, he later consoled himself by soliloquizing—"I like to tell myself that that one short passage of mine which he incorporated into the script must have been good; and that without doubt, I fared better than any of those many others whose botched beginnings he wrote bodily."[240] *Démons et Merveilles,* the French edition containing the story, ignores Price as a collaborator.

The story was "Through the Gates of the Silver Key," and it appeared in *Weird Tales* for July, 1934. It tells what happened to Randolph Carter when he disappeared in Arkham, in the cave near his ancestors' home. A violent dislocation in time, space, and personality

---

237. E. Hoffmann Price, "The Man Who Was Lovecraft," *Something About Cats,* p. 279.
238. Ibid., pp. 279–82.
239. [Even if relatively little of Price's prose was left in "Through the Gates of the Silver Key," many of his conceptions were retained.]
240. Ibid., p. 282.

took place. Randolph Carter lost his identity and confronted the diverse manifestations of the entity Carter—the supreme archetype Carter. "There were Carters in settings belonging to every known and suspected age of Earth's history, and to remoter ages of earthly entity transcending knowledge, suspicion, and credibility; Carters of forms both human and non-human, vertebrate and invertebrate, conscious and mindless, animal and vegetable."[241] Unhappily for the fearless Randolph Carter, he chose to be placed on Yaddith—a planet not yet born—and was there changed into one of the local denizens, a clawed, tapir-snouted creature, but a Carter for all of that. A Dr. Jekyll and Mr. Hyde relationship ensues as the Randolph Carter part struggles to release himself from the non-humanoid which houses him. Finally, by incantation and rocketship, Randolph Carter returns to earth, much the worse for wear, bearing the visible, ugly appurtenances of his life on Yaddith. His fate remains unsettled.

Four characters in the story assemble to decide whether to apportion the estate of the vanished Carter. One of these is Ward Phillips—Lovecraft's self-caricature. He is "an elderly eccentric of Providence, Rhode Island,"[242] a harmless old dreamer, "lean, gray, long nosed, clean shaven, and stoop shouldered."[243] Opposite him in temperament is the apoplectic-faced and portly Ernest K. Aspinwall. He is a lawyer, a cousin of Randolph Carter, though he is a practical man who is scornful of mysticism. This apoplectic gentleman dies from a stroke before the story ends. If Ward Phillips is incidentally based on Lovecraft, did he also have a real person in mind for Aspinwall?

Sometime in 1884, or thereabouts, Lovecraft's grandfather, Whipple V. Phillips, had organized the Snake River Company, a venture in farming and cattle raising in Idaho. The three directors of this invest-

---

241. H. P. Lovecraft, "Through the Gates of the Silver Key," *The Outsider*, p. 50.
242. Ibid., p. 41.
243. Ibid., p. 42.

ment company were Whipple V. Phillips, Charles H. Sawyer, and L. Aspinwall.[244] Let us now recall that the name of the man who had his legs cut off in "In the Vault" was "the vicious Asaph Sawyer."[245] One may assume from this that Messrs. C. H. Sawyer and L. Aspinwall probably swindled Lovecraft's grandfather or ruined the company in some way and that Lovecraft was taking a vicarious revenge by appropriating their surnames to unpleasant characters and then murdering and mutilating them. But this would be wrong. For if we speculate in this fashion, we raise ticklish problems. For example, Dr. Elihu Whipple in "The Shunned House" and Professor George Gammell Angell in "The Call of Cthulhu" were suggested in part by Dr. Clark, Lovecraft's uncle, and a person for whom he felt the deepest affection. Yet Drs. Whipple and Angell are killed in their respective stories. It is not a gratuitous act; nor are the deaths of Aspinwall and Sawyer gratuitous acts. Their deaths contribute to the integrity of the story, its plot advancement or climax. Thus, even if we could find real persons whom Lovecraft knew or heard of, people whose generic names he used in his stories, we can in no wise conclude that Lovecraft's tales are in some strange way a private and perverse psychodrama.

Before leaving the matter of names, that of Randolph Carter deserves a glance. To some extent he was Lovecraft's "hero." That he named him Carter is more likely a carefully made choice than a random pick. Lovecraft as a student of Rhode Island history knew the history of the Carters in Providence. Indeed, on at least one occasion, he wrote a correspondent a detailed account of John Carter: how he had served as an apprentice to Benjamin Franklin before coming to Providence in 1767 to print *The Providence Gazette* and *Country Journal*,[246] and

---

244. Prospectus for the Snake River Company, circa 1881, RM.
245. H. P. Lovecraft, "In the Vault," *The Outsider*, p. 168.
246. [The paper was founded in 1762 by William Goddard. Carter (1745–1814) took over the paper in 1767.]

how his children and grandchildren had married to advantage to place them in Providence's patrician class.[247]

A solo effort of more ambitious scope than "Through the Gates of the Silver Key" was the thirty thousand word "The Shadow out of Time," which Lovecraft wrote in 1934/35.[248] In its panoramic sweep it belongs with Olaf Stapledon's *Last and First Men* (1930), and the 1937 sequel, *Star-maker*. Yet where Stapledon is optimistically concerned with tracing the vicissitudes and mutations of man through eighteen species and some 2,000,000,000 years into the future, Lovecraft calculatingly treats humanity in casual fashion. Reigning homo sapiens are but one of the assemblages of life which this planet has and will support—a common observation, certainly, but few writers have exploited this fact and its possible consequences for mankind as dramatically as Lovecraft. Lovecraft does not envision the evolution of a "new man" infinitely suave and daring, who will lead us to colonize other worlds. To the ego's cry, Lovecraft points to his poem "Nemesis":

> Where the black planets roll without aim—
> Where they roll in their horror unheeded
>   without knowledge or lustre or name.[249]

This attitude was born in Lovecraft, he wrote, from "a very potent & visual and imaginative concepts. The primary concept is one of vast nighted worlds holding unimaginable concepts known to no other parts of space, & so hideous that any one of them would explode with horror if made conscious of the other's hellish arcana."[250]

A similar note opens "The Shadow out of Time" when the narrator, Dr. Nathaniel Wingate Peaslee, advocates the abandonment of archeological digging in Western Australia, lest "a specific, lurking peril

---

247. H. P. Lovecraft, MS. letter to Elizabeth Toldridge, dated June 10, 1929, JHL.
248. [The story runs to 25,600 words.]
249. H. P. Lovecraft, "Nemesis," *Beyond the Wall of Sleep*, p. 386.
250. H. P. Lovecraft, MS. letter to Kenneth Sterling, dated August 8–9, 1935, KS.

V. Home

... though it will never engulf the whole race, may impose monstrous and unguessable horrors upon certain venturesome members of it."[251] Peaslee, a professor of political economy at Miskatonic University, was lecturing to his class one day in May, 1908, when he quite suddenly slumped into a coma. He awoke the next morning, but without recalling either his name or past history. "My eyes gazed strangely at the persons around me, and the flexions of my facial muscles were altogether unfamiliar."[252] In 1913, Peaslee recovered and concluded the sentence he had begun speaking five years earlier to his students. In the interim his wife had obtained a legal divorce because of the odd change which had come over him. With the aid of his faithful son, Wingate, Peaslee attempted to reconstruct those five lost years. There were two, not one, Nathaniel Peaslees to deal with. One, Dr. Peaslee himself to all outward appearances, had gone on a strange quest for occult knowledge, consulting esoteric books, studying at American and European universities, and traveling to such remote places as the Himalayas, the deserts of Arabia, and the north of Spitzbergen, Artica. Of this globetrotting Peaslee, the professor could remember nothing. What he fitfully recalled in fragments was a quite different existence. He dreamt, if dreams they were, that a transference of minds had occurred and that he had gone back into time "somewhat less than 150,000,000 years ago."[253] An alien being had usurped his body while he was forced to inhabit a strange rugose, conical body. Despite the shock and resentment at this metamorphosis, he acknowledged that the conical Great Race, of which he was a temporary member, "was the greatest race of all because it alone had conquered the secret of time."[254] The Great Race knew all that had or would occur on our

---

251. H. P. Lovecraft, "The Shadow Out of Time," *The Outsider*, p. 400.
252. Ibid., p. 401.
253. Ibid., p. 418.
254. Ibid., p. 417.

planet. Superior mental beings, they could project their mind "forward in time, feeling its dim extrasensory way till it approached the desired period."[255] Once this was achieved, "it would enter the organism's brain and set up therein its own vibrations, while the displaced mind would strike back to the period of the displacer, remaining in the latter's body till a reverse process was set up."[256] While living with the Great Race, Peaslee was asked to write out in English an account of mankind. After this knowledge had been secured, "his captive mind was returned to its own body in the future after being purged by mechanical hypnosis of all it had learned in the Great Race's Age."[257]

At various times during 1928 and 1929, Professor Peaslee in the *Journal of the American Psychological Society* minutely described his dreams. A mining engineer from Australia wrote to him to say that certain designs and hieroglyphics which he (Peaslee) had described were to be found etched on incredibly old stones lying at a point 22° 31′ 14″ South Latitude, 125° 0′ 39″ East Longitude. (This would place it one hundred miles south of Joanna Springs.) An expedition under the auspices of Miskatonic was sent to explore the ruins. Dr. Peaslee and his son accompanied the scientific party. One night, Peaslee "afflicted as usual with that strange feeling regarding the northeastern terrain," walked out from camp alone.[258] He looked at those disordered ruins, glowing beneath the fungoid moon. With "pseudomemories" tugging his brain, Peaslee entered the crumbled edifice, electric torch in hand, and moved with uncanny sureness to an inner chamber where he adroitly opened a locked cabinet.[259] Inside he found what he feared he would find. But before he could safely take it away, a shrill whistling

---

255. Ibid., p. 411.
256. Ibid..
257. Ibid., p. 412.
258. Ibid., p. 426.
259. Ibid., p. 427–29.

V. Home

sound, reminding him of a demon subterranean race in his dreams, sent Peaslee on a mad scramble. Somehow, he staggered back to camp. In his flight he dropped the crucial object he had sought. Perhaps mercifully, for after taking the thing from its shelf, Peaslee had glanced inside to see his greatest fear confirmed—he had looked into a book written in English in his own handwriting.

The vivid description of Peaslee's bolt out of the hoary building remains among Lovecraft's successfully realized scenes. The annals of the Great Race are recorded with the imagination and wealth of detail which had earlier showed itself in *At the Mountains of Madness* and to somewhat a lesser degree in "The Call of Cthulhu." Their physical appearance, if anything, is more grotesque than that of Cthulhu. They are described as being ten feet tall with four flexible, cylindrical members at the apex. Two of these terminated in enormous nippers, which, when clicked or scraped, served as speech instruments. At the end of the third were four red, trumpetlike structures. The fourth, ending in a yellow globe, had three dark eyes along its central circumference. Surrounding this head rose "four slender gray stalks bearing flowerlike appendages, whilst from its nether side dangled eight greenish antennae or tentacles."[260] These conical creatures were asexual, reproducing by spores, germinated under water. As might be guessed, their government was a sort of fascistic socialism.[261]

Edmund Wilson, after noting Lovecraft's account of the Great Race and something of their organization, wrote as follows: "Now, when the horror to the shuddering revelation of which a long and prolix story has been building up turns out to be something like this, you may laugh or you may be disgusted, but you are not likely to be terrified—though I confess, as a tribute to such power as H. P. Lovecraft possesses, that he at least, at that point in his series, in regard to the

---

260. Ibid., p. 415.
261. Ibid., p. 419.

omniscient conical snails, induced me to suspend disbelief."[262] If so practical a critic as Wilson suppressed his disgust or laughter, one may presume that the ordinary reader will also do so. But Wilson immediately goes on to say: "It was the race from another planet which finally took their place, and which Lovecraft evidently relied on as creations of irresistible frightfulness, that I found myself hard to swallow: semi-invisible polypous monsters that uttered a shrill whistling sound and blasted their enemies with terrific winds."[263] This is curious. Why—after accepting the Great Race—quibble here? Especially since the "polypous monsters" are dealt with cautiously. Little is given of their history or physiology; they do not have a proper name because the Great Race, which regarded them with fear, avoided mentioning them. Although the Great Race had driven the "polypous monsters" underground, they knew that one day in the future these subterraneans would liberate themselves. If one is inclined to laugh at outlandish creations, the description of the Great Race—rather than the "polypous monsters"—should be jolly reading. What could be more anomalous than them? A look through the microscope at a drop of tap water, perhaps. Many nasty-looking organisms there.

The Great Race came to Earth from the dying planet Yith. These pilgrims usurped and appropriated to themselves the cone bodies of an unnamed race, and later waged war against the polypous entities, who had some six million years ago dominated this and three other planets. After driving them underground, the Great Race established a complex civilization. Towering buildings were constructed, one of the most important being Central Archives, where the past and future histories of this planet and others were recorded on imperishable material. The Great Race, foreseeing that the defeated polypous ones would eventually leave their caverns to retaliate successfully, forsook their conical bodies

---

262. Wilson, p. 287.
263. Ibid., p. 287–88.

V. Home

and projected themselves into the two-hundredth century A.D. into the bodies of "hardy Coleopterous species"—beetles who will dominate this world immediately after man's demise.[264] By 5,000 A.D. the cruel empire of Tsan-Chan is established.[265] This gradual retrogression to Oriental barbarism and civil disorder may mean that mankind will go gently into the night like the dodo bird. When the earth cools, the Great Race will abandon its post-human beetle existence, and this time migrate to Mercury. There these transferred minds will lodge in the bodies of bulbous vegetables. Arachnids are to rule Earth's last age.[266]

When Donald Wollheim edited the Viking Portable *Novels of Science*, he selected Lovecraft's "The Shadow out of Time" and three other distinguished works: H. G. Wells' *The First Men in the Moon,* John Taine's *Before the Dawn,* and *Odd John* by Olaf Stapledon. Less concerned with scientific speculation than the other three writers in the collection, Lovecraft combined geology and astronomy, along with bizarre theories of evolution, and turned these into the terror tale. He employs, nevertheless, the stock accessories of science-fiction, viz., space and time travel, invasions from space, remarkable inventions, and intellectually superior non-anthropoids. Despite this, he seems to be antipodal to the popular notion of what constitutes science-fiction. Purists will insist that Lovecraft never wrote science-fiction because he is not really concerned with technology. Space ships, for example, are to Lovecraft merely handy devices for moving a character from one place to another. A witch doctor and a physician both administer quinine, but they do it for different reasons. To the witch doctor, the curative power lies with the Great Rain Maker while the quinine is but an incidental part of the ceremony. It is the magical aspect of science which fascinates Lovecraft. He lacks the ebullience, the assurance that

---

264. H. P. Lovecraft, "The Shadow Out of Time," *The Outsider,* p. 416.
265. Ibid.
266. Ibid., p. 416–17.

science is opening up a wonderful world.

It is not easy to settle on a definition that will satisfy everyone of what, properly speaking, is science-fiction. As nearly everyone knows by now, the term was coined by the then-editor of *Amazing Stories,* Hugo Gernsback. Since then the genre's ancestry has been traced to such respectable progenitors as Plato's *Timaeus* and *The Republic,* and to Lucian of Samosata, the Greek satirist who, in 250 B.C., wrote of spacemen riding on the backs of swans over the Atlantic on their way to the moon. More, Bacon, and Swift have also been yoked as forbearers.

Today, the usual impression of science-fiction is arrived at from random exposure to comic strips, movies, and television, as well as magazines. It is optimistic of the future and solemnly preoccupied with gadgets, spacewarping, and planting colonies. Unbowed men and girls confront their destinies with nimble fortitude. Admittedly much of this type of science-fiction has proved trivial, although it has all served to prepare the public for scientific and technological advancements even if some science-fiction writers in their prognostications are fifteen years behind the scientists in their laboratories.

A more significant trend at present is the novel of social criticism, which has also attracted some first-rate "non-professional" science-fiction writers. Social criticism in the mode of science-fiction has created serious literature and brought distinction to the genre—C. S. Lewis' trilogy, Huxley's *Brave New World,* Bradbury's *Fahrenheit 451,* Orwell's *1984,* Vonnegut's *Player Piano,* and even, perhaps, John Hersey's *The Child Buyer* may be included.

Does "The Shadow out of Time" belong with the anti-utopian novels? Among other things, these other works show a deepening concern over the tyranny which will accrue from technology, subliminal advertising, strong centralized governments, etc. In most, there is at least one character who is either fighting against the encroachments on his liberty and sanity or is acutely aware of the many perversions taking place around him. Lewis, Huxley, and the others are involved

V. Home

with the human condition, whereas Lovecraft, as I never tire of repeating, treats man with what may be called calculated neglect. Few writers have so profoundly weighted their work with such pessimism. A. E. Housman's

> I a stranger and afraid
> In a world I never made

could serve as the epigraph for any or all of the stories in the Cthulhu mythos. Most certainly *At the Mountains of Madness* and "The Shadow out Time" do have a place in science-fiction literature, however removed they are from the optimistic or anti-utopian novels. "The Shadow out of Time" superbly met Wollheim's criteria that "the ideal science-fiction novel . . . is the book which manages to combine a sound imagination and believable prognostication with a sincere desire to set the reader thinking along concepts vaster than his own petty life, concepts as large at least as the movement of Earth's inhabitants as a whole."[267]

"The Shadow out of Time" went to market in the steps of *At the Mountains of Madness*. Submitted to *Weird Tales,* it was rejected by Farnsworth Wright.[268] Donald Wandrei saw the typescript, urged Lovecraft to mail it to *Astounding Stories,* where it was procured by editor F. Orlin Tremaine and published in June, 1936.[269]

There was no open hate between Lovecraft and "Pharaoh," as Wright was dubbed by the Lovecraft circle. During the summer of 1935, Robert Bloch visited Wright in Chicago and reported to Lovecraft that "Compliments flowed your way throughout the two interviews I had, and the consensus of opinion is that you should submit something as soon as you can. Needless to say, Wright again expressed

---

267. *Novels of Science,* ed. Donald A. Wollheim, New York, Viking, 1945, pp. xii–xiii.
268. [The story was never submitted to *Weird Tales.*]
269. Moskowitz, p. 49. [Wandrei himself took the ms. of the story to Tremaine, who accepted it without reading it.]

a wish to see you out here and meet you personally."[270] How much nicer it would have been, Lovecraft must have thought at some time, if, as in the eighteenth century, there were patrons who could free the artist from haggling in the market place, could bestow ample funds, and observe his work with lively appreciation. And as for that *Weird Tales*, it was "simply too trivial for notice . . .";[271] "the trash one dabbles in—W.T. etc. that really has no relationship to solid reading . . .";[272] "Skimm'd thro last month's WT and found it uniformly lousy."[273] The last two remarks were made to his youthful confident, Robert Barlow.

Early in 1935, Barlow asked Lovecraft to visit him and his parents again. After the usual "Are you sure I wouldn't be in the way"—"No, of course not, we'd love to have you" letters had been exchanged, not once, but a dozen times, it was finally settled that Lovecraft should spend June, July, and part of August with the Barlows in Cassia, Florida. Sometime during those leisure days, the conversation had turned to genealogy and Lovecraft made a discovery which pleased him very much. It appeared that he and Robert Barlow were sixth cousins by virtue of common descent in the seventh generation from a gentleman born in 1658, i.e. John Rathbone of Block Island. "Although Bob is young enough to be my son," said Lovecraft, "he is descended from old John of 1658 in exactly the same number of generations."[274]

Another thing which delighted Lovecraft while visiting his distant cousin was the news that the N.A.P.A. convention at Oakland, California had elected him (Lovecraft) as one of its three executive judges. He had held the post before and reelection meant more work: manuscripts

---

270. Robert Bloch, MS. letter to H. P. Lovecraft, n.d., circa June, 1935, AK.
271. H. P. Lovecraft, MS. letter to Richard Ely Morse, dated February 9, 1936, TOM.
272. H. P. Lovecraft, MS. letter to Robert H. Barlow, dated July 9, 1936, JHL.
273. H. P. Lovecraft, MS. letter to Robert H. Barlow, dated July 23, 1936, JHL.
274. H. P. Lovecraft, MS. letter to Margaret Ronan, n.d., circa 1936, MR.

to be corrected *gratis,* and officers who would seek advice on their new duties. Even in the seclusion of Cassia, letters marked "H. P. Lovecraft, % Barlow, Box 88, DeLand, Florida" (Cassia did not have mail delivery) continued in a steady flow. Amateur affairs seemed to dominate his correspondence. Miss Toldridge was still sending him envelopes stuffed with newspaper clippings on science and "odd ball" fillers.[275] A young *Weird Tales* writer wrote thanking him for all his help. Another young man, William Crawford, was eager to print Lovecraft's hitherto unpublished novelette, "The Shadow over Innsmouth." Lovecraft consented, though he had reservations whether the book would sell.[276]

Yet another request came from Julius Schwartz, editor of *Fantasy Magazine,* a science-fiction "fan" type publication. The third anniversary of the magazine was approaching and to celebrate Schwartz asked Abraham Merritt, Lovecraft, C. L. Moore, Robert E. Howard, and Frank Belknap Long, Jr. to participate in writing a round-robin weird fantasy story to highlight the special issue. Lovecraft concurred with the others' decision to accept.

After extracting a promise from Cousin Robert that he would come to Providence next year, Lovecraft bid farewell to the Barlows. On the way north he hastily wrote out his section of the composite story, "The Challenge from Beyond." He regarded the whole thing as "merely an amusing stunt."[277] He used two thousand words—slightly more than the other four since he had the difficult central section that demanded a maximum of plot development. Lovecraft played with an idea he had used in "The Thing the Doorstep," "Through the Gates of the Silver Key," and "The Shadow out of Time." The narrator's mind is kidnapped and sent hurtling through time and space until it is

---

275. Eighteen letters from Elizabeth Toldridge to H. P. Lovecraft, dated June through July, 1935, AK.
276. H. P. Lovecraft, MS. letter to Margaret Ronan, n.d., circa 1936, MR.
277. H. P. Lovecraft, MS. letter to Richard Ely Morse, dated January 16, 1936, TOM.

housed into an alien body where it can be interrogated. Lovecraft's portion of the story ends with the narrator staring at a mirror which is giving back the reflection of a gigantic, pale centipede. Stylistically, Lovecraft was here dismally undistinguished, e.g. "Meanwhile the sense of forward, outward motion grew intolerably, incredibly, cosmically swift."[278] Through some caprice, editors believed such redundancies left the reader agog. When Lovecraft called "The Challenge from Beyond" "hack junk of the rankest sort,"[279] he perhaps spoke truer than he knew.

Once Lovecraft completed his portion of the hack mosaic, he was free to write a story in friendly retaliation to Robert Bloch's "The Shambler from the Stars." Bloch's story, which he dedicated to Lovecraft, appeared in the September, 1935, issue of *Weird Tales*. In that, he left Lovecraft as a shapeless mass of bloody pulp (something like *Weird Tales* perhaps) in the clutch of an abyss-evoked monster. Lovecraft now returned the compliment in "The Haunter of the Dark." Dedicated to Bloch, it left Bloch, called Robert Blake in the story, as a glassy-eyed corpse, seated at a window, dead from stark fear.

Blake, described as a writer and painter devoted to myth, dream, and superstition, finds himself drawn to a deserted church which had been the meeting place for the Starry Wisdom sect, a darkly evil cult whose members were ostracized from the community in 1877. Entering the church, Blake discovers in the rear vestry room an oppressive collection of sinister books: a Latin version of the *Necronomicon*, the sinister *Liber Ivonis*, *Cultes des Goules*, the *Unaussprechlichen Kulten*, and old Ludvig Prinn's hellish *De Vermis Mysteriis*. Clearly, "this place had once been the seat of an evil older than mankind and wider than the known universe."[280]

---

278. H. P. Lovecraft, "The Challenge from Beyond," reprinted in *Fantastic Science Fiction Stories* (May 1960), p. 51.
279. H. P. Lovecraft, MS. letter to Richard Ely Morse, dated January 16, 1936, TOM.
280. H. P. Lovecraft, "The Haunter of the Dark," *The Outsider*, p. 184.

V. Home

A small chamber in the steeple containing a skeleton and a strange trapezoidal object raises the question, "What, anyway, was this abandoned lair of cosmic evil?"[281] But apparently it was not so abandoned, for Blake's meddling rouses the "Haunter of the Dark" monster to stalk abroad for sacrifices and, not unexpectedly, he comes to call at Mr. Blake's house.

"The Haunter of the Dark" is set in Providence. The house and the view described in the story are authentic—66 College Street and what Lovecraft himself could see as he glanced over his desk through his westward window.[282] In this familiar setting Lovecraft writes with old assurance about the noxious church and its neighborhood. As in "The Dreams in the Witch House," Catholic immigrants are present; superstitious, they gather by candlelight around the haunted church and recite their ineffectual prayers.

"The Haunter of the Dark" is one of the last professional stories that Lovecraft worked on. It is the last which comes under the Cthulhu classification, but it is not the consummation of the twelve Mythos stories that preceded it. Much remained to be written. There were lacunas to be sketched in and inconsistencies awaiting correction when Death unexpectedly intervened.

This terminus point in the Cthulhu mythology may be the appropriate time to touch on influences and sources. So far as is known, Lovecraft did not bequeath anything resembling Miller's *The Books in My Life*,[283] nor has there come to light a notebook penned by Lovecraft that would tell us which books he incorporated into his mythos. In lieu of such evidence, source speculation has been lively.

The situation, however, is far from muddy. Enough snips and

---

281. Ibid., p. 187.
282. H. P. Lovecraft, letter to Nils H. Frome, dated December 15, 1936, reprinted in *Science Fiction Critic,* May, 1937, p. 95.
283. [Henry Miller, *The Books in My Life* (1952).]

scraps can be culled from extant letters to show that Dunsany, Poe, and Machen were vital influences, possibly the most important; Dunsany so much so in the beginning that the years 1919 through 1921 may quite properly be called his "Dunsanian" period. Poe followed as a mixed blessing. He is one of the easiest figures in world literature to parody, yet his distinct melody is not played so well by others. Most of Lovecraft's stories from "Dagon" (1917) to "The Horror at Red Hook" (1925) fail to realize the tension or the pressure of awareness embodied in Poe's styles. If Lovecraft were writing an enormous novel, his often tasteless quasi-Poe style would participate in the energy of the book. But a short story lacks this latitude, and the flaws are painfully discerned. As for plot ideas, a reading of "Cool Air" with Poe's "The Facts in the Case of Mr. Valdemar" will reveal the most obvious instance of this.[284] A favorite word of Poe and Lovecraft (Baudelaire, also) is *putrescence*. There is also a scene of dissolution in "The Thing on the Doorstep" which, for a literal description of bodily decay, said Lovecraft, "is not surpassed in Poe's Mr. [*sic*] Valdemar."[285]

Arthur Machen must be reckoned an inspiration in Lovecraft's fiction. If Poe is the romantic archetype of the artist, reeling down the street with his brain stewed in alcohol, Machen's early career was no less typical of the artist serving his literary apprenticeship. For years he starved in London, living on green tea, stale bread, and tobacco.[286] His early years spent at his father's Llanddewi rectory in Wales are curiously similar to Lovecraft's years along the Seekonk River. One wonders whether the pattern holds for other writers of fantasy and weird literature. Machen wrote: "My father and mother apart, I loved to be by myself, with untold leisure for mooning and loafing and roaming and

---

284. [The influence of Poe's story on HPL's seems clear, but he himself stated that he had been thinking of Machen's "Novel of the White Powder."]
285. H. P. Lovecraft, MS. letter to Margaret Ronan, n.d., circa 1936, MR.
286. William Francis Gekle, *Arthur Machen, Weaver of Fantasy*, New York, Round Table Press, 1949, pp. 1–33.

wandering ... Solitude ... woods ... deep lanes and wonder; these were the chief elements of my life."[287] Lovecraft's debt to the Welsh author was very great. When asked to enumerate his ten favorite weird short stories, Lovecraft had listed three by Machen—"The Novel of the White Powder," "The Novel of the Black Seal," and "The White People." From these stories he assimilated into the Cthulhu Mythos the Aklo letters, the Dols (changed to Dholes), the Jeelo, and the voolas.

From Machen, Lovecraft learned to fashion a non-human "language" of spells and incantations which, in turn, the Lovecraft circle borrowed. Peter Penzoldt, I believe, was the first to indicate this distinctive feature in Machen's and Lovecraft's stories. In discussing the diction or "descriptives" wielded in the horror tale, Penzoldt arranged four types. Type A consists of words which taken separately carry no horrible signification: "soft," "wet," or "cold," for example; but the three words in a phrase do evoke horror, as when a soft, wet, and cold hand touches you in the dark. Type B words contain unpleasant associations even in isolation. To cite Penzoldt's example from Machen's "The Novel of the White Powder": "There upon the floor was a dark and putrid mass seething with corruption and hideous rottenness." Closer to Type A than B, Type C *suggests* horror. This is subtler and examples are less satisfactorily excised from the body of the story. The climax of Monty James' "The Ash Tree" comes in a phrase: "... it seems as if Sir Richard were moving his head rapidly to and fro with only the slightest possible sound." The reader of this story will guess that Sir Richard's head is actually a cluster of enormous spiders.[288]

Writers of weird literature employ one or all of these descriptive techniques in a story. Type D, on the other hand, seems to be used only by a few. Machen, first, then Lovecraft to a greater degree used it. Type D words are not real words, but rather "phonetic transcriptions

---

287. Arthur Machen, *Far Off Things,* London, Martin Secker, 1923, p. 22.
288. Penzoldt, pp. 180–81.

of hideous idiotic cries."[289] Machen, imbued with Welsh folklore and language from his infancy, was sentient of the eerie effect which a sentence or two in Welsh could have on the eye and ear of one who did not know the language. In *The Great Return*, Machen describes the priest celebrating the Mass of the Sangraal: "*Ffeiriadwyr Melcisidec! Ffeiriadwyr Melcisidec!* shouted the old Calvinistic Methodist deacon with the grey beard. Priesthood of Melchizedek! Priesthood of Melchizedek!"[290] Lovecraft created a limited idiom of his own by joining dislodged syllables and words from several languages including Welsh, Gaelic, Latin, and Middle English.

> It's voodoo, I tell you . . . that spotted snake . . . Curse you, Thornton, I'll teach you to faint at what my family do! . . . 'sblood, thou stinkard, I'll learn ye to gust . . . wolde ye swynke me thilka wys? *Magna Mater! Magna Mater! Atys* . . . *Dia aghaidh's ad aodaum* . . . *agus bas dunach ert! Dhonas's dholas ort agus leat-sa! Ungl* . . . *ungl* . . . *rrlh chchch* . . .[291]

Lest one is prone to smile, let me hasten to say that these cries are the climax to a perfectly constructed tale, "The Rats in the Walls," and the full power of the conclusion is appreciated best when the story is read in its entirety. The outburst cited above comes from a twentieth century man, hitherto urbane and rational, someone like you, gentle Reader, who is slipping back, back through the centuries to rejoin in spirit and deed his slightly human, anthropophagical kinsmen.

Machen's simple, lucid prose was an influence in curbing Lovecraft's occasional tendency to be led unawares into a prosaical luxuriance. His best stories, such as "The Shunned House," *The Case of Charles Dexter Ward*, "The Colour out of Space," *At the Mountains of Madness*, and "The Shadow over Innsmouth," have that sparse Machen manner which makes them read like good journalism. One also thinks of the laconic New England writer, Mary Wilkins Freeman, whose

---

289. Ibid., p. 181.
290. Ibid., p. 182.
291. H. P. Lovecraft, "The Rats in the Walls," *The Outsider*, p. 85.

short stories were known and praised by Lovecraft.[292]

He credited the genesis of his Cthulhu mythology to Dunsany, but August Derleth believes, correctly I am persuaded, that Lovecraft "got no more than the idea" from the baron.[293] None of Lovecraft's major deities are derived from *The Gods of Pegāna*. The latter is more of a rogues gallery rather than a story of extraterrestrial assault. One would like to know what Lovecraft thought of Carl Spitteler's epic poem *Olympian Spring*, which won him the Nobel Prize for literature in 1919—the year that Lovecraft was reading Dunsany and perhaps thinking about a mythology of his own. Spitteler had dramatically remoulded the accepted mythology surrounding the birth and adventures of the Greek gods to permit his personal vision of life. Of course Lovecraft could not have read *Olympian Spring* since it has yet to be translated into English, but newspapers and magazines must have reviewed the epic of this neglected Swiss poet. Perhaps the discovery that contemporary writers were boldly forging or recasting mythologies, might have encouraged Lovecraft to dream in similar areas. Was he not, after all, an inveterate myth builder in his youth?

One Lovecraft enthusiast, George Wetzel, believes that Greek mythology was instrumental in the formation of Lovecraft's mythos. As evidence of this he notes that the child Lovecraft built altars to the classic gods; several early specimens of his poetry and prose poems deal with ancient Greek life or religion; the book appearing in so many stories is the *Necronomicon*, a compound of two Greek words, probably meaning "guide to the regions of the dead."[294] Also in stories such as "The Statement of Randolph Carter" and "Through the Gates the Silver Key" there are openings in the earth leading to the underworld.

---

292. H. P. Lovecraft, *Supernatural Horror in Literature*, p. 72.
293. August Derleth, *H. P. L.: A Memoir*, p. 73.
294. [Whereas HPL believed erroneously that the Greek word *Necronomicon* meant "Image [or Picture] of the Law of the Dead," its actual meaning is "A book concerning [or classifying] the dead."]

(The Greeks believed specific sites were entrance ways to Hades.) When he lived in New York, Lovecraft and his wife frequented a Greek restaurant decorated with tiled walls depicting scenes from the Greek classics.[295] One could add to Wetzel's list of things Hellenic several that he overlooked, but it would not appreciably strengthen his hypothesis. A moment's reflection will show how extraneous the mythologies are to each other. The Greek way of life, as Edith Hamilton has overstressed, was one of equipoise. Nothing in excess. But there was another side to the Greeks. We sometimes forget that the statues of their gods, which have come to us in cold marble, were painted in vibrant colors. The goddesses could be jealous, fickle, or petulant. The gods themselves, even Zeus, were often absurdly, distressingly human. They cast off their Olympian detachment more than once to intercede in the affairs of men. Compare the Acropolis with the cyclopean ruins of the Old Ones or the physical perfection of the Hellenic deities with Cthulhu or the Great Race and we shall perceive the distance to be very great in letter and spirit.

Lovecraft himself did not attribute a Grecian influence in the conception or growth of his mythology. He had spoken in the generalist manner: "All of my stories, unconnected as they may be, are based on the *fundamental lore or legend* that this world was inhabited at one time by another race who, in practising black magic, lost their foothold and were expelled, yet live on outside ever ready to take possession of this earth again."[296] I emphasized "fundamental lore or legend' because Lovecraft saw the underlying unity of mythologies, religious epics, even fairy tales and nursery rhymes. The great basic drama which the human mind has rationalized out of the behavior of nature has been the primeval opposition of cosmic light and dark forces. The one rep-

---

295. See George Wetzel, "The Cthulhu Mythos: A Study," *Howard Phillips Lovecraft: Memoirs, Critiques, & Bibliographies*.

296. *Best Supernatural Stories of H. P. Lovecraft*, p. 8. [The quotation is spurious. See Ch. III, n. 33.]

V. Home

resented life and goodness, the other death and evil. Much of the world's mythology and folklore consists of accounts of their struggles. They appear under the many names of racial folk heroes and devils. Death and evil always triumph for a time, but usually are vanquished in the end, just as night inevitably succumbs to day. Lovecraft has his forces of good and evil. The Elder Gods[297] are the benign deities living peacefully at or near Betelgeuse in the constellation Orion. They rarely intervene between the struggle of the powers of evil and Earth's denizens. With some resultant confusion for readers, his powers of evil are variously called the Great Old Ones or the Ancient Ones. Unlike the Elder Gods, the Great Old Ones are named. Supreme among them is the blind, idiot god, Azathoth who rules with Yog-Sothoth. Nyarlathotep is their messenger. Others in their camp include Cthulhu, Hastur the Unspeakable,[298] and Shub-Niggurath, "the Goat with a Thousand Young." There is nothing in the Cthulhu mythology to show that light will eventually prevail. Lovecraft puts an ironic or perverse twist on certain essential themes running through the earth's chief legends. Consider the story of the human hero who crosses water or climbs a tree and thus returns to the magical other world, where he rescues or carries off the imprisoned daughter of a giant or magician. When Randolph Carter or Gilman is transported into another world, the one returns in squamous disarray, while the other meets a crone whose avenger tears out his heart. Or, compare "The Shadow over Innsmouth" with stories of mermaids or Undines who fall in love with a mortal, acquire a soul and feet in place of their scaly tails. The *Necronomicon* has its antecedents as well. Michel Deutsch suggests Genesis—"Signalons au passage le curieux rapprochement qu'on peut faire entre le symbolisme du *Nécro-*

---

297. [There are no Elder Gods in HPL's work. The term never occurs in his stories. The conception was grafted onto HPL's mythos by August Derleth.]
298. [Hastur is mentioned glancingly in "The Whisperer in Darkness," but it was Derleth who made the entity a member of HPL's pantheon of "gods."]

nomicon et la tradition biblique de l'arbre maudit de la connaissance."[299]

I have often wondered whether Soame Jenyns' *Free Inquiry into the Origin and Nature of Evil* (1757) was in any way influential in shaping Lovecraft's mythopoeic powers[300] for Jenyns' view of the universe and Lovecraft's fictional world are curiously alike. Jenyns, "a witty trifler— or at least a trifler who hoped to be witty,"[301] set out in his essay to justify the ways of God to man, even though—as he acknowledged more than once—"the human mind can comprehend but a small part of the great and astonishing whole."[302] Undaunted, Jenyns stated that we are living in the best of all possible worlds. Sickness, poverty, and natural calamities are but part of a larger order. The belief in "plenitude," the great chain of being theory, was dragged to its *reductio ad absurdum* when Jenyns wrote: "I am persuaded that there is something in the abstract nature of pain conducive to pleasure: that the sufferings of individuals are absolutely necessary to universal happiness."[303] Everything is for the best. *Dei gratia.* Everyone has his station in life. Man is only a link in the vast chain descending by imperceptible degrees from God, to "Superior Beings," to man, insensible matter, to nothing.

> As we receive a great part of our pleasures, and even subsistence from the sufferings and deaths of lower animals, may not these superior Beings do the same from ours, and that by ways as far above the reach of the most exalted human understandings, as the means by which we receive our benefits are above the capacities of the meanest creatures destined for our service?[304]

---

299. Deutsch, p. 262. ["We point in passing to the curious parallel that can be made between the symbolism of the *Necronomicon* and the biblical tradition of the cursed tree of knowledge."]

300. [There is no evidence that HPL was familiar with this work.]

301. Joseph Wood Krutch, *Samuel Johnson,* New York, Henry Holt, 1944, p. 163.

302. Soame Jenyns, *Free Inquiry into the Nature and Origin of Evil,* London. J. Dodsley, 1773, p. 92.

303. Ibid. p. 89.

304. Ibid. p. 94.

And, further:

> there may be numberless intermediate Beings, who have power to deceive, torment, or destroy us for the ends only of their own pleasure or utility, who may be vested with the same privileges over their inferiors, and as much benefit by the use of them, as ourselves.[305]

This could have come from Abdul Alhazred's *Necronomicon*. Throughout his essay Jenyns reiterated, "He [God] has given many advantages to Brutes, which Man cannot attain to with all his superiority, and many probably to Man which are denied to Angels; amongst which his ignorance is perhaps none of the least."[306] Jenyns is here saying what Lovecraft was to say in virtually all of his stories.

Jenyns' best-possible-world argument aimed at increasing complacency with society's ills, results in the very pessimism it hoped to dispell. "When he [Jenyns] suggests that man might well be tormented by superior creatures just as men themselves torment animals he is simply revealing the whole universe as a carefully designed torture chamber for all except the Supreme Torturer."[307] Samuel Johnson, a Grub Street hack at the time Jenyns' book was published, wrote an anonymous review of it. With great vigor he logically exposed Jenyns' absurdities. To a person such as Johnson, pained by the misery of his fellow creatures, Jenyns' persiflage summoned up his wrath and, incidentally, one of his best reviews. With superb restraint, he dryly advised Jenyns "to distrust his own faculties, however large and comprehensive."[308]

In suggesting Jenyns as a possible influence on Lovecraft's fiction, I confess that I cannot recall seeing his name mentioned among the million or more words of Lovecraft's correspondence that I have read.

---

305. Ibid. p. 96.
306. Ibid. p. 63.
307. David Daiches, *A Critical History of English Literature,* New York: Ronald Press, 1961, 2.769.
308. Anon. rev. (Samuel Johnson) "A Review of *A Free Inquiry into the Nature and Origin of Evil,*" Oxford, 1796.

Nor is there any proof that he owned a copy of the *Free Inquiry into the Origin and Nature of Evil*. A very real possibility exists, however, that Lovecraft did read Jenyns and probably long before he came across Dunsany. From an early age Lovecraft was well read in eighteenth century English literature. Even a person who is reasonably familiar with the Enlightenment would know of Soame Jenyns' controversial essay. If Lovecraft did not know the essay first hand, he may well have heard of it from the Great Cham's ten thousand word review—Lovecraft possessed ten volumes by or about him[309]—since Johnson meticulously described the salient features of Jenyns' thesis and illustrated those points with examples of his own which were more graphic than Jenyns himself would have dared to present.

Among other influences, that of Charles Fort deserves brief mention. Fort was called by a staunch admirer, the late Tiffany Thayer, "the one sane man in a mad, mad world—and for that reason very lonely."[310] Fort, writing mainly in the 1920s and 1930s, was not antiscience, but he was against the smug, dogmatic tone which so many men of science assume. Accept, but only temporarily, anything scientists say, said Fort, for there is a great deal that they do not know and cannot explain, yet they will not admit ignorance.[311] To support this contention, Fort wrote five books[312] crammed with tens of thousands of unusual occurrences which have been reported in newspapers the world over. Such unexplained phenomena as human vampirism, people who burned to death through spontaneous combustion, although their clothes remained unscorched (apparently Dickens and C. B. Brown knew what they were about), ships which have disappeared

---

309. See *List of Books in H. P. Lovecraft's Library*, comp. Mary Spink, JHL.
310. Charles Fort, *The Books of Charles Fort*, New York: Henry Holt, 1941, p. xxi.
311. Ibid., p. xiii
312. [Fort (1874–1932) published four books of nonfiction and a novel. HPL read the first, *The Book of the Damned* (1919), in 1927.]

V. Home

suddenly without a trace, teleportation, poltergeists, lights flashing on the moon, mysterious airships, and more, much more. (Psychologists, who have theories on why people *really* buy all those paperbacks, should have something merry to say about Mr. Fort and his mania for compiling myriad bits of odd news.) Fort delighted in showing how scientists themselves occasionally cross up each other. There is a classic instance, buried somewhere among Fort's items, which tells of an astronomer who "discovered" a new star. Other astronomers rushed to their telescopes and breathlessly reported seeing it. Busy mathematicians confirmed it. Later, the discoverer admitted that what he had thought was a star was only a piece of dust on his lens.

Lovecraft was very much aware of Mr. Fort's lively speculations. He had often talked of him, even mentioned him by name in a few stories, and referred to him in letters. In March, 1927, he urged August Derleth to read Fort's *Book of the Damned*—". . . there never was a more gloriously provocative sourcebook of breath-taking notions about Earth's relations with Outside Things."[313] This remark most likely refers to Fort's belief that other planets are observing us, and are landing their agents—disguised as humans—on our earth.

Dimly seen in the background of Lovecraft's stories is the Gothic novel. Gothicism has to do, among other things, with chains, isolated dim castles, catacombs, candles guttering in the dark, strange shrieks, owls and bats, and seemingly unmotivated chases through the night. These are not far from Lovecraft's explorer who enters the ruins of an aeon old civilization with an electric torch that threatens to extinguish. Reprocessing old material is not unusual. Science-fiction has depended on myth, legend, and the fairy tale. The magic carpet has been converted into a rocket ship.[314]

---

313. August Derleth, "Lovecraft As Mentor," *The Shuttered Room*, p. 144.
314. John Chambers, "The Cult of Science Fiction," *The Dalhousie Review* (Spring 1960), p. 85.

The Cthulhu Mythos was evolved piecemeal. To know all the sources and influences which muscled their way into Lovecraft's imagination is a vain expectation. That his debt to others was great, is clear. Yet, and this must not be overlooked, like an artist, he took his material where he found it and never failed to make it his own.

In late December, 1935, Lovecraft received a manuscript titled "Well-bred Speech." It was from Anne Tillery Renshaw, who operated a speech/charm school in Washington, D.C. She was an Amateur Journalist, had met Lovecraft, and knew of his revisionist work. Would he, please, read her manuscript and offer suggestions? Lovecraft made "rather cursory"[315] corrections since his aunt's illness that winter and other necessary duties had kept him busy. "I have done some wholesale correction on historical, mythological, and other points which I doubt if the average reviser would be likely to have paralleled. Not that I am better informed than others, but that I have the dull, plodding patience to *look closely* for slips and make very sure that nothing erroneous or misleading remains."[316] He planned to return the manuscript. Back shot her reply: "Don't you dare send my ms. home! Sir."[317] She wanted him to overhaul it. Miss Renshaw knew from previous clients of Lovecraft's that he was adept at various prose styles and could thus revise without unevenness. He must have been a virtuoso to have ranged from short stories "not unworthy of Poe," to the flatulence and banality of a David V. Bush.

Students of human nature who have wondered what the relationship between a ghostwriter (for that is what Lovecraft's revisions, *in extenso,* made him) and his client must be like, would find Miss Renshaw's letters interesting. In the beginning, when Lovecraft pointed out the errors and deficiencies of her manuscript, she was properly ap-

---

315. H. P. Lovecraft, MS. letter to Anne Tillery Renshaw, dated March 30, 1936, JHL.
316. Ibid.
317. Anne Tillery Renshaw, MS. letter to H. P. Lovecraft, dated April 6, 1936, JHL.

V. Home

preciative of the task which lay before him. In her later letters—they are actually notes written "in haste"—she is terribly busy, it has been a hectic week, she is teaching, must attend her cardiac stricken brother, will visit Father, ill in Mexico. The implication in all of this is that Miss Renshaw is capable of writing her own book if only she could pluck a few moments of leisure. As the months roll by in 1936, her missives tend to minimize his contribution. His handwriting is atrocious, she complains. She intends to edit and cut the book to suit the needs of her school. He probably won't recognize her book. And why the delay?

Several events delayed completion of the Renshaw textbook. On June 11, 1936, Robert E. Howard committed suicide. He drove into the desert and shot himself in the head the day his mother died. Lovecraft wrote a long obituary which was belatedly printed in the September *Fantasy Magazine*. Four months after Howard's passing, Lovecraft, writing to a friend, ventured his explanation of Howard's last crisis.

> I doubt whether there was any *definite* cause aside from Mrs. Howard's approaching death. As I see it, it was simply the disastrous combination of a certain kind of temperament with one sharp blow. Probably it would never have occurred if good old Two-Gun hadn't been watching sleepless by his mother's bedside for endless weeks. He was nervously & physically exhausted by those weeks of overwork, sleeplessness & tension—brooding deeply (as shown by poems like 'The Tempter') even though putting up a brave front to the outside world. Then came despair—& the consciousness that the fight for his mother's life was hopeless. With no energy to resist the shock—no fund of healthy life-clinging left after the weeks of force-sapping, nerve-twisting strain—poor REH reacted in what must have seemed the shortest & simplest way. And what a damned shame! But of course I suppose general temperament was a factor. Despite his violent, assertive contempt for the "artistic attitude," Two-Gun was essentially of the neurotic aesthetic type—that is, a person filled with imaginative concepts of certain conditions unrelated to reality

which he would like to see around him, correspondingly resentful of the pressure of the actual world.[318]

Social duties that summer cut into his ghostwriting chores. Robert Barlow arrived and stayed through the month of August. His host put him up in a nearby rooming house. The smiling boy came into Lovecraft's home every morning, demanding good naturedly, to see something new in Providence; and Lovecraft, good soldier, obliged. Barlow departed on the first of September.[319] Two weeks later arrived an old friend, James Ferdinand Morton, curator of the Paterson Museum. He remained three days. Both had a craving for ice cream that would have been suspect even in a pregnant woman tormented by the Spleen. On September fourteenth they went to Warren and ate two quarts apiece of ice cream at Maxfield's—Lovecraft's varieties being orange, pineapple, lemon, raspberry, chocolate, banana, grape, and loganberry. They stopped eating not because they were full, but because their cash was running low.[320]

Meanwhile, Miss Renshaw was waiting. To meet her deadline, Lovecraft was obliged to labor, he said, sixty hours without sleep.[321] For this wakeful session and all the others required to complete the book, he received one hundred dollars.[322]

Barlow said that Lovecraft had shaped his intellectual life and many of his tastes and habits more than anyone else. Lovecraft, to Barlow, "was much more than a story writer . . . he [was] more important as a man who had the integrity to ignore the Machine Age and its frenzied leveling-out-to-rubble of life's rich irregularities, who had the courage to study and think and converse and write, in accordance with

---

318. H. P. Lovecraft, MS. letter to Margaret Ronan, n.d., circa October, 1936, MR.
319. Ibid.
320. Ibid.
321. H. P. Lovecraft, MS. letter to Kenneth Sterling, dated October 18, 1936, KS.
322. Anne Tillery Renshaw, MS. letter to H. P. Lovecraft, dated September 15, 1936, JHL.

V. Home

the deeper traditions of a more orderly age. He was the twin of the 'Last Puritan,' except that he knew what he wanted, and frankly admired that character."[323]

This last statement had been endorsed by Lovecraft in a letter which he had written to Barlow in 1936. He urged all his young correspondents to read Santayana's brilliant comic novel, *The Last Puritan*.

> The character I most respected, without question [in the novel] was Oliver Alden himself. Admitting his grotesque one-sidedness—his indifference to the formal arts & his exaggeration of the sense of duty—we must acknowledge that in his basic attitude toward the universe he represents a principle so valuable & important, & so tragically missing from the cheap breed of moderns, that its existence justifies almost any overdevelopment or misapplication of it . . . the principle of *art in life,* or aesthetic selectiveness as applied to personality & behaviour. A man with this principle is fortified against the cheaper aspects of his environment & really extracts more from life than does a commonplace stallion . . . Oliver is the one real man amidst a fantastic menagerie . . . Out of it [Anglo-Saxon Puritan race] have come the leaders & educators & statesmen, & historians of ten generations—& that the spark has not quite flickered out is proved by the encouraging number of solid men of Oliver's age & even younger—men like Pres. Conant of Harvard (in his middle 40's), the LaFarge brothers (in their 30's), & so on. A degenerate commercial psychology with whorishly vulgar & saddened values has done much to kill the essential human ability roughly describable as "Puritanism," but if ever a sounder social & economic system is achieved under socialism, we may see something of a return. Santayana, steeped as he is in the Popish-Mediterranean tradition, is not the man to judge the thought-&-feeling stream of a purely Northern people . . . I spit upon the low ideals of the shrewd Yankee-trader class . . . a class which in the past was recognized as inferior by its New England betters, & which has only in the last half-century dared to pose before a gullible public as *representative* of our law & people.[324]

---

323. Robert H. Barlow, "The Wind That Is in the Grass," *Marginalia*, p. 349.
324. H. P. Lovecraft, MS. letter to Robert H. Barlow, dated September the Last, 1936, JHL.

When Barlow asked Lovecraft what he thought of Walt Whitman, Whitman with his—

> A woman waits for me, she contains all, nothing is lacking,
> Yet all were lacking if sex were lacking, or if the moisture of the right man were lacking.[325]

Lovecraft recoiled:

> I don't know anything about Walt Whitman's career, but he was a half-crazed old slopover anyhow. And when it comes to making a thorough fool of oneself over women—hell! Compare the millions of high-grade men who *don't* with the relatively insignificant handful who do ... we'd all like to kiss pretty girls till our dying day—but we know damn well that it would be only a repellent & sordid mockery except with the very few women who really had affection for us when we were young. Therefore the man of taste & dignity cuts off that side of his personality in toto as he ages—until the excision comes to be really natural & he is able to converse with young women just as cooly & impersonally as if they were lampposts, hydrants, men, old women or no-parking signs ... Novels could be—& probably have been—written about the tragedy of rich old men who are made to believe that they have another chance at life in all its fulness—that once more they may become linked with female youth & beauty on dignified terms, so that the future will again glow with adventurous expectancy, & the common events of life take on an added significance. The higher they soar, the harder they fall—& the aftermath is ghastliness & horror. Poor old duffers. Their fate ought to cheer the socialist who argues that the cosmos is against private wealth![326]

Lovecraft's concern with the cultured individual in society is worth exploring a bit further. The cultured individual to Lovecraft's way of thinking was the person, like himself, who did not necessarily accept the world in which he found himself, but who, on the contrary, swept away from his sight all that was irrelevant, sordid, and ugly, and through his imagination created a reality of his own. This, in essence,

---

325. Walt Whitman, *Leaves of Grass*, Random House, 1921, p. 117.
326. H. P. Lovecraft, MS. letter to Robert H. Barlow, dated September the Last, 1936, JHL.

V. Home

was the end of culture: books, art, and nature in all her vibrant colorations nurtured the interior life of the individual. A cultured being, Lovecraft took pride in his individuality. The reading of a favorite book or the exploration of Colonial homes caught him in the bowels and left him trembling afterwards, so attuned was he to the spirit of the artistic creation. He experienced in such moments the same exultation, the ecstasy of a Daedalus by the seashore, or of children "tumbling in the streets, and playing ... moving [like] jewels,"[327] although he never associated his experiences with mysticism. There was a Lord Chesterfield courtesy in his behavior of an essentially aristocratic complexion. In the difficult art of adjusting one's culture to human relationships, Lovecraft found this mannerism a great help. The Welsh writer John Cowper Powys advanced the idea in all seriousness that since Christian humility was too far above most of mankind to attain, and since the passive religions of the East were uncongenial to us, we Westerners should try to acquire a Lord Chesterfield courtesy toward one another. Out of a show of etiquette, genuine feeling and sympathy for one another might eventually result. "Christians have," thought Powys, "very often the worst manners in the world."[328] We must begin somewhere. Let us at least polish our manners *à la* Lord Chesterfield suggested Powys.

Lovecraft's *laissez faire* attitude toward his fellow men was the gesture of a cultured person. If he was incapable of feeling sorrow for their sufferings, he at least was never a party to inflicting pain. Culture for Lovecraft was a substitution for the lack of love and religion in his life. In his life, culture served as an acoustical tile, deadening the loud coarse laughter which echoed from empty heads, the city with its mechanical contraptions which lacerated the air with their hums and

---

327. Thomas Traherne, "Centuries of Meditations," *Anthology of English Prose,* ed. Eirian James, Cambridge, England: Cambridge University Press, 1956, p. 47.
328. John Cowper Powys, *The Meaning of Culture,* New York: W.W. Norton, 1929, p. 247.

buzzes. Lovecraft was able to attain a modicum of happiness above that of the modern society with its pleasures and ennui, its lonely crowds and status seekers.

In the fall and winter of 1936, Lovecraft returned to an early love—astronomy. He began attending club meetings of "The Skyscrapers," a local organization under the auspices of Brown University. With his delectable no-nonsense reportage, he told of a recent lecture on early Rhode Island astronomy given by "an amiably ignorant grammar-school principal, in a toupee too brown for his graying fringe, who didn't know what an *orrery* is!"[329] His keen interest in astronomy may have been rekindled by something he learned that previous spring. "I've just stumbled on a whale of a *genealogical* discovery; one which gives me a bigger kick than any other I've made! Believe it or not, *I find I am the great-great-great-great-great-great-great-great-great-grandson of the astronomer who introduced the Copernican theory into England!* It sure gave me a kick to get a real *man of science* in my pedigree."[330] Lovecraft was referring to John Field, born between 1515 and 1525, who died in May, 1587. John Field was called "The Proto-Copernican of England" since his *Ephemeris* (1557) was the first English account of the true motions of the heavenly bodies. An Oxonian, he spent much time abroad, especially in Germany. Information concerning Lovecraft's distinguished ancestor is to be found in *Gentleman's Magazine* for May, 1834, and November, 1862.[331]

Along with astronomy, Lovecraft maintained a very spry interest in politics through the fall and autumn of 1936. When Rabbi Wise spoke in Providence on behalf of the Democrats, Lovecraft hurried to hear him. "An astonishingly brilliant speaker & epigrammatist—well worthy of his reputation."[332] Naturally, when President Roosevelt appeared on

---

329. H. P. Lovecraft, MS. letter to Margaret Ronan, n.d., circa 1936, MR.
330. H. P. Lovecraft, MS. letter to Kenneth Sterling, dated May 25, 1936, KS.
331. Frederick Clifton Pierce, *Field Genealogy*, 1901, I.42.
332. H. P. Lovecraft, MS. letter to Margaret Ronan, n.d., circa 1936, MR.

V. Home

the terrace of the State Capitol on the morning of October twenty-first, Lovecraft quickened his steps in that direction. "I had several fine glimpses of him ... Ordinarily I'm not much for seeking personal glimpses of the great—but the sight of the only first-rate, forward-looking leader in the United States was too much for an old man to resist!"[333] The change from a Tory to a bare-headed FDR supporter is surprising, yet, in his mind, Lovecraft was picturing the New Deal in regal dress—the "Hyde Park aristocracy," and an intellectual elite, culled from our universities, all gathered around the Great One. Lovecraft was all in favor of a president who guaranteed each person security and opportunities commensurate with his skill.

> There ought not to be any rallying around the standards & ideals of the contemporary workman, together with a massed hatred of the standards & ideals of the contemporary aristocrat. Standards & ideals should not be associated with any one "class" any more than with any other "class". Keeping well-groomed & talking grammatically & enjoying Horace & possessing sensitive honour—in brief, being a gentleman—ought not to be associated with the inheritor of a fortune any more than with an intelligent mechanic or miner. *We must learn to divorce the idea of human status & attributes the relatively trivial concepts of remunerative occupation & financial position.* There will always be *natural* aristocrats & men of taste, & there will always be crude clods; but in a rational society it may be that the aristocrats will include people whose *purely economic* activities are relatively insignificant—miners, mill-hands, 'bus-drivers, &c—whilst crude clods will include highly-paid industrial administrators. The big idea is *to substitute the idea of personal excellence for that of economic position*—& in order to do that, we must not encourage any hatred or repudiation of those high qualities which are at present (through long injustice) ideals associated with the "ruling class."[334]

The business of "class consciousness" was excessive. sometimes absurd. "Why in newspapers do they always write "John Smith, grocer," and never "John Smith, admirer of Greek sculpture, or John Smith,

---

333. Ibid.
334. H. P. Lovecraft, MS. letter to Kenneth Sterling, dated December 14, 1936, KS.

student of astronomy"? he wanted to know.[335]

During most of the winter Lovecraft's long-standing susceptibility to cold weather kept him indoors. The radiators at 66 College Street chugged and gurgled. In this steam bath atmosphere his nerves relaxed. Occasionally he would walk out among conservative snowflakes and swing through the apple chevron doors of the cafeteria at the foot of Federal Hill.

Christmas he celebrated with his aunt. He personally decorated the tree and placed "a cupboard full of surprises" under it.[336] One of Lovecraft's correspondents presented him a human skull which had been excavated from an Indian burial mound. "Alas, poor Yorick! Well—the able sachem's dome will always be regarded with veneration around here."[337]

In January, Lovecraft became ill. He started a journal and jotted into it the symptoms of his disease. He wrote briefly and repeatedly of abdominal pains, a feeling of being bloated, alternate periods of torpor and light-headedness, loss of appetite, snatches of sleep, increasing lassitude, and the difficulty of concentrating.[338] He sent Barlow one of his rare typed letters, complaining, "This goddam grippe or whatever the hell I've got has got me so Yuggoth-cursed weak that my script can't be depended upon."[339]

The "grippe" worsened. In early March, Mrs. Gamwell summoned Dr. William L. Leet. He came and was taken not to her nephew's bedside, but to the bathtub. Lovecraft was inside. He explained that the pressure of the water made him feel more comfortable. Remaining in

---

335. Ibid.
336. H. P. Lovecraft, MS. letter to Margaret Ronan, n.d., circa December, 1936, MR.
337. 310. H. P. Lovecraft, MS. letter to Robert H. Barlow, dated January 5, 1937, JHL. [The correspondent was the young Willis Conover.]
338. Donald Wandrei, MS. letter to Arthur Koki, dated May 22, 1961, AK.
339. 312. H. P. Lovecraft, MS. letter to Robert H. Barlow, dated January 27, 1937, JHL.

V. Home

the tub for his interview and examination, Lovecraft spoke easily and softly, but clearly, about the symptoms of the past two months. Dr. Leet, sensing a serious and possibly terminal condition, placed him in the Jane Brown Memorial Hospital. This was done on March 10, 1937. Dr. Leet remembers that Lovecraft was "always gentle, polite, and soft spoken, receiving special sympathy from the nurses ... He took his illness as it came, managing as best he could with grace and courtesy."[340]

Lovecraft's hospital record follows:

Mr. Lovecraft, 46 yrs of age, entered the JBM Hosp. on March 10, 1937 for observation. Presents a story of increasing weakness, listlessness, loss of weight, nausea and vomiting, & pallor. At present vomiting most everything taken even to liquids. Complaining also of pain in abdomen & back. Abdomen distended. Edema of ankles.

3-11 pt compl. of pain in bed, vomiting even liquids.

3-12 Condition no better.

3-14   "   poor. Vomiting even liquids.
      Drowsy & weak.
      Paracenteiis abdomen yielded 6¾ qts of amber fluid.

3-15 Discharge Note

      Pts condition has been a steady downhill one since admission. It is felt that he has a generalized carcinomatosis and chronic Nephritis with impending Uremia.
      Did not respond to Symptomatic measures.
      Died on 6th Hosp. day.

Condition on Discharge—Dead.[341]

Mrs. Gamwell telegraphed Robert Barlow: HOWARD DIED THIS MORNING NOTHING TO DO THANKS.[342]

---

340. Dr. William L. Leet, MS. letter to Arthur Koki, dated March 31, 1961, AK.

341. Hospital Record of H. P. Lovecraft, History #20703 N. 760 (microfilm) Jane Brown Memorial Hospital.

342. Telegram from Mrs. Annie E. P. Gamwell to Robert H. Barlow, dated

The day after, *The New York Times* had the following notice:

WRITER CHARTS FATAL MALADY

Providence, R.I. March 15 (AP) Howard Phillips Lovecraft, 46 years old, a writer of horror tales, died early today of an illness from which he had suffered from childhood. During the past month, when his condition became serious, he devoted his writing to a minute clinical study of his disease as an aid to science, continuing the daily chart until he could no longer hold his pencil. His sole survivor is an aunt, Mrs. Phillips Gamwell of this city.[343]

The funeral was held on March eighteenth. The service was read at noon at the chapel of Horace B. Knowles Sons. Some forty persons attended. There were friends from Amateur Journalism.[344] A few Brown University students who had shared his antiquarian interests also came. Burial was in the Phillips plot at Swan Point Cemetery.

No special article on H. P. Lovecraft appeared in the Providence newspapers.[345] The attention of Providence and the entire country was centered on the school explosion in New London, Texas, which killed four hundred twenty five children and teachers. The cause of the explosion remains a mystery to this day.

The front pages also carried a statement by Father Teilhard de Chardin that there is no conflict between evolution and the Church. Man is made in God's image said the Jesuit geologist. "The great, the tremendous, the significant fact about man is the coming of thought with and through him."[346]

It was an eminently hopeful position.

March 15, 1937, JHL.

343. *The New York Times,* March 16, 1937, p. 5.

344. In telephone conversation with Edward C. Cole on November 11, 1961.

345. [In fact, obituaries appeared in both the *Providence Evening Bulletin* (15 March) and *Providence Journal* (16 March). It was from the former item that the *New York Times* derived the information for its brief notice.]

346. "Jesuit Backs Evolution Theory; Finds No Conflict With Church," *The Providence Journal* (March 19, 1937), p. 1.

VI. The Story Thus Far

> Lovecraft ... une des figures les plus tragiques de l'histoire littéraire.[1]

Lovecraft's death at the age of forty-six came as a shock to his many friends and correspondents and to the readers of *Weird Tales*. For months after his unexpected death, letters arrived to the editor of that publication expressing sorrow and, in some instances, anger:

> Reading your magazine habitually, I sometimes wonder whether you ever realized how great a contributor you had in H. P. Lovecraft. Whether you ever gaged the fineness of his stories, the originality of his genius? Of course, you published them, alongside of others. You sent him his cheque, and that was that. But has it ever occurred to you that in Lovecraft you had the greatest genius that ever lived in the realm of weird fiction?[2]

Still others wrote asking that his stories and poems be collected in permanent book form. This possibility was seriously considered by Lovecraft's eighteen year old literary executor, Robert H. Barlow, who permitted August Derleth and Donald Wandrei to publish a giant omnibus edition of Lovecraft's best work. To do this, Derleth and Wandrei invested their savings to establish a publishing house (in Sauk City, Wisconsin) which they named Arkham House, after the legendary town Lovecraft used in a number of his stories. Two years later, in 1939, Arkham House released

---

1. Deutsch, p. 266. ["Lovecraft ... one of the most tragic figures in literary history."]
2. "The Eyrie," *Weird Tales* (July 1937), p. 125.

The Outsider and Others containing thirty-six stories. It was a large, attractive volume of 553 pages, or some 330,000 words. Despite lengthy and favorable[3] reviews in *Publishers' Weekly* and *The New York Herald Tribune,* this limited edition of twelve hundred copies sold very slowly, going out of print in December, 1943. When the book had appeared, there were grumblings that five dollars was too high a price. Today (1962) a mint copy of *The Outsider and Others* commands as much as one hundred twenty five dollars. Those libraries that did not take the precaution of removing their copy to their Rare Book department, no longer have it.

In the year that *The Outsider and Others* was published, Lovecraft's literary heir left the country and enrolled at the Escuela de Antropologia of the Institute Nacional de Ciencas Biológicas in Mexico City where he became impressed with Mexican anthropology. Showing an extraordinary talent for languages, Barlow mastered classical Nahuatl and developed a deep interest in Mexican prehistory. He returned to the States to obtain an A.B. degree from the University of California, Berkeley in 1942. While a senior, he won the Emily Chamberlain Cook Prize in poetry. He wrote an intense, disturbing poetry alien to Lovecraft's neoclassical mimicry. Such a poem was "For D."

> My thoughts and pillows are disarranged;
> I seem to confuse your wrists with the line
>   of a Kwan-Yin scroll,
> Your mouth with a brown triangular butterfly,
> Your belly with good linen
> Spread on a hedge from dawn.
>
> I will shut the window of my rained-on heart,
> Since you occupy the bed which is almost
>   legitimately yours.
> I will not think of the sliding hands.
> I will read a book
> Or walk on Van Ness Avenue screaming.[4]

---

3. See *New York Herald Tribune,* December 17, 1939.
4. Robert H. Barlow, *Poems for a Competition,* Sacramento, Cal.: The Fugitive Press, 1942.

VI. The Story Thus Far

Barlow, one of the most intellectually brilliant of the young men in Lovecraft's circle, received a fellowship from the Rockefeller Foundation in 1944 for work in the collection of old Mexican documentary materials. This was followed in 1946 by a two-year Guggenheim Foundation grant for research at the Bibliothèque Nationale. Although he did not speak French at the time of the award, he told his colleague, Dr. Ignacio Bernal, that "pensaba por tan to aprenderlo. Faltaban unas dos semanas para su partida, lo que consideró suficiente y en efecto, se fué hablando un francés que, si no parisno, era cuando perfectamente correcto."[5] Upon his return to Mexico he immersed himself in the history, pre- and post-Conquest, of the Maya civilization. He also served as acting chairman of the department of anthropology at Mexico City College.

On January 1, 1951, he committed suicide in his home in Azcapotzalco by taking sleeping pills.[6] He was only thirty-two years old, yet the scholarship he left behind would have honored a scholar twice his age—seventy monographs, articles, and a dozen book-length works, most of them written in Spanish. His obituary in *American Anthropologist* concluded: "Never robust in health, sensitive to the world around him to an uncommon degree, unable to devote himself blindly and exclusively to his love of knowledge for its sake alone, he succumbed to the *mal du siécle* which in one way or another has touched us all. His place will not soon be filled."[7]

The death of Lovecraft's literary executor did not halt publication of Lovecraft's works. While Barlow was living and teaching in Mexico, a fair amount of Lovecraftiana appeared. In 1943, Arkham House is-

---

5. Bernal, p. 3. ["he had been intending to learn it. He was leaving in around two weeks, which he considered enough time, and, indeed when he parted he was able to speak a French that, though not Parisian, was perfectly accurate." (translation by Ovidio Cartagena).]

6. Dr. Ignacio Bernal, MS. letter to Arthur Koki, dated May 9, 1961, AK.

7. Norman A. McQuown, "Obituary: Robert H. Barlow," *American Anthropologist* 53, No. 543 (1951).

sued a second volume, *Beyond the Wall of Sleep,* which contained prose poems, some early stories, collaborations, a large selection of poetry, and an "Appreciation" by W. Paul Cook.[8] Like *The Outsider and Others,* this was a limited (1,217) edition also. Through these two books as well as reprints in *Weird Tales* and anthologies, interest in Lovecraft grew. To satisfy this curiosity, three books—*Marginalia* (1944), *Something About Cats* (1949), and *The Shuttered Room* (1959)—have been published, containing juvenilia, recollections and reflections by those who knew Lovecraft personally, and essays on the Cthulhu mythology.

It is not possible in this introductory work to assess the articles on Lovecraft which have appeared, a few in national publications, most in science-fiction "fanzines"—mimeographed or hectographed amateur publications that seldom survived beyond vol. 1, no. 1. Generally speaking, the articles on Lovecraft, as a person, have had an unfortunate tendency to make him a recluse. "Lovecraft, a semi-invalid, a recluse, and an antiquarian ..."[9] Not surprisingly, this type of statement has been picked up and echoed halfway across the world—"Malade, pauvre, émigré par la pensée dans le dix-huitième siècle américain, il n'a guère quitté sa maison de Providence (Rhode Island)."[10] "Krótkie życie Lovecrafta (1890–1937) tak jak i życie jego XIX wiecznego antenata [Edgar Allan Poe] przeszło pod znakiem nieszęścia. Nędza, słiabe zdrowie nieudane małżeństwo ... Z zakątka w Nowej Anglii ..."[11]

---

8. [Cook's appreciation had first appeared as a booklet, *In Memoriam: Howard Phillips Lovecraft* (1941).]

9. Vincent Starrett, *Books and Bipeds,* New York: Argus Books, Inc., 1947, p. 119.

10. Andre Billy, "Lovecraft: Edgar Poe du XXe siecle," *Le Figaro, Litteraire,* October 28, 1961, p. 4. ["Sick, poor, exiled by thought in the American eighteenth century, he barely left his house in Providence (Rhode Island)."]

11. H. P. Lovecraft, "Koszmar z Innsmouth," trans. Andrzej Wermer, *Prze Kroj,* Numer 766–68, p. 18 (1959). Excerpt cited, translated from the Polish: "Lovecraft's short life (1890–1937), like that of his 19th century predecessor [Edgar Allan Poe] passed in the shadow of misfortune. Poverty, poor health, and an unhappy marriage ... In his hiding place in New England ..."

Vincent Starrett flatly confesses that "Lovecraft the man is more interesting than his work."[12] But the man was not the "creep" that others would have him be. What, for example, does it mean to say that Lovecraft was a "recluse"? The *American College Dictionary* defines a recluse as "a person who lives in seclusion or apart from society, often for religious meditation."[13] It would appear that this is an unsatisfactory description of Lovecraft. Eight years ago, Helen Worden Erskine wrote a fascinating book called *Out of this World* which dealt with a dozen recluses in the New York City area. The home of a recluse is usually easy to detect, Miss Erskine said. The doorbell has been yanked out, there is no mailbox, the blinds are always lowered, the doors bolted, no lights or telephone.[14] Hardly 66 College Street. The reasons that drive a person to seclusion are an inability to withstand misfortune, overdevotion to person or place, loss of perspective brought about by emotional rather than intellectual unbalance, probably suspicious in early life, no sense of humor, constantly living in fear.[15] Some of these desiderata are found in Lovecraft—or anyone. To call Lovecraft a recluse is to overlook his correspondence, his willingness to meet with and help writers, his frequent trips, and love for good conversation. A brusque appraiser of Americana, an Outsider, an uneasy Augustan—these may be more acceptable tags if by them one means that Lovecraft was in the world but not involved in his times to the extent that most people are.

There are more hopeful signs of Lovecraft's growing importance than the stagily written articles in fanzines and elsewhere might suggest. "The Music of Erich Zann" is now included in a college textbook of short stories for study, placing Lovecraft in company with Heming-

---

12. Starrett, p. 203.
13. *The American College Dictionary*, ed. Clarence L. Barnhart, New York, Random House, 1947. p. 1012.
14. Helen Worden Erskine, *Out of this World*, New York: G. P. Putnam, 1953, pp. xi–xii.
15. Ibid., pp. xi–xiii.

way, Faulkner, Kafka, and Poe.[16] This is not the final proof of greatness, but it is an acknowledgement that Lovecraft is, if not a master, at least a skilled practitioner in the Gothic and fantastic mode of literature. His stories in the past two decades have been widely anthologized in such collections as Dashiell Hammett's *Creeps By Night* and *Great Tales of Terror and the Supernatural*, the popular Modern Library Giant, edited by Wise and Fraser.[17] Five paperbacks containing Lovecraft's stories exclusively have appeared. The latest, *Cry Horror!*, sold 54% of its 150,000 copy printing—a fair sale as paperbacks go.[18] In November, 1961, Roddy McDowall recorded two of Lovecraft's stories: "The Hound" and "The Outsider." Hollywood has not yet discovered Lovecraft (*At the Mountains of Madness* would make an exciting film), though Hollywood has discovered one of Lovecraft's protégés—Robert Bloch. Bloch's novel *Psycho* was made into cinema history by Alfred Hitchcock. (Only Griffith's *Birth of a Nation* has grossed more money in the black-white film category.) In a recent letter to me, Bloch wrote to say:

> I've never made any secret of my debt to HPL, and regard him as a definite seminal source in American fantasy—he helped, influenced directly or indirectly so many writers. What he lacked was a critical "break" . . . If he'd received some kind *imprimatur* from a spokesman for the intelligentsia, I feel that he might have taken his rightful place as a writer of importance.[19]

If Lovecraft is "une des figures les plus tragiques de l'histoire littéraire" it is the old, recurring story of neglect, misunderstanding, and belated recognition.

---

16. *The Short Story*, ed. James B. Hall and Joseph Langland, New York: Macmillan Go., 1956, pp. 150–59.
17. [The Hammett volume appeared in HPL's lifetime, in 1931. The Wise and Fraser anthology appeared in 1944.]
18. In private conversation with sales manager, Avon Publications Inc., on November 18, 1960.
19. Robert Bloch, MS. letter to Arthur Koki, dated April 28, 1961, AK.

VI. The Story Thus Far

World-wide acquaintance is spreading through Polish, French, Swedish, Portuguese, and Spanish translations. In England, two books, *The Haunter of the Dark and Other Tales* (1951) and *The Case of Charles Dexter Ward* (1952), were published by Victor Gollancz, Ltd. Reviewed by some eighty newspapers and literary journals in the British Commonwealth nations, they met with, for the most part, very favorable reviews.[20]

In the past decade it has been the French, more than the British, or even the Americans, who have enthusiastically hailed Lovecraft. Most recently, André Billy, de l'Academie Goncourt, devoted his column in *Le Figaro* to Lovecraft. Although M. Billy committed a number of inexcusable errors of biographical fact concerning "Edward Philippe [*sic*] Lovecraft," the title of his article was portentous— "Lovecraft: Edgar Poe du XXe siècle."[21] Five books containing Lovecraft's short stories have been published in France. Éditions Denoël is responsible for four of the books, and Jacques Papy for translating three of those volumes. Monsieur Papy's personal opinion of Lovecraft?

> I am afraid I am going to disappoint you. But the truth is, strange as it may seem, that I don't like H. P. Lovecraft, and that I consider him as one of the worst *writers* that ever put pen to paper . . . It is a fact that my translations of his stories are better (though I am saying it) than his prose, be it only for the very simple reason that I have had to prune, to weed, and even to cut savagely to make some of his stories legible in French. I find that he writes in a ponderous manner, that he must needs use 3 adjectives when one would be quite enough, and that, on the whole, to put things in a nutshell, his stories are uncommonly good but uncommonly badly told.[22]

Papy did not permit his judgement to affect his translations which were distinguished enough to excite encomiums from Jean Cocteau:

---

20. Press clippings of *The Haunter* and *Case of Charles Dexter Ward*, gathered by Durance Press Cuttings, London, England, AK.
21. Billy.
22. Jacques Papy, MS. letter to Arthur Koki, dated September 19, 1961, AK.

"Votre traduction est plus belle qu'une simple traduction. Elle conserve le pouvoir de convaincre." "Je me demandais si la langue de Lovecraft était aussi belle que la nôtre."[23]

Lovecraft improved for French sensibility has given him a new bid for recognition. I suspect from the very stimulating French critiques that have thus far been written by Bergier, Ernoult, and Deutsch, among others, that we shall, in the future, look to France to tell us about our American author. Is the nation that put Poe on a pedestal now ready to do the same for H. P. Lovecraft?

---

23. Ibid. ["Your translation is lovelier than a simple translation. It retains the power to convince." "I wonder if Lovecraft's language was as lovely as ours."] Cocteau also publicly praised Papy's translations. Scott in *Exiles and Fabrications* gives the publication as *The London Observer* in 1954, but this is incorrect.

Bibliography

I. BOOKS

Allen, Walter. *The English Novel.* New York: E. P. Dutton, 1958.

Amis, Kingsley. *New Maps of Hell.* New York: Ballantine Books, 1960.

Bailey, J. O. *Pilgrims Through Space and Time.* New York: Argus Books, Inc., 1947.

Barlow, Robert H. *Poems for a Competition.* Sacramento, Calif.: The Fugitive Press, 1942.

Barnhart, Clarence L., ed. *The American College Dictionary.* New York: Random House, 1947.

Baugh, Albert C., ed. *A Literary History of England.* New York: Appleton-Century-Crofts, Inc., 1948.

Bayles, Richard M., ed. *History of Providence County, Rhode Island.* New York: W. W. Preston and Co., 1871.

Birkhead, Edith. *The Tale of Terror,* London: Constable and Co. Ltd., 1921.

Bishop, Zealia. *The Curse of Yig.* Sauk City, Wis.: Arkham House, 1953.

Burke, Edmund. *Works,* vol. I. Boston, Little, Brown and Co., 1901.

Bush, David V. *Affirmations and How to Use Them.* Washington, D.C.: D. V. Bush, 1923.

———. *Applied Psychology and Scientific Living.* St. Louis, Mo.: David V. Bush Pub. Co., 1923.

———. *How to Put the Subconscious Mind to Work.* Chicago: David V. Bush Pub., 1924

———. *Inspirational Poems.* St. Louis, Mo.: David V. Bush Pub., 1921.

College Hill: A Demonstration Study of Historic Area Renewal, Providence, R.I., 1959 (Conducted by the Providence City Plan Commission in cooperation with the Providence Preservation Society and the Housing and Home Finance Agency).

Cook, W, Paul. *In Memoriam: Howard Phillips Lovecraft.* North Montpelier, Vt.: Driftwood Press, 1941.

Crane, Hart. *The Letters of Hart Crane,* ed. Brom Weber. New York: Hermitage House, 1952.

Daiches, David. *A Critical History of English Literature,* 2 vols. New York: Ronald Press, 1961.

DeCamp, L. Sprague. *Science-Fiction Handbook.* New York: Hermitage House, 1953.

De la Mare, Walter. *Collected Poems.* New York: Henry Holt and Co., 1941.

———. *The Return.* New York: Alfred A. Knopf, 1922.

Derleth, August. *H. P. L.: A Memoir.* New York: Ben Abramson, 1945.

———. *Some Notes on H. P. Lovecraft.* Sauk City, Wis.: Arkham House, 1959.

Dunsany, Lord. *The Gods of Pegāna* Boston. J. W. Luce Co., n.d.

Erskine, Helen Worden. *Out of this World.* New York: G. P. Putnam, 1953.

Fiske, John. *Myths and Myth Makers.* Cambridge, Mass.: Riverside Press, 1902.

Fort, Charles. *The Books of Charles Fort.* New York: Henry Holt, 1941.

Freud, Sigmund. *Collected Papers.* 5 vols. New York: Basic Books, Inc., 1959.

———. *The Interpretation of Dreams.* London: Hogarth Press, 1953.

Gekle, William Francis. *Arthur Machen, Weaver of Fantasy.* New York: Round Table Press, 1949.

Gissing, George. *The Private Papers of Henry Ryecroft.* New York: E. P. Dutton, 1927.

Guiney, Louise Imogen. *The Letters of Louise Imogen Guiney,* ed. Grace Guiney, 2 vols. New York: Harpers, 1926.

Hall, James B., and Joseph Langland, ed. *The Short Story.* New York: Macmillan Co., 1956.

Hawthorne, Nathaniel. *The House of the Seven Gables* New York: A. L. Blunt, 1851.

———. *The Portable Hawthorne,* ed. Malcolm Cowley. New York: Viking Press, 1948.

Howard, Robert E. *Skull-Face and Others.* Sauk City, Wis.: Arkham House, 1946.

Huxley, Aldous. *The World of Aldous Huxley,* ed. Charles Role, New York: Universal Library, 1947.

Jenyns, Soame. *A Free Inquiry into the Nature and Origin of Evil.* London: J. Dodsley, 1773.

Knight, Damon. *In Search of Wonder.* Chicago: Advent, 1956.

Knoles, George Harmon. *The Jazz Age Revisited.* Stanford, Calif.: Stanford University Press, 1955.

Krutch, Joseph Wood. *Samuel Johnson.* New York: Henry Holt, 1944.

Levin, Harry. *The Power of Blackness.* New York: Vintage Books, 1960.

Lord, Walter. *The Good Years.* New York: Harper and Bros., 1960.

Lovecraft, H. P. *Best Supernatural Stories of H. P. Lovecraft,* Cleveland and New York: World Publishing Co., 1945.

———. *Beyond the Wall of Sleep.* Sauk City, Wis.: Arkham House, 1943.

———. *Démons et Merveilles,* trans. Bernard Noel. Paris, Deux Rives, 1955.

———. *Marginalia.* Sauk City, Wis.: Arkham House, 1944.

———. *The Outsider and Others.* Sauk City, Wis.: Arkham House, 1938.

———. *The Shunned House.* Athol, Massachusetts, Recluse Press, 1928.

———. *The Shuttered Room and Other Pieces.* Sauk City, Arkham House, 1959.

———. *Something About Cats and Other Pieces.* Sauk City, Arkham House, 1949.

———. *Supernatural Horror in Literature.* New York: Ben Abramson, 1954.

Macdonald, George. *The Visionary Novels of George Macdonald: Lilith and Phantastes.* New York: Noonday Press, 1954.

Machen, Arthur. *Far Off Things.* London: Martin Secker, 1923.

Maugham, W. Somerset. *The Summing Up.* New York: International Collectors Library, 1938.

Morris, Joe Alex. *What a Year!* New York: Harper and Bros., 1956.

Newman, Cardinal John Henry. *The Idea of a University.* New York, Doubleday, 1959.

O'Brien, Edward J., ed. *The Best Short Stories of 1928.* New York: Dodd, Mead, and Co., 1928.

Penzoldt, Peter. *The Supernatural in Fiction.* London: Peter Nevill, 1952.

Pierce, Frederick Clifton. *Field Genealogy.* 2 vols. 1901.

Poe, Edgar Allan. *Tales of Mystery and Imagination.* New York: Heritage Press, 1941.

Powys, John Cowper. *The Meaning of Culture.* New York: W. W. Norton, 1929.

Scarborough, Dorothy. *The Supernatural in Modern English Fiction.* New York: G. P. Putnam and Sons, 1917.

Scott, Winfield Townley. *Exiles and Fabrications.* New York: Doubleday, 1961.

Shipley, Joseph T., ed. *The Dictionary of World Literature.* New York: Philosophical Library, 195J.

Simms, William Gilmore. *The Letters of William Gilmore Simms.* Ed. Mary C. Simms Oliphant, Alfred Taylor Odell, T. C. Duncan Eaves, 5 vols. Columbia, S.C.: University of South Carolina Press, 1958.

Spencer, Truman J. *The History of Amateur Journalism* New York: The Fossils, Inc., 1957.

Starrett, Vincent. *Books and Bipeds.* New York: Argus Books, 1947.

Unger, Leonard, and William Van O'Connor, ed. *Poems for Study.* New York: Rinehart Co., 1957.

Varma, Devendra. *The Gothic Flame.* London: Arthur Baker, Ltd. 1957.

Wetzel, George, ed. *The Lovecraft Collectors Library,* 5 vols. North Tonawanda, New York: SSR Publications, 1952–55.

———, ed. *Howard Phillips Lovecraft: Memoirs, Critiques, & Bibliographies.*

North Tonawanda, NY: SSR Publications, 1955.

Whitman, Walt. *Leaves of Grass.* New York: Random House, 1921.

Wilson, Colin. *The Outsider.* Boston: Houghton Mifflin Co., 1956.

Wilson, Edmund. *Classics and Commercials.* New York: Farrar, Straus and Co., 1950.

Winwar, Frances. *The Haunted Palace.* New York: Harper and Bros., 1959.

Wise, Herbert A., and Phyllis Fraser, ed. *Great Tales of Terror and the Supernatural.* New York: Random House, 1944.

Wollheim, Donald A., ed. *The Portable Novels of Science.* New York: Viking, 1945.

Woodford, Jack. *Unwilling Sinner.* New York: Woodford Press, 1952.

II. PERIODICALS

Bernal, Ignacio. "Necrologia: Robert H. Barlow." *Sobretiro del Torno XIII del Boletin Bibliografico de Antropologia Americana,* 1950.

Bradbury, Ray. "Pillar of Fire." *Planet Stories* III, 38–58 (Summer 1948).

Chambers, John. "The Cult of Science Fiction." *The Dalhousie Review* (Spring 1960): 78–86.

Deutsch, Michel. "Lovecraft ou la Mythologie." *Esprit* (September, 1957): 256–66.

Ernoult, Claude. "Lovecraft ou le mythe en révolution." *Les Lettres Nouvelles,* XXI (November, 1954): 664–71.

Eisler, R. "The Fish As Sexual Symbol." *The Psychoanalytic Review,* VI (1919): 460–64.

"The Eyrie." *Weird Tales,* XXX, No. 1 (July 1937): 122–28; XXXV, No. 9 (May 1941): 120–21.

"Howard Phillips Lovecraft Memorial Symposium." *Fresco, University of Detroit Quarterly,* VIII (Spring 1958).

Johnson, Samuel. "A Review of *A Free Inquiry into the Nature and Origin of Evil,*" Oxford, 1796.

"Koezmar z Innsmouth," trans. Andrzej Wermer, *Prze Kroj,* Numer 766–68, 17–23 (1959).

(Lovecraft, H. P.) "Letter to Editor." *All-Story Weekly*, XXIX ((March 7, 1914): 223–24.

Mabbott, Thomas O., review of *The Outsider and Others*. *American Literature*, XII (March, 1940): 136.

McQuown, Norman A. "Obituary: Robert H. Barlow." *American Anthropologist*, LIII (1951): 543.

Mencken, H. L. "The New Architecture." *American Mercury*, XXII (February, 1931): 164.

Morey, C. R. "The Origin of the Fish Symbol." *The Princeton Theological Review*, VIII, No. 3 (July, 1910): 401–33; IX, No. 2 (April, 1911): 268–89.

Moskowitz, Sam, "A Study in Horror: The Eerie Life of H. P. Lovecraft." *Fantastic*, IX, No. 5 (May 1960): 35–50.

Sturtevant, Ethel G. "Dunsany on Gods and Men." *Columbia University Quarterly*, XXI (July 1919): [186]–99.

"The Supernatural in Horror Literature," anon. rev. *Dial*, LXIII (6 December 1917): 590–91.

III. NEWSPAPERS

Billy, André. "Lovecraft: Edgar Poe du XXe siecle." *Le Figaro Litteraire* (28 October 1961).

"The Case of Charles Dexter Ward," anon. rev. *The Observer* (10 February 1952).

"The Case of Charles Dexter Ward," anon. rev. *Times Literary Supplement* (22 February 1952).

"Century-Old Firm Fails." *New York Times* (22 February 1924).

"Deaths." *Providence Daily Journal* (21 July 1898).

"Disrobing, Vandalism at Cemetery Probed." *Camden Courier Post* (29 September 1961).

"Historic House Taken on a Journey." *Providence Journal* (21 September 1959).

"Jesuit Backs Evolution Theory; Finds No Conflict with Church."

Providence Journal (19 March 1937).

Matthews, Brander, rev., "The Cabinet of Gothic Tales of Terror," *New York Times Book Review* (25 September 1925).

"The Outsider and Others," rev., *New York Herald Tribune* (17 December 1939).

"When a Neighborhood Is in Trouble." *The Worcester Evening Gazette* (1 December 1959).

"Writer Charts Fatal Malady." *New York Times* (16 March 1937).

IV. MANUSCRIPTS

Davis, Sonia H. "The Private Life of Howard Phillips Lovecraft," 194-, John Hay Library.

Gamwell, Annie E. P. Letters and telegrams to Robert Barlow, 11 pages, 12 March to 15 December 1937. Relating to H. P. Lovecraft's final illness. John Hay Library.

Lovecraft, H. P., "The Horror at Red Hook," dated 2 August 1925, Manuscript Division, New York Public Library.

———. Juvenile periodicals, 123 items, 1899–1909, John Hay Library.

———. Letters to Elizabeth Toldridge, 448 pages, 1928–1937, John Hay Library.

———. Letters to Kenneth Sterling, 1935–1937, Private collection, Dr. Kenneth Sterling.

———. Letters to Margaret Ronan, 1936–1937, Private collection, Margaret Ronan.

———. Letters to Mrs. Annie E. P. Gamwell. 19 pages, 1921–1928, John Hay Library.

———. Letters to Mrs. Lillian D. Clark, 990 pages, 1921–1931, John Hay Library.

———. Letters to Robert Barlow, 463 pages, 1931–1937, John Hay Library.

———. Letters to Richard Ely Morse, 1932–1937, 14 pieces, Manuscript Division, New York Public Library.

———. Letters to Richard Ely Morse, 1933–1936, Private collection, Thomas O. Mabbott.

———. "The Terrible Old Man," dated January 28, 1920, Private collection, Arthur Koki.

Spink, Mary. *List of Books in Howard Phillips Lovecraft's Library."* n.d., John Hay Library.

Toldridge, Elizabeth. Eighteen Letters to H. P. Lovecraft, June–July, 1935, private collection, Arthur Koki.

V. OTHER SOURCES CONSULTED

Crane, Hart. *123 Original Letters of Hart Crane to Gorham B. Munson, from 1919–1928* (microfilm) Columbus: Ohio State University Libraries.

Lovecraft, H. P. High school transcript, Grades 9 through 11 (1904–1908). Issued by Central Records Office, Department of Public Schools, Providence, R.I.

Lovecraft, H. P., vs. Sonia Haft Greene, Petition for Divorce, No. 23118. Includes Citation for Deposition and Final Decree, March, 1929, Superior Court, Providence, R. I.

Lovecraft, H. P. Hospital Record of Lovecraft. History #20703 N. 760 (microfilm) Jane Brown Memorial Hospital.

Lovecraft, H. P. "Commonplace Book" from 1919 to 1934, 43 pages, "presented to R.H. Barlow, Esq. on May 7, 1934," John Hay Library.

Lovecraft illustrations. A collection of original crayon drawings, and one oil painting by several artists, 19—. John Hay Library.

Lovecraft, Sarah Susie Phillips. "Commonplace Book," n.d., John Hay Library.

———. Death Certificate (Bk. 27, p. 158). Issued by the City Registrar's Office, Providence, R. I.

Lovecraft, Winfield Scott. Death Certificate (Bk. 20, p. 262). Issued by the City Registrar's Office, Providence, R.I.

Ollendorff's New Method of Learning to Read, Write, and Speak the Spanish Language. New York: Appleton and Co., 1905. Copy autographed and dated by H. P. Lovecraft, Private collection, Arthur Koki.

Press clippings of *The Haunter of the Dark and Other Tales* and *The Case of Charles Dexter Ward*, gathered by Durance Press Cuttings, London, W.C. I. England, Private collection, Arthur Koki.

Rathbone Family Historian 1, No. 7 (July 1892).

Renshaw, Anne Tillery. "Well-bred Speech." Typescript with corrections by H. P. Lovecraft, John Hay Library.

Scott, Winfield. Townley, Reportorial notes for an article on H. P. Lovecraft, John Hay Library.

ADDENDA

Margulies, Leo, ed. *The Unexpected.* New York: Pyramid Books, 1961.

Phantastique—Science-Fiction Critic, II (March, 1938).

Index

After Many a Summer Dies the Swan (Huxley) 85
Age of Fable, The (Bulfinch) 35
Alhazred, Abdul 86, 243
All-Story Weekly 49–50
"Amateur Journalism: Its Possible Needs and Betterment" 74
Amazing Stories 170, 230
American Anthropologist 259
American College Dictionary 261
American Notebooks (Hawthorne) 150
Amis, Kingsley 172
Argosy 50n5
Arkham House 9–10, 257–58, 259
"Arthur Jermyn." *See* "Facts concerning the Late Arthur Jermyn and His Family"
"Ash-Tree, The" (James) 237
At the Mountains of Madness 190–95, 196, 198, 227, 231, 262
Atlas Shrugged (Rand) 163
Auden, W. H. 163
Austen, Jane 130–31

Baird, Edwin 25, 90, 91, 211
Barlow, Bernice L. 212, 214
Barlow, R. H. 18, 209–10, 211–14, 232, 233, 248–50, 254, 257, 258–59
Beard, James Franklin, Jr. 19
"Beast in the Cave, The" 32–34
"Berenice" (Poe) 148–49
Bergier, Jacques 158
Berkeley Square (film) 26
Bernal, Ignacio 212n214, 259
Best Short Stories of 1928 (O'Brien) 172

"Beyond the Wall of Sleep" 62–63
Beyond the Wall of Sleep 10, 25, 260
Bierce, Ambrose 124, 167
Billy, André 17, 260n10, 263
Birkhead, Edith 129–30, 132–33
Birth of a Nation (film) 262
Bishop, Zealia 197, 216–17, 218
"Black Cat, The" (Poe) 69
Bloch, Robert 157, 231–32, 234, 262
"Boarded Window, The" (Bierce) 124
Book of the Damned, The (Fort) 244n312, 245
Books in My Life, The (Miller) 235
Boston, Mass. 155–57
Bradbury, Ray 95n1
Bridge, The (Crane) 189
Brown, Charles Brockden 135
Brown, Harrison 19
Brown University 36, 41, 73, 207, 256
Bryan, William Jennings 113
Bulfinch, Thomas 35
Bullen, John Ravenor 182–83
Burke, Edmund 132
Burroughs, Edgar Rice 50
Burton, Robert 217
Bush, David Van 88–90, 99–100
Byrd, Richard E. 185

"Call of Cthulhu, The" 163–67, 223, 227
Carey, Henry 22
Carter, Lin 19
Carter, William H., Jr. 19
Case of Charles Dexter Ward, The 154, 167–70, 194
Castle of Otranto, The (Walpole) 132–33

"Cats of Ulthar, The" 63, 147, 208
"Challenge from Beyond, The" (Lovecraft et al.) 233–34
Chambers, Robert W. 60, 86
Charleston, S.C. 188
Chaucer, Geoffrey 79
Chesterfield, Philip Dormer Stanhope, Earl of 251
Chivers, Thomas Holley 79
Clark, Franklin C. 41–42, 103, 223
Clark, Lillian D. 8, 18, 19, 39, 105–6, 135, 146, 200–201
Cleveland, Ohio 79–80, 141
Cocteau, Jean 17, 263–64
"Colour out of Space, The" 170–72
Condie, Thomas Gray, Jr. 51
"Confession of Unfaith, A" 56
Conover, Willis 254n337
Conservative 52, 53–54
Cook, W. Paul 38, 41, 116, 129, 141, 145, 188, 189–90, 260
"Cool Air" 236
Coolidge, Calvin 185
Cosmopolitan 185
Cox, George Benson 92, 93
Crane, Hart 80, 97–98, 109–10, 122, 189, 209
Crawford, William L. 233
Cry Horror! 262
Cthulhu Mythos 36, 154, 163–67, 170–71, 235, 237, 239–46
Cummings, Ray 151

Daas, Edward F. 50
"Dagon" 57–61
Davis, Sonia H. 10. *See also* Greene, Sonia H.
de Camp, L. Sprague 9
de Castro, Adolphe 167, 174
de la Feld, Hubertus 21
de la Mare, Walter 66, 69
"De Triumpho Naturae" 45–46
Démons et Merveilles 158, 221
Denoël, Éditions 263
Derleth, August 115, 214, 219, 239, 245, 257

Deutsch, Michel 163nn64, 72, 241–42, 257n1
Dexter, Lord Timothy 116
"Doom That Came to Sarnath, The" 63–64
Doorways to Poetry (Moe) 182
Dowdell, William J. 82
Dream-Quest of Unknown Kadath, The 65, 157, 160–63
"Dreams in the Witch House, The" 203–6, 208, 235
Dunsany, Lord 61–62, 63, 64, 65–66, 70, 73, 104, 134, 147, 155, 156, 160, 236, 239, 244
"Dunwich Horror, The" 9, 190

Eddy, C. M., Jr. 175, 177
Edison, Thomas Alva 51
Eliot, T. S. 181
Erckmann-Chatrian 135
Ernoult, Claude 203n191
Erskine, Helen Worden 261
Exiles and Fabrications (Scott) 20
"Expectancy" (Toldridge) 180

Fables (Gay) 26
"Facts concerning the Late Arthur Jermyn and His Family" 72
"Facts in the Case of M. Valdemar, The" (Poe) 236
Fadiman, Clifton P. 191
Faig, Kenneth W., Jr. 9
"Fall of the House of Usher, The" (Poe) 136, 206
Fantasy Magazine 233
"Festival, The" 86–87, 121
Field, John 252
Figaro 17, 263
Fiske, John 104
Fitzgerald, F. Scott 186
Fort, Charles 244–45
Free Inquiry into the Origin and Nature of Evil, A (Jenyns) 242–44
Freeman, Mary E. Wilkins 238–39
Freud, Sigmund 132, 139
Fungi from Yuggoth 183–84

Index

Galbraith, John Kenneth 185
Galpin, Alfred 79–80
Gamwell, Annie E. P. 18, 39, 105, 146, 175, 177, 207, 254, 255
Gamwell, Phillips 39
"Gaudeamus" 68n58
Gay, John 26
Gernsback, Hugo 230
Ghelderode, Michel de 17
Gissing, George 96
Goddard, Robert H. 200
Gods of Mars, The (Burroughs) 50
Gods of Pegāna, The (Dunsany) 65, 239
Gogol, Nikolai 119
Goldsmith, Oliver 181
Gollancz, Victor 263
"Good Anaesthetic, A" 36
Gothic Flame, The (Varma) 133
Great Meadow Country Clubhouse 40
Great Return, The (Machen) 238
Greek mythology 35, 40
Greene, Florence 99n18
Greene, Sonia H. 9, 81–82, 88, 89, 90–93, 95–102, 105, 106, 137–41, 142–43, 144, 173–74, 175–78, 203, 206, 216. *See also* Davis, Sonia H.
Griffith, D. W. 262
Grill, Jack 19
Guest, Edgar A. 23, 89
Guiney, Louise Imogen 25

"H. P. Lovecraft" (Koki) 8
"H. P. Lovecraft: The Outsider in Legend and Myth" (St. Armand) 9
Hamilton, Edith 240
Harrison, Benjamin 23
"Haunter of the Dark, The" 234–
Hawthorne, Nathaniel 35, 51, 111–12, 150, 203
"He" 120–22, 153–54
Henneberger, J. C. 98n13
"Herbert West—Reanimator" 77–79, 83
Hess, Clara 47
Hitchcock, Alfred 262

Hitler, Adolf 116–17
Holmes, Oliver Wendell 25
Home Brew 76–77, 83, 88
Hoover, Herbert 185
Hope Street High School 37–38
"Horror at Red Hook, The" 106–8
"Horror in the Museum, The" (Lovecraft–Heald) 208
Houdini, Harry 90, 91, 93, 99
House of the Seven Gables, The (Hawthorne) 111–12, 203
Housman, A. E. 231
Houtain, George Julian 76
Howard, Robert E. 219–20, 247–48
"Howard Phillips Lovecraft: A Self-Portrait" (Thomas) 9
Huxley, Aldous 85, 117

"Idealism and Materialism: A Reflection" 127, 159
"Imprisoned with the Pharaohs" (Lovecraft–Houdini). *See* "Under the Pyramids"
"In the Vault" 123–25, 223

James, M. R. 85, 135, 237
Jenyns, Soame 242–44
Johnson, Samuel 26–27, 33, 181, 243
Jones, C. H. 29–30
"Journal of a Solitary Man, The" (Hawthorne) 150
Juvenile Port-Folio and Literary Miscellany 51

Kalem Club 110, 140, 141
Keller, David H. 29
King in Yellow, The (Chambers) 60
Kirk, George 110–11
Kleiner, Rheinhart 100, 101
"Knight's Tale, The" (Chaucer) 79
Knopf, Alfred A. 212
Knowles, Horace B., Sons 256
Koki, Alfred S. 8
Koki, Philip 8

Last Puritan, The (Santayana) 249

"Last Test, The" (Lovecraft–de Castro) 174
Lawrence, D. H. 18
Leet, William L. 254–55
"Ligeia" (Poe) 149
"Little Glass Bottle, The" 27
Long, Frank Belknap, Jr. 10, 75, 90, 91, 103, 111, 116, 141, 174, 178, 187, 209
Long, Frank Belknap, Sr. 110, 174
Lovecraft, H. P.: and amateur journalism, 50–56, 69–70, 73–74, 75–76, 82–83; ancestry of, 21–22, 252; and astronomy, 36–37, 252; childhood of, 21, 25–28, 30–42; commonplace book of, 125, 150–51; divorce of, 175–78; education of, 30–31, 37–38, 41–42; employment of, 90, 97–98, 100–101; French criticism of, 17, 163, 166, 263–64; health of, 254–56; letters by, 18, 135, 180, 198–200, 214–19; marriage of, 90–144; poems by, 44–47, 53, 181–84; politics of, 252–54; racism of, 10, 113–17; readings of, 26–27, 32, 49–50, 96–97, 135, 242–45; and religion, 56, 112–13; as revisionist, 88–89, 99–100, 123, 174–75, 221–24, 233–34, 246–47, 248; and science fiction, 60, 230–31; stories by, 27–28, 32–34, 57–62, 67–69, 70–73, 76–79, 83–87, 89, 102–5, 106–8, 120–22, 146–73, 190–95, 196–98, 202–7, 208–9, 224–32, 234–42, 245–46; travels of, 79–82, 87–88, 174, 178–79, 187–90, 200–201, 209–14, 232–33; and World War I, 54–56
Lovecraft, Sarah Susan Phillips 22, 24–25, 31, 38–39, 41, 46–47, 56–57, 70, 73–75
Lovecraft, Winfield Scott 23–25, 28–29
Lovecraft: A Biography (de Camp) 9
"Lovecraft's Manual of Explosions" 36

Loveman, Samuel 10, 54, 71, 80, 90, 101, 109–10, 111, 129, 189, 209
Lucian of Samosata 230
"Lurking Fear, The" 83–84

Mabbott, Thomas Ollive 19, 136, 147
Macaulay, Thomas Babington 26
McDowall, Roddy 262
Machen, Arthur 60, 134–35, 236–38
Matthews, Brander 130
Maugham, W. Somerset 64–65, 197, 217
Mencken, H. L. 43
Miller, Henry 235
Modern Treatment of Syphilis, The (Moore) 29
Moe, Maurice W. 54, 79, 182
Monk, The (Lewis) 133
"Moon-Bog, The" 151–52
Moore, J. Earle 29
Morton, James F. 248
Mortos Podem Voltar, Os 169
Moskowitz, Sam 60, 172n92
Munroe, Harold Bateman 40–41
"Music of Erich Zann, The" 261
"Mystery of the Grave-Yard, The" 32
Myths and Myth-Makers (Fiske) 104

Narrative of Arthur Gordon Pym, The (Poe) 192
National Amateur Press Association 51–52, 82–83, 232–33
Necronomicon (Alhazred) 86, 87, 239, 241, 243
"Nemesis" 224
New York, N.Y. 80–82, 90–126, 145–46, 178, 189, 209
New York Times 256
Newburyport, Mass. 87
Newman, John Henry 215
"Nietzscheism and Realism" 56
Northanger Abbey (Austen) 131
"Novel of the White Powder" (Machen) 237

Index

"Nymph's Reply to the Modern Business Man, The" 53

O'Brien, Edward J. 172, 191
Ollendorff's New Method of Learning to Read, Write, and Speak the Spanish Language 217
Olympian Spring (Spitteler) 239
"On a New England Village Seen by Moonlight" 181–82
"On the Creation of Niggers" 46
On the Sublime and Beautiful (Burke) 132
Out of This World (Erskine) 261
"Outsider, The" 147–51
Outsider and Others, The 9–10, 258
Overcoat, The (Gogol) 117

"Pacificst War Song—1917" 54
Papy, Jacques 17, 172, 194, 263
Pascal, Blaise 162
Penzoldt, Peter 85–86, 237
Philips, Ambrose 21–22
Phillips, Emma 24
Philips, John 21
Phillips, Whipple Van Buren 22–23, 25, 29, 38, 116, 222–23
"Pickman's Model" 155–57
"Picture in the House, The" 72–73
Pigafetta, Filippo 73
Plato 230
Poe, Edgar Allan 21n1, 43–44, 69, 79, 102, 136, 148–50, 151, 192, 206, 236
"Polaris" 61n40, 62
Pope, Alexander 26, 181
Portable Novels of Science, The (Wollheim) 229
Powys, John Cowper 251
Price, E. Hoffmann 157, 220–21
"Private Life of H. P. Lovecraft, The" (Davis) 10
Private Papers of Henry Ryecroft, The (Gissing) 96
Progress of the Soul, The 202
Providence, R.I. 42–44, 47, 102–3, 142–45, 169, 207–8

Providence Evening Bulletin 256n345
Providence Gazette and Country Journal 223
Providence Journal 36, 114, 256n345
Psycho (Bloch) 262
Putnam's Sons, G. P. 201–2

Radcliffe, Ann 133, 135
Rainbow 81
Rand, Ayn 163
Rathbone, John 232
"Rats" (James) 85
"Rats in the Walls, The" 85–86, 238
Read, Herbert 162
Recluse 129
Regnum Congo (Pigafetta) 73
Renshaw, Anne Tillery 246–47, 248
Return, The (de la Mare) 66–67, 69
Rhode Island Journal of Astronomy 36
Rhode Island National Guard 52n10, 54–55, 159
Rhode Island School of Design 115
Robinson, Edwin Arlington 184
Roerich, Nicholas 191–92
Roosevelt, Franklin D. 252–53
Roulet, Jacques 104

St. Armand, Barton L. 9
St. Augustine, Fla. 195–96
Salem, Mass. 87–88
Santayana, George 249
Scarborough, Dorothy 129, 130–31, 133–34, 135
Schwartz, Julius 233
Scientific Gazette 36
Scopes trial 112–13
Scott, Winfield Townley 20, 57, 74–75, 184, 188, 215–16
Scribner, Charles 51
"Secret Cave or John Lees Adventure, The" 27–28
"Shadow out of Time, The" 224–31
"Shadow over Innsmouth, The" 196–98, 233, 241
"Shambler from the Stars, The" (Bloch) 234

"Shunned House, The" 102–5, 165, 206–7, 223
"Silver Key, The" 157, 158–59, 221
Smith, Charles W. 53, 123n83
Smith, Clark Ashton 219
"Some Causes of Self-Immolation" 56
"Some Notes on a Nonentity" 25
Souplaut, Philippe 133
Spectator 51
Spencer, Truman J. 82–83
Spitteler, Carl 239
Stapledon, Olaf 224
Starrett, Vincent 260n9, 261
"Statement of Randolph Carter, The" 71–72, 157, 158
Sterling, Kenneth 29
"Strange High House in the Mist, The" 155
"Strange Island of Dr. Nork, The" (Bloch) 157
"Supernatural Horror in Literature" 129–37
Supernatural in English Fiction, The (Scarborough) 129, 130–31
Sweeney, Ella 31
Swift, Jonathan 26, 117

Tale of Terror, The (Birkhead) 129–30
Talman, Wilfred B. 111
Teilhard de Chardin, Pierre 256
"Terrible Old Man, The" 152–53
Thayer, Tiffany 244
"Thing on the Doorstep, The" 31n38, 202–3, 236
Thomas, James Warren 9, 10
Thomson, James 181
Three Impostors, The (Machen) 60, 134
"Through the Gates of the Silver Key" (Lovecraft–Price) 157, 221–24
Time Machine, The (Wells) 34
Titanic 55, 185
Toldridge, Elizabeth 18, 180–82, 187, 199–200, 201, 210, 219, 233
"Tomb, The" 66, 67–69, 147
Tombaugh, C. W. 190
Transatlantic Circulator 60–61
Trilling, Diana 18

Tryout 53, 123, 152
Tucker, Gertrude 90, 92, 97
"Two Bottles of Relish, The" (Dunsany) 156

"Ulalume" (Poe) 192
"Under the Pyramids" (Lovecraft–Houdini) 90
United Amateur 51
United Amateur Press Association 50, 51–52, 69–70, 73, 75, 83
Unterecker, John 7, 10, 20

Vagrant 57, 72–73, 147
Varma, Devendra P. 133
Vathek (Beckford) 162

Wandrei, Donald 170, 231, 257
Washington, George 199
Weird Tales 85, 90, 91, 97, 98, 123, 145, 147, 151–54, 157, 170, 180, 187, 195, 196, 197, 198, 208, 219, 221, 231, 232, 233, 234, 257, 260
Well Bred Speech (Renshaw) 246
Wells, H. G. 34, 166
Wetzel, George T. 239–40
"Whisperer in Darkness, The" 190, 203
"White Ship, The" 63
Whitehead, Henry S. 195, 201
Whitman, Sarah Helen 42–43, 102
Whitman, Walt 181, 250
"Why I Am Not a Free Thinker" (Moe) 54
Wickenden, Mr. 61
Williams, Roger 42
Wilson, Colin 126–27
Wilson, Edmund 17, 134–35, 166, 172, 188, 227–28
Wilson, Woodrow 52
Wise, Stephen Samuel 252
Wollheim, Donald A. 229, 231
Wormius, Olaus 87
Wright, Farnsworth 170, 196, 197–98, 220, 231–32

"Yellow Sign, The" (Chambers) 86

www.ingramcontent.com/pod-product-compliance
Lightning Source LLC
Chambersburg PA
CBHW060113170426
43198CB00010B/880